LANGUAGE AND LITERACY SE...
Dorothy S. Strickland and Celia Genish..., ...

DRAMATIZING LITERATURE
in
Whole Language Classrooms

SECOND EDITION

John Warren Stewig
Carol Buege

Teachers College, Columbia University
New York and London

Published by Teachers College Press, 1234 Amsterdam Avenue
New York, NY 10027

Library of Congress Cataloging-in-Publication Data
Stewig, John W.
    Dramatizing literature in whole language classrooms / John Warren
Stewig, Carole Buege. — 2nd ed.
      p.   cm. — (Language and literacy series)
    Includes bibliographical references and index.
    ISBN 0-8077-3307-5 (pbk. : alk. paper)
    1. Drama in education. 2. Language arts. I. Buege, Carol.
II. Title. III. Series: Language and literacy series (New York,
N.Y.)
PN3171.S788   1994   94-429
372.6'6—dc20

ISBN 0-8077-3307-5

Printed on acid-free paper

Manufactured in the United States of America

99 98 97 96 95 94 8 7 6 5 4 3 2 1

(*Copyright page continued on p. xi*)

Contents

Foreword

Oral language and the art of drama are closely intertwined, and both are important to the development of our children. As John Warren Stewig and Carol Buege point out, oral language is the most important facet of language. Oral language is a primary means of making and conveying meaning, the most used of the language arts skills, and the basis for reading and writing. Most of the oral message is conveyed through vocal overlays of pitch, stress, and juncture and by accompanying facial expressions. The process of making drama is a highly motivating method for bringing oral language learning into the classroom.

In addition to the value of mastering the art of oral communication, drama as an art form is important to the lives of all children and should be a part of their classroom culture. Richard Riley, the U.S. Secretary of Education, released a statement on February 23, 1993 supporting the role of the arts in education reform.

> As we work to improve the quality of education for all children, the arts must be recognized as a vital part of our effort. The arts . . . are a unique medium for communicating what is special to each of us as human beings and what is special to each of us as creative individuals. The arts provide valuable opportunities for understanding our cultural heritage and that of all other civilizations. The arts also enhance our nation's economic competitiveness by developing creative problem solving skills, imagination, self-discipline and attention to detail.

With *Dramatizing Literature in Whole Language Classrooms*, the authors have written a text that clearly, carefully supports classroom teachers so that they may guide children to use their minds, bodies, and voices to create individual responses within the social *process* of creating drama. This is a very special text for several reasons. The writing is inviting, lucid, engrossing. The organization illustrates a clear understanding of the classroom process and a sensitivity to the strengths and hesitancies of teachers trying out new methodology—but I would quickly add that the book holds numerous examples drawn from classroom experience and a wealth of knowledge of children's literature that will be helpful to more experienced teachers. The annotated reading lists are very helpful.

Looking at the book in a more detailed fashion, Chapter 1 defines spontaneous drama, explaining its values and placing it—with many useful experiences—as an important element of the language arts curriculum. Chapter 2 presents the "what" of spontaneous drama, illustrating the nature of a lesson—the motivation, the planning, playing and evaluating with the children. The rich use of children's literature to illustrate the basic components of a drama session is a particular strength of this text. Chapter 3 is also a jewel. The authors' years of work with teachers is apparent as they lead the reader through the "how" of conducting drama sessions. For example, the sets of leading questions are excellent models for teachers who wish to master the art of flexibly guiding activities in which children have real creative input. The section on working with the exceptional learner is practical and helpful. There is even a short section on advocacy—often important in schools that have yet to learn of the values of truly creative work through drama in the language arts. Chapters 4 through 6 bring even more practical materials and structures to the reader. Chapter 4 masterfully illustrates drama in reading and literature programs, as a part of verbal and nonverbal development and as motivation for creative writing and an activity based on creative writing. Chapters 5 and 6 specifically address drama used across the kindergarten to third- and fourth- to eighth-grade curricula.

This book is a gift to the teaching profession. John Warren Stewig and Carol Buege have created a richly detailed, carefully structured text that leads teachers step by step through the complex process of fostering creative expression in the medium of drama. *Dramatizing Literature in Whole Language Classrooms* is particularly timely in these days of educational reform when we seek methods to teach all of our children to survive, succeed, and be happy in an ever more complex world.

Lyn Wright
Chair, Department of Theater
Arizona State University, Tempe
Past President, American Alliance
for Theater and Education

Preface

Teachers throughout the United States are involved in an exciting effort to reshape elementary and middle school curricula so that they will look far different tomorrow than they do today. These efforts go by many different names: whole language, integrated teaching, and literature-based instruction, among others. As is usual when schools change, the rate of change varies widely. Some districts have made such significant system-wide changes that the ways in which boys and girls learn are dramatically different than they were ten years ago. In other districts, a few teachers are beginning to take hesitant first steps—often without much district level support—to move away from a textbook driven curriculum. These efforts will go on for a long time, and the final look of curriculum cannot be envisioned.

Our goal in this text is to examine the role of informal classroom drama as one part of the changes taking place. Have you tried doing drama with children in your classroom? If you are among the small number who have, did the experience make you want to do it more often? Many teachers have heard about informal dramatics for children, but balk at the idea of trying it, because drama in the classroom is so different from more conventional academic activities. Perhaps you've not experimented with informal drama experiences simply because what you knew about drama was too unclear to you. Or perhaps you have not known what to do, or why to do it.

In contrast, perhaps you're a teacher who has been using informal classroom drama with students. Many such teachers, convinced of the values of drama and skilled in leading it, are nonetheless being called on by parents and administrators to concentrate on measurable outcomes of teaching. In counterbalance to the innovation described above, there is another force at work in shaping curriculum. That is an increasing attempt, often at the statewide level, to do paper-and-pencil assessment of what are often called "basic skills." Many capable teachers using drama are being pressed to spend less time on such activities, in favor of teaching the kind of segmented, sequential skills measured on some statewide assessment programs. Drama is as a consequence a valid technique in danger of being crowded out of the curriculum.

Our purpose here is to convince you, as we are convinced, that all children should have regular, recurring experiences in spontaneous drama in schools. This book is for you, the classroom teacher, whether you have been teaching many years or are only now approaching student teaching. It is for you, whether you are working in the most revamped whole language curriculum or if you are only now beginning to think about how to change the ways you teach. We want to show you the many ways teachers can use children's books as a basis for drama. This book was written as a result of our many years of elementary and middle school teaching, and our conviction that you can learn how to do drama with children. This book can start you on a study of the ways dramatizing literature can become an integral part of your curriculum, and it will lead you to other helpful books as you develop your ability to do drama with boys and girls.

The book's focus is on classroom drama, a vehicle for encouraging, extending, and enhancing the imagination children bring to your classroom. It spells out in detail the growth in language creativity that results when youngsters work with teachers who provide informal drama experiences. The book describes carefully *what* drama is, *how* it is done with children, and *why* it should be part of elementary curricula. In addition, this book includes a chapter focused on kindergarten through third grade, and another on fourth through eighth grade, with many specific suggestions about lesson ideas that can help you begin implementing drama. If you are a teacher who already uses drama with confidence, these specific lesson ideas may suggest some possibilities new to you.

All this was done with one idea in mind—to encourage teachers, including those who have never had a drama experience themselves, to set forth boldly on an experiment with children. When teacher and students work together in improvised drama, important social, intellectual, and emotional goals can be attained. An important natural resource, children's imaginative ability, can receive the encouragement it deserves. As a teacher concerned with human resources, you can do something. As an articulate educator, you can include drama in the curriculum and convince parents and administrators that such experiences are vital for all students.

We would like to express our gratitude to Carol Joppe, a primary teacher at Wilder Elementary School, a whole language school in Green Bay, Wisconsin, who provided ideas for Chapter 5.

Acknowledgments

(This is a continuation of the copyright page.)

Grateful acknowledgment is made for permission to reproduce the following illustrations:

Figure 1.2: Photograph courtesy of Eileen Littig of Northeastern Wisconsin In-school Telecommunication, Green Bay, WI. From the television series, "Creative Dramatics: Drama as an Important Classroom Tool."

Figure 1.3: Illustration from *Jiggle Wiggle Prance* by Sally Noll. Copyright © 1987 by Sally Noll. Reprinted by permission of Greenwillow Books, a division of William Morrow & Company, Inc.

Figure 1.4: Illustration reprinted with the permission of Charles Scribner's Sons, an imprint of Macmillan Publishing Company from *Stone Soup* by Marcia Brown. Copyright © 1947 Marcia Brown; copyright renewed © 1975 Marcia Brown.

Figure 2.1: Photograph from *Look, Think and Write* by Hart Day Leavitt and David A. Sohn. Copyright © 1985; used by permission

Figure 2.2: Photograph courtesy of the Waukesha (WI) Public Schools and Richard D. Bradley, photogtrapher

Figure 2.3: Illustration from *Little Red Riding Hood* illustrated and retold by Trina S. Hyman. Copyright © 1983; used by permission of Holiday House.

Figure 2.4: Illustration from *The Three Billy Goats Gruff*, copyright © 1987 by Janet Stevens, reproduced by permission of Harcourt Brace & Company.

Figure 3.1: Illustration reprinted with the permission of Atheneum Publishers, an imprint of Macmillan Publishing Company from *Red Riding Hood* by Beatrice Schenk de Regniers, illustrated by Edward Gorey. Illustrations copyright © 1972 Edward Gorey.

Figure 3.2: Illustration from *The Missing Tarts* by B. G. Hennessy, illustrated by Tracey Campbell Pearson. Copyright © 1989 by Tracey Campbell Pearson for illustrations. Used by permission of Viking Penguin, a division of Penguin Books USA Inc.

Figure 3.3: Margot Tomes's illustration from *The Fisherman and His Wife* by John Stewig. Copyright © 1988; used by permission of Holiday House.

Figure 4.3: Illustration from *Puss in Boots* by Gail E. Haley. Copyright © 1991 by Gail E. Haley. Used by permission of Dutton Children's Books, a divsion of Penguin Books USA Inc.

Figure 4.4: Illustration from *Harriet the Spy* by Louise Fitzhugh. Copyright © 1964 by Louise Fitzhugh. Reprinted by permission of HarperCollins Publishers.

Figure 4.5: Photograph courtesy of the Racine (WI) Public Schools and Richard D. Bradley, Photographer.

Figure 4.7: Illustration by Robin Jacques from *A Book of Witches* by Ruth Manning-Sanders. Copyright © 1966. Reproduced by permission of Robin Jacques.

Figure 5.2: Photograph courtesy of the Racine (WI) Public Schools and Richard D. Bradley, Photographer.

Figure 5.3: Illustration reprinted with the permission of Macmillan Publishing Company from *The Three Little Pigs and the Fox* by William H. Hooks, illustated by Steven D. Schindler. Illustrations copyright © 1989 S. D. Schindler.

Figure 5.8: Illustration by Jan Brett reprinted by permission of G. Putnam's Sons from *The Mitten*, copyright © 1989 by Jan Brett.

Figure 5.9: Checklist of objectives and behaviors from *Theatre Arts in the Elementary Classroom: Grade 4 Through Grade 6* (1986) by Barbara Salisbury. Used by permission of Barbara Salisbury Wills.

Figure 6.1: Illustration from *A Medieval Feast* by Aliki (1983) reprinted by permission of HarperCollins Publishers.

Figure 6.3: Illustration from *Motel of the Mysteries* by David Macaulay. Copyright © 1979 by David Macaulay. Reprinted by permission of Houghton Mifflin Company. All rights reserved.

Grateful acknowledgment is also made for permission to reproduce the following poems:

"Some One." The Literary Trustees of Walter de la Mare and The Society of Authors as their representative.

"Wind Weather." Used by permission of Virginia Brasier

"April Rain Song." From *The Dream Keeper and Other Poems* by Langston Hughes. Copyright 1932 by Alfred A. Knopf, Inc. and renewed 1960 by Langston Hughes. Reprinted by permission of the publisher.

"Galoshes," from *Stories to Begin On* by Rhoda W. Bacmeister. Copyright 1940 by E. P. Dutton, renewed © 1968 by Rhoda W Bacmeister. Used by permission of Dutton Children's Books, a division of Penguin Books USA Inc.

"Snakes and Snails," from *Bird in the Bush* by Grace Taber Hallock. Copyright 1930 by E. P. Dutton, renewed © 1958 by Miss Grace Taber Hallock. Used by permission of Dutton Children's Books, a division of Penguin Books USA Inc.

CHAPTER 1

Introduction and Definitions

The little boy, in no way good looking, too large for his grade—and, therefore, gawky—was memorable only for the amount of disruption he caused in the class. Yet, as we worked over the course of several weeks through a sequence of drama experiences, I thought I detected some changes. The loud voice was at times less penetrating, and the impulses to act the clown or to misbehave for attention seemed less frequent.

Yet it was not until the day we began work on Jay Williams's *The King with Six Friends* (1968) that the changes became clearly apparent. The class was divided into several small groups to involve each child, because the story has only nine characters. We worked on interpretations of the story and then redid them so the children could be different characters. Tom, who previously had been on the edge of the group, was chosen to be king in one group this time. When his group shared its interpretation with the rest of us, the way in which Tom had become the king was striking. In bearing and demeanor, in voice and every action, he portrayed for us the regal monarch. Later that day, as we were walking out to recess, he came up beside me and confided shyly that the real reason he liked drama was "because everybody gets to be king."

Something in the series of drama experiences we had been doing touched this child, drawing out qualities of which the class and I were unaware. The experiences had not "taught" him anything—in the conventional sense of the word. He had learned no new facts and memorized no new dates. But he, indeed, had learned some things about himself and his relations to others that affected his behavior in positive ways. He came to an understanding of his role as a contributing member of the group, needing to be neither withdrawn nor aggressive to be accepted.

This is only *one* example of *one* way in which children can grow through continued contacts with drama. There are many other ways, and we will be exploring them in this book. But to understand what drama can

1

do for children, we first need to understand the nature of informal classroom drama.

Drama, an ancient art form, shares one characteristic with all the other arts. All art forms, whether painting, sculpture, dance, writing, or drama, are alike in that they are an artist's individual reaction to a stimulus. These individual expressions or comments by artists take different outward forms but share the unique quality of being a response to or a statement about something an artist felt was important. The painter sees an arrangement of objects and creates a still life. The writer contemplates an aspect of human nature and fashions a story about someone who embodies this trait. The dramatist observes a recurrent human problem and writes a play in which the characters deal with this problem.

In all these instances, when the public finally experiences the art work, it is in finished form. By the time a painting is hung in a gallery, the artist's work is finished. By the time the playgoer reaches the theatre, the play-wright's work is finished. Drama—meaning a play—is a polished form with a script the actors must follow. This is in contrast to *spontaneous drama*, an art form for children that emphasizes process instead of product. In classroom drama, students use their bodies and voices to create a response to a stimulus material. The motivation may be visual, aural, or related to another sense. The child is challenged to create an individual response, a personal reaction to the stimulus material (see Figure 1.1).

An educator of much perception, whose career was devoted to using drama techniques with teenaged delinquent boys, summarized a major concern of informal drama.

> A great deal of education is concerned basically with putting something into the child's mind, with storing facts, and making it memorize and retain. . . . But surely this "putting in" side of education is only a part of the matter and should be subsidiary to the development outwards of the child's personality and character from within the child himself. (Barnfield, 1968, p. 14)

Putting in or taking out, which shall it be? As with all dichotomies, this one is artificial. Surely no one vitally concerned with educating children would seriously argue that *all* of education should be either cramming ideas in or pulling them out. However, there is danger that many people—perhaps too many—see the former as the most crucial aspect of education. Within the past several years, there has been increased tension between demands for a return to the "basics" (Hirsch, 1987), however inadequately defined, and more innovative approaches (Pappas, Kiefer, & Levstik, 1990). This is in spite of the fact that people who have studied children have produced powerful statements about the significant work children can do if motivated successfully to draw upon their inner resources.

	Scripted Drama	Spontaneous Drama
Involvement	A few children can be involved; the rest must take backstage or other supportive jobs.	Involves all children in a variety of active roles.
Creativity encouraged	Close adherence to the script by the playwright is mandatory.	Children use story or other motivation as a springboard for their own creation.
Pressure to perform	High; children know audience is watching, done in surroundings with which child is often unfamiliar.	Low; if audience exists at all, it is small group of children's peers in the classroom situation with which they are familiar.
Need for props and equipment	Extensive; often these are not things children can create, but must be made for them by others.	Minimal or nonexistent; child uses creative imagination to evoke needed equipment, emphasis on refining movements (e.g., picking up a fork) to convey ideas.
Language learnings	Few; children are limited to understanding the uses the author has made of language.	Many; the situations presented challenge children to create use of language, both verbal and nonverbal.

FIGURE 1.1. Distinctions between scripted and spontaneous drama.

Many years ago, Natalie Robinson Cole, a gifted master teacher (who happened to lack a "proper" degree in teaching), wrote a compelling book describing how she freed children to produce expressive art, music, dance, and writing, using very simple motivations. *The Arts in the Classroom* (1940) is interesting because it is one of the first works presenting methods of teaching children from "disadvantaged" backgrounds. Cole, who worked in southern California with Mexican-American children, displays an enviable empathy for her students. The book is one of the few in education that is well worth reading despite its advanced age. The reason Cole's first and her more recent (1966) books seem so pertinent today to those of us interested first in children's welfare and then in teaching them academic subjects is that so much of what she wrote long ago is still waiting to be put into widespread effect by most teachers.

WHY IS DRAMA A LANGUAGE ART?

This heading asserts that dramatics is one of the language arts, and few would argue that point. Although it would seem to follow then that drama should be part of the language arts program in elementary schools, an examination of these programs shows otherwise. A curious aspect of the programs is that their emphasis is somewhat out of touch with the way people use language as adults. To support this statement, we need to be aware of the nature of both adult use of language and language arts programs.

Linguists have long pointed out the primacy of oral language, that is, the importance of speech. Most adults, whether a college professor leading a class discussion or an automobile mechanic discussing with the service manager the reason for performing a particular repair, use language orally. The majority of us use whatever oral proficiency we have developed. A look at elementary language arts programs, however, reveals that this fact of life is generally not reflected in these programs.

Language arts programs have become so codified that it is possible to predict what one might be like without ever visiting the classroom or talking with the teacher. Recently, interest in whole language programs has been widespread. Despite this, many teachers use one of the nationally distributed hardbacked basic language texts from a major publisher. How a teacher uses it depends on a variety of elements within the classroom: the teacher's interest in the book, the students' response to it, the amount of time devoted to language arts, and the available supplementary materials. Quite frequently teachers also use a spelling book that ranges from a rather traditional story or interest-topic approach to a more innovative linguistically organized one. Somewhat less frequently teachers give either cursory or compulsive attention to one of the many handwriting series.

You'll notice that in the foregoing description *oral* language, the most important facet of language, receives only minimal attention. It is difficult to find a language arts program that emphasizes the oral arts—listening and speaking.

Several writers have commented on the need to develop sequential programs in listening (Norton, 1989), oral language (Jalongo, 1992), and dramatics (McCaslin, 1990), but too little has been accomplished in these areas. It is these areas, and the speech skills so crucial to most adults, that are, paradoxically, most frequently ignored in elementary language arts curricula. Although most primary grade children do get some experiences in oral language during the show-and-tell period (Stewig & Jett-Simpson, in press), it is rather limited. Regular dramatic experiences are too seldom a part of the ongoing language arts program.

Because of the widespread view among linguists that language is primarily a spoken art, language programs that do not give children frequent and varied chances to talk should be viewed as inadequate. It is our contention that adding drama to the language arts curriculum can provide the necessary opportunities for development of language and language-related abilities. Some of the specific language skills that drama develops are discussed later in the book.

COMPONENTS OF CLASSROOM DRAMA

All informal classroom drama experiences are made up of four basic components, which will be introduced briefly here and explained more fully in Chapter 2.

1. *The material.* This is the idea used to motivate the sessions, the stimulus material around which a session is built. Motivations that appeal to the senses of the child should usually be selected. They should be structured to provide continuity, but open-ended so they provide opportunities for students to create responses (see Figure 1.2).
2. *The discussion-questioning segment.* After the leader presents the motivating material, and sometimes as this is going on, discussion occurs. This is directed by the teacher through judicious use of questions, but because children's responses are spontaneous, the teacher shifts questioning strategies while working to make the most of student ideas.
3. *The playing of an idea.* This stage varies in complexity depending on the age and previous drama experience of the boys and girls. Sometimes it includes initial "warm-up" activities. These may or may not be directly related to the main enactment of the session. Some exploration of rhythmic movement might lead into the dramatizing. This could be a simple pantomime of a single activity, for example, opening a box containing a birthday present. It could be movement through space, as fish (leaping), bees (flying), chicks (hopping), squirrels (fleeing), or seals (diving), some of the movements explored by Jean Marzollo in her book *Pretend You're a Cat* (1990). Sally Noll, in her vividly pictured book *Jiggle Wiggle Prance* (1987), presents 33 action verbs that will have youngsters up and moving

FIGURE 1.2. Introductory rhythmic movement experiences challenge children to think about the different ways in which their bodies can be moved, either in place or through space.

(see Figure 1.3). Myriad movement possibilities also spring from Michelle Koch's *Hoot. Howl. Hiss.* (1991), in which bright watercolor illustrations show animals and give the words for the noise each makes. This can encourage initial exploratory verbal activity, linked to movement. At other times playing is more complex, for example, enacting an entire story that the students have created (O'Shea & Egan, 1978).

4. *Evaluation.* This is an important element in drama because the children are encouraged to consider what they have done and to decide which aspects they were pleased with and which could have been done more effectively.

These components vary in importance depending on the group of children involved, the ideas used for the drama session, how long the children have been having drama experiences, and the purposes for the particular session.

TERMINOLOGY

There are various terms peculiar to dramatics, especially the drama experiences discussed in this book. The most common title for what this book is about is *creative drama*, although the term presents two problems:

1. "Creative" has been so misapplied to such a variety of different phenomena that it is almost impossible to establish a clear, denotative meaning for the word (Wagner, 1978).
2. Drama should *always* be creative, so as an adjective the word is redundant. If we accept different types of creativity, then all drama, from the informal dramatic play of preschool children to the finely disciplined Shakespearean performance (and including such technical activities as lighting and scenery construction), is creative.

Another term sometimes used to describe drama experiences with children is *developmental drama* (McCaslin, 1990, pp. 9–10). Used widely by Canadian drama leaders, the term emphasizes that as a child lives with this art form throughout the elementary school years, regularly recurring drama experiences develop abilities in characterization, plot creation, mood and conflict establishment, and other facets of dramatics. This term implies that a leader is present, planning carefully to provide for children a sequence of experiences in each of these drama aspects. Through these experiences each child develops that variety of abilities, attitudes, outlooks, and understandings that come from a sustained contact with drama. Other terms

FIGURE 1.3. The bright, full-color illustrations in Sally Noll's *Jiggle Wiggle Prance* (1987) depict animals of all sizes from elephants to frogs, each presenting useful movement possibilities.

for this activity include *drama in the classroom*, *educational drama*, and *improvisational drama*.

However, this book emphasizes that the making of classroom dramas is *spontaneous*. An intuitive, flexible, adapting, and dramatic experience that is truly spontaneous is necessary. Dictionaries list *natural*, a good word to describe the drama experience we are considering here, as one synonym for spontaneous. Leaders are concerned with evoking in children a natural, or spontaneous, response to the chosen motivation. This is akin to the free, unstructured response of young children's imaginative play, so respected in the preschool but often discouraged in first grade and beyond. Swartz (1992) explains why he feels the term *spontaneous* is particularly appropriate.

The teacher does not formulate ahead of time what the children's response to the material ought to be, but rather plans a motivation and then builds a dramatic experience as the children's natural responses to that motivation come forth. This does not mean, however, that the drama *program* is spontaneous or unplanned.

Earlier in this century a group of educators believed that elementary school programs should evolve from the needs of the children; that is, the curriculum should be emergent and the teacher's major role should be to follow the expressed interests of the children. A recently republished, notable statement about this is *I Learn from Children* (Pratt, 1990). This delightful account is by a courageous and innovative educator, who experimented many years ago with "progressive" ideas, among them an *emergent* curriculum. Though now primarily of historical interest, the book demonstrates conclusively the benefits gained from this approach to curriculum planning. People who held this philosophy believed that teachers should not present an idea to stimulate an interest but rather should help children study something after an interest was expressed.

This is not the role of the informal drama leader. Many writers on the nature of creativity have pointed out that children cannot create in a vacuum but must be exposed to some sort of stimulus. So the role of the drama teacher is one of locating and selecting from among the available materials the ones that he or she thinks will be most effective in accomplishing the particular purpose for the session. This requires preplanning, but not of the entire lesson.

Another term widely used throughout this book is *leader*, a term we use interchangeably with the word *teacher*. For many people teacher is largely a didactic role, occupied mainly with dispensing information. No dictionary says the role of the teacher is that of standing in front of a group of children and talking *at* them. Yet, this is a too common picture, among those in the profession and outside it. This role is not congruent with the goals of drama, or the philosophy of whole language. Becoming a spontaneous drama leader requires some abilities different from those customarily used when teaching more conventional subject matter. These differences should become more apparent later in the book.

Throughout the book we will be talking about drama *sessions*, another purposeful change in terminology. This is used to avoid calling them lessons, for too many people bring negative connotations to the word *lesson*. Alice and her friends, in their discussion of lessons, illustrate this problem.

> "We had the best of educations—in fact, we went to school every day—" . . .
> "And how many hours a day did you do lessons?" said Alice.
> "Ten hours the first day," said the Mock Turtle: "nine the next, and so on."
> "What a curious plan!" exclaimed Alice.
> "That's the reason they're called lessons," the Gryphon remarked: "Because they lessen from day to day."
> This was quite a new idea to Alice, and she thought it over a little before she made her next remark. "Then the eleventh day must have been a holiday?"
> "Of course it was," said the Mock Turtle.
> "And how did you manage on the twelfth?" Alice went on eagerly.
> "That's enough about lessons," the Gryphon interrupted in a very decided tone. [Browne (Ill.), 1988, pp. 88–90; Weevers (Ill.), 1989, pp. 95–98]

The idea of lessons becoming shorter is pleasant to many people, for too many students are convinced that lessons are unpleasant, to be endured until escape is possible. Thus, instead of lessons, we refer to drama sessions. There are two other reasons as well.

1. There is not a specific "chunk" of material that must be covered in a given time span (a single session, a month's experience, or a year's work). The teacher does have a plan, but, as will be pointed out later, it must remain flexible so adjustments can be made as the session progresses. A higher degree of flexibility must be present than is usually possible in more academic lessons, the learning dimensions of which are all too frequently established by curriculum planners, subject matter experts, textbook writers, and the teacher in the next grade.
2. The mental "set" of both leader and students is different than in a conventional academic lesson where children too frequently "take in" whatever is presented. Admittedly, in a drama session the leader is presenting something, but only for the purpose of motivating the children. While some children invariably remember details in the material, that isn't the major goal. Confronted with a visual image, an aural message, or a tactile sensation, children draw from within themselves responses and reactions. They select the most appropriate of these, playing them out while

interacting with other children doing the same thing. If, after using the material in a session, children do remember details of names, occurrences, and sequences, this is a dividend, not the purpose of the session.

INTERPRETING VERSUS IMPROVISING

To some the term *improvising* seems a cumbersome way to say "act out." Frequently teachers respond by saying, "But I do that all the time in my reading classes." However, there is a rather subtle distinction between interpreting a story and improvising one.

It is true that many elementary school teachers make extensive use of interpreting literature in traditional reading classes. This takes many forms. It may vary from simply assigning certain children to read each of the character parts in a story to allowing a group to enact the story without using the book as a cuecard. In these activities, a crucial element is successful and accurate interpretation, enactment, or re-creation of the author's statement and intent.

For example, in working with "The Fox and the Grapes" by Heidi Holder (1981), a teacher may talk with children about how they can convey the anger of the thwarted fox and what sounds and bodily movements they can use to show this. In this case, the group is working with interpreting, not improvising.

However, when the teacher asks, "Can you imagine what might have happened if the grapes *had* fallen into the fox's paws?" *then* he or she is asking children to extend, extrapolate, enrich the basic materials with ideas of their own. This, then, is the point at which one moves from interpreting to improvising and begins doing spontaneous drama with children.

Perhaps another example will clarify the distinction. Allowing children to choose parts and read a story as they want is doubtlessly valuable. In such a story as "The Midas Touch" by Eleanor Farjeon and William Mayne (1965), children revel in impersonating the greedy king and his pathetic daughter. But too often teachers, even though they may sense that children are learning from such an experience, would probably move to more practical considerations. The results of such impersonation wouldn't be tangible enough. The problem of teaching for tangible results has intensified recently as dissatisfied adults have clamored for more teaching of "basics."

Creative improvisation is the major emphasis in dramatics. It is defined here as entirely different from interpretation, as it involves going *beyond* the basic material. Taking the theme of the Midas Touch story, there are a variety of possible questions to which children could easily respond.

- Why do you imagine the king was so greedy? What might have made him this way?
- How did his daughter happen to be so sweet, having been raised alone in the castle with her father as an example?
- How did the king react to other people? (You will recall that in the story we do not see him interacting with other people.) What do you think he was like to his servants? The people of the town?
- In what other ways could he have solved his problem?

Children would enjoy improvising these ideas. The teacher might use some of these questions to stimulate discussion, others to encourage children to "act out" their responses and to create other episodes that could occur before, during, and after the basic story. For other ideas about using this story, and 18 others, see the very fine *Improvisation with Favorite Tales*, by Ruth Beall Heinig (1992) in which this respected drama leader gives suggestions about how to move from literature into dramatizing. Each unit on a story includes pantomime and verbal activities, organized helpfully into those for solo and for paired or group playing.

No matter what specific questions the teacher uses to begin a session, he or she easily could move from interpretation to improvisation and provide an experience in spontaneous drama for children. In essence the teacher asks children to draw from within themselves ideas, thoughts, feelings, and conclusions based on, but not found in, the basic material.

Another incident illustrates the essential difference between the processes. Recently, while working with a group of students on the poem "The Sandhill Crane" by Mary Austin (Sutherland, 1976), we were thinking together about the words and examining what ideas the word *scuttle* brought to our minds. We tried scuttling, some on stomachs stretched flat on the floor, some as small four-legged animals moving rapidly in ways the word suggested to them. Soon one of the students commented that minnows wouldn't scuttle in many different directions, but would rather travel in a school until something made them "scuttle away in fear," as the poem describes it. Another girl suggested she could be a stone, and another student could throw her into the midst of the school of fish. This idea appealed to the group, and so they formed a compact school swimming on their stomachs across the room until the girl who was the stone was "thrown" into their midst. Then such a scuttling was seen!

The students had developed the idea beautifully and, in addition, provided an example of how to build an incident spontaneously. None of this was included in the poem; the minnow is only one of the small animals mentioned incidentally by the poet as she built upon the idea of fear. Yet, since our goal was not simply literal interpretation of what was there, but rather *improvisation*, which is the essence of drama, we decided it was well worth the time to act out the scuttle incident. The same students began to create ideas based on the poem but not found in it, as they saw there were endless suggestions within the bounds of this simple poem, as is indeed the case with any bit of motivational material.

Dramatics Is Not Theatre

One aspect of creative or improvisational drama must be emphasized at this point. Though dramatics may lead into creative theatre by children, it is a completely separate entity. There should be no intent, for example, that simple improvisation on a new ending for a favorite fairy tale lead into a fully costumed and lighted adaptation of a scripted play for parents. Children may eventually mature from simple spontaneous creation of a new character in the story *Stone Soup* by Marcia Brown (1947) (see Figure 1.4) or John Warren Stewig (1991) to authorship of a new version of Cinderella. But if that does occur, it must be because of the children's desire to do so. The leader, in fact, must be constantly wary to succumb to neither his or her own need nor that of the principal or PTA president to mount a production for an audience.

Sometimes a semi-finished play does evolve based on the poem or story introduced by the leader. When this happens naturally, as an expression of interest by the children, there are additional learnings that occur as the sessions progress in this direction. It is, however, imperative that leaders continually examine their own motivations to make sure that it is the children's ideas that are making a formal "play" seem important.

An excerpt from Louise Fitzhugh's *Harriet the Spy* will be useful in helping children understand what drama is, and what it is *not*. The short, ten-page excerpt (pp. 248–258) is the section where Miss Elson is announcing the necessity to plan the children's part in the Christmas pageant. The section represents Fitzhugh at her funniest: The despair of Harriet, Sport, and Pinky when the children line up behind Beth Ellen's inane suggestion that they should all be part of the Christmas dinner, is quintessential Fitzhugh. "In a minute they would all be assigned to be things like giblet gravy" (p. 251). Events only get worse when they go to Miss Berry, the dance teacher, whose job it is to transform them into things like a bowl of cranberries. The selection is included in *The Random House Book of Humor for Children*, selected by Pamela Pollack and illustrated by Paul O. Zelinsky (1988). Ramona's dramatic play is equally funny in an excerpt from *Beezus and Ramona* by Beverly Cleary, also included in this collection. After Beezus reads her "Hansel and Gretel," Ramona role plays being Hansel, leaving a trail of cracker crumbs across the living room floor. Later, disaster strikes

FIGURE 1.4. Marcia Brown's *Stone Soup* (1947) is an old tale that can easily be pantomimed in several short scenes. The villagers, because of their selfishness, push sacks of barley, lower buckets of milk, spread old quilts, hang meat in cellars, and perform other activities in an effort to delude the soldiers.

when a terrible rubbery smell proves to be Ramona's doll's head, in a birthday cake for Beezus in the oven. The reason? Ramona was being Gretel and pushed her doll (the witch in the story) into the oven! This is a convincing example of a child getting caught up in an exciting story and enacting it on her own. It's a contrast with the teacher's misunderstanding of play-giving in the excerpt by Fitzhugh.

QUALITIES OF SPONTANEOUS DRAMA

There are several qualities of spontaneous drama that are unique. A brief introduction will be given here, and more complete explanations will follow in Chapter 2.

Spontaneous drama is *inclusive*. This means all children can participate. Because the emphasis is not on preparing finished productions for performance, all children in a group should be encouraged to take part, regardless of the amount of "skill" or lack of it they show. We do this through the strategy of simultaneous playing, setting up many small groups that involve children all at once. McCracken and McCracken (1987) comment that "many children need assistance in beginning dramatization and . . . [it is] helpful to have the class as a whole practice being a single character. Inhibition is lost in the crowd" (pp. 66–67).

Spontaneous drama is *ongoing*. The drama leader does have a purpose in mind for each session, but because the emphasis is on the *process* and not on the *product*, if a particular purpose is not accomplished in one session, it may be accomplished in a later session.

Spontaneous drama is *recurring*. Several elements prevail during all drama experiences, whether they involve kindergarten children ferociously stomping around their room as monsters when dramatizing part of Maurice Sendak's *Where the Wild Things Are* (1963) (see Figure 1.5) or a group of teenagers tensely enacting a drug-use problem as in S. E. Hinton's *That Was Then, This Is Now* (1971). In drama, participants work at varying times with mood, plot, conflict, characterization, rhythm, unity, and dialogue. These drama elements are of concern no matter what the stimulus material may be.

Spontaneous drama is a *process*. While there are some definite, though different, advantages to be gained from involving children of any age in formal play production, the teacher is aware that this process is unlike the spontaneous drama process. Spontaneous drama emphasizes the children being involved in expressing their reaction to a stimulus material, not in presenting something finished for an audience.

Figure 1.1 at the beginning of this chapter summarizes some major

FIGURE 1.5. Exploring the movement of characters from a story is one way to begin simple enactments. Here children are being the monsters in Maurice Sendak's *Where the Wild Things Are* (1963).

distinctions between the two related but different art forms we have been considering

PSYCHOLOGICAL VALUES OF DRAMATICS

Many other writers have described effectively and at some length the social and emotional values that accrue when children do drama on a regular basis (Hoetker, 1969). Almost all of the books mentioned include a rationale for establishing dramatics as part of a child's education. An early pace-setter, Geraldine Siks (1958) presents a very readable, convincing statement of the values of drama. It can be read for the humane approach it expresses and the confidence in children it exudes. Sadly, this consummate belief in the ability of children to draw ideas from within themselves is not universal among teachers. The grade-oriented college students we encounter in classes are unwitting witnesses to elementary school experiences with teachers too often more interested in "putting in" rather than in "drawing out."

While the Siks book is but one of several basic books dealing with creative drama, it is mentioned because the author describes at length the following values that children develop when they are involved in a drama program:

1. Confidence and the ability to express themselves creatively
2. Positive social attitudes and relationships
3. Emotional stability
4. Bodily coordination
5. A philosophy of life (wonderment about the individual ways of living)

As explained previously, a child's *creativity* can be developed by exposure to drama. Several people have called for the need to encourage creativity, identified the means of doing so, and described the conditions necessary for encouraging creativity (May, 1975). Such empirical studies as the one by Schmidt, Goforth, and Drew (1975), done with matched groups of kindergarten students, have demonstrated conclusively that children's creativity can be enhanced through creative drama.

An important social value developed by dramatics is *teamwork*, which is the very heart of drama (Yawkey et al., 1981). As a child works with other children, he or she learns to modify ideas, plans, and thoughts as a result of exposure to the ideas, plans, and thoughts of others (Barsky & Mozenter, 1976; Bolton, 1980). The teacher encourages this interaction, as children discover that the group, with candor and impartiality, exerts the discipline necessary for effective playing.

Drama also provides children with healthy channels for the *expression of emotions*. When working *on* ideas in drama, a child can also work *out* frustrations, fears, and inhibitions that ordinarily must be kept in during more conventional school classes. Seeing that characters in motivational materials share some common problems can encourage a child to be more open in expressing feelings.

The leader must be aware, however, of the necessity to protect a child whose emotional problems are too intense for exposure to the group. Teachers should never see themselves as therapists or the drama session as a catharsis or therapy that will help a disturbed child. Drama is considered a language art, and its purpose as described here is to develop communication abilities. While some highly trained psychologists do use role playing (in ways similar to drama) to achieve therapeutic ends, this is different from informal drama in the classroom (Boyd, 1975). So, if during a session a child reveals severe emotional problems, the teacher should work with the school psychologist or other professional personnel in providing individualized help for the child, apart from the drama experiences in the classroom. Jennings (1987) comments further on this issue.

Drama also provides for the development of *reasoning powers*. As children analyze the appropriateness of what has been done in the session, they begin to evaluate, formulate alternatives, and develop the ability to choose the most appropriate of the alternatives.

All the abilities mentioned above are crucial, but because they have been so well explicated elsewhere by other writers, they will not be developed more fully here. A unique aspect of dramatics—the *language learning* that this art form can foster—is the focus of this book and is described in detail in Chapter 4.

In what ways might drama be included in elementary classrooms? The answer to that question is determined largely by the type of classroom. In traditional classrooms, teachers interested in drama often incorporate it as a separate strand, often part of the reading/language arts program. But in the last five years, more and more teachers have been moving from traditional ways of working with children, into more innovative language and literature-based approaches, which are often called whole language. Because this term is frequently used imprecisely, to mean different things to different people, it is critical to describe what this approach to teaching involves.

WHAT IS WHOLE LANGUAGE?

Philosophy, Not a Method

Kenneth Goodman (1986), the best known proponent of this approach, states that "whole language is firmly supported by four humanistic-scientific pillars. It has a strong theory of learning, a theory of language, a basic view of teaching and the role of teachers, and a language-centered view of curriculum" (p. 26). It reverses the "bottom-up" theory of reading instruction that has been in vogue for so many years. It concentrates on the "whole" picture of language and views it as a total system comprising several components. Linguists have long pointed out that when children first enter school, they do so with a basic understanding of this system. They understand stories, speak in sentences, and possess a large vocabulary on which to base future learning. It is therefore sensible to capitalize on this knowledge and immerse children in all the facets that make language an entity. Linek (1991) regards literacy as "valuing what children already know and immersing them in all aspects of community—they learn by doing" (p. 125).

Students and Authentic Uses of Language

Concrete examples of authentic uses of language include using experience stories and hands-on projects to write stories. Multisensory involvement in such activities is a ready-made vehicle to convert such experiences into written language. Children naturally accept the fact that their words can be recorded on paper and read by themselves and others. Their words will have personal meaning and give them ownership of their written stories.

There is an abundance of children's books available today that are rich in vocabulary, language, and culture. Whole language experiences abound in this literature, in contrast to basal texts, which are too often written with contrived, watered down vocabularies. The question is not "*Should* one use children's literature as a basis for learning language?" but rather "*Which* stories from children's literature should be used?" According to Meek (1990), "Literacy emerges in print rich environments" (p. 3).

Changing Teacher Roles

When teachers begin using whole language methods of teaching, they no longer depend on basal reading texts to provide opportunities for children to learn to read. Instead they become language facilitators, providing and making accessible a multitude of reading materials for children to use. The gamut runs from storybooks to cereal boxes to beginning dictionaries to telephone directories to anything else in between. A variety of methods of seeing words in print make children aware of the many places that language is used in today's world.

The teacher's role shifts from knowledge "dispenser" to knowledge "provider" in a whole language classroom. Teachers develop flexible activity centers, use thematic units, involve students in authentic speech and literacy events, and assist them in selecting appropriate activities for learning language. The teacher becomes a professional decision maker instead of following programmed "teacher questions" from a basal reading manual. The teacher applies methodology to fit the immediate situation and becomes a support person encouraging students to take more responsibility for their own learning (Watson, 1989).

Where Drama Fits

Wells (1990) states, "Although actual acts of reading and writing are necessarily individual, the context in which such acts occur is always inherently social" (p. 13). Creative drama is a perfect vehicle for enhancing language development. Children as young as three years of age very naturally act out a variety of roles when playing "house" or "cops and robbers" or "shopping." Such experiences involve all the senses and the use of real language. Pretending needs a basis from which to begin, and the most immediate role models are other people in their lives: older siblings, parents, TV characters, among others. Children are extremely observant and reflect what they see and hear in re-enacting snippets of the real world in their particular environment.

The continuation of this natural skill works well in school. Children must be encouraged to participate in dramatizing characters and events, while utilizing fully the vocabulary and language skills they inherently possess. A brief brochure produced jointly by the National Council of Teachers of English and the (then) Children's Theatre Association of America (n.d.) states that "informal classroom drama helps participants develop improved skills in reading, listening, speaking, and writing." Whether from real life or children's literature, drama enhances understanding of the way language works, thereby emphasizing the essentially social nature of literacy. Pearson (1989) states that "the goal in whole language curricula seems to be to eliminate the gap between school literacy tasks and real world literacy tasks" (p. 234). Monson and Pahl (1991) state it another way: "Learning is a process of meaning making and problem solving" (p. 52). Creative drama is an important means of assisting teachers in accomplishing this purpose.

SUMMARY

The purpose of this brief introduction to the nature of informal classroom drama, the terminology involved, and the values children derive from such experiences was to interest you in providing drama experiences for your students. You can provide such experiences for children, whether you work in a traditionally organized classroom or use one of the variations of whole language approaches with which teachers are experimenting. The purpose of Chapter 2 is to detail more completely the scope of informal drama experiences for children.

RELATED READING

Berghammer, G., Federlein, A. C., & Nielson, L. (1991). *Developmental drama: The curricular process for pre-kindergarten–grade 6*. Des Moines: Iowa Department of Education.

It is possible to select a topic, such as pantomime, movement, or story drama, and follow it through this guide, moving, for example, from the identification of general objectives and learner outcomes in pantomime (p. 15) to later development of specific lists of suggested activities (p. 44), and then on to examples of these embedded in actual lesson plans (pp. 51–66). The opening philosophical statement points out the need for teachers to see drama in two ways: first, as an expressive art form in its own right and, second, as a means of achieving outcomes in subject matter areas. The authors identify critical themes (i.e., critical thinking, problem solving, literacy, and socialization), which the guide develops. This is made more practical for teachers attempting to use drama, through the contrasting examples of traditional approaches and creative drama provided in each of these four themes. Appendix A is a glossary of terms, especially useful for those classroom teachers with minimal or no technical theatre/drama background, and Appendix B directs readers to other print materials about drama. Appendix C documents that many states are generating curriculum guides in drama.

Courtney, R. (1989). Culture and the creative drama teacher. *Youth Theatre Journal, 3*(4), 18–23.

In this final of a series of four articles, Courtney brings what he has learned from years of observing drama as used in many different cultures into the context of the drama teacher in schools today. Beginning with his awareness that he was not a member of the native or tribal group he was observing, he extends this to the teacher in school, who must be aware that many minority children fail in "programs designed by whites." The author points out that participating in drama transforms children from who they are into who they wish to be, but that this varies with culture. Most teachers' expectations are culture bound, and children who do not conform to these expectations are liable to fail. Therefore, teachers working with minority children must re-evaluate their expectations, while at the same time trying to meet institutional expectations. Many inner city teachers work in situations in which the wide variety of children coming to them don't share common cultural milieus that provide them with a shared way of perceiving the world, including even what roles they may take in a drama. Courtney says that the first task, then, is to find out what cannot be done in the class. To do this, teachers must understand the fundamental differences among the cultures of the children they teach.

Feistritzer, P. (1979, May). Entering the world of children. *Momentum*, pp. 11–23.

Drama as it could be—integral, not peripheral—to education, is described in this article telling of the work of the Austrian philosopher Dr. Rudolph Steiner. In the Waldorf schools, numbering 165 around the world, based on his ideas, the arts of storytelling and creative drama are basic. In addition to their use in language arts and history, they are part of the content and methods of science and math. A class may spend as much as eight weeks (daily classes) on a single story, as the teacher uses the material to challenge curiosity and aid concentration. Children use drama techniques to illustrate, among other things, grammatical concepts. Another part of this experience is Eurthmy, a language of gesture originated by Steiner.

Gourgey, A. F., Bosseau, J., & Delgado, J. (1985). The impact of an improvisational dramatics program on student attitudes and achievement. *Children's Theatre Review, 34*(3), 9–14.

This chapter mentioned the effects of drama on student attitude, and this article reports the results of a drama program for economically disadvantaged elementary school children, comprising 150 black and Hispanic students. The Arts Alternatives Program emphasizes improvisational drama, including role playing as well as story making and play writing. Student responses to seven different aspects of attitude were measured, and a teacher rating scale of children was also used; both were administered as a pretest in October and as a posttest in May. Significant gains in attitude were reported, from both students and teachers.

Hornbrook, D. (1992). Can we do ours, Miss? Towards a dramatic curriculum. *The Drama/Theatre Teacher, 4*(2), 16–20.

In this article, the author takes on many of the tenets commonly held about creative drama, seeing them as the "worst characteristics of . . . [a] progressivist legacy" (p. 16). He says that in casting aside learning about theatre, important drama leaders like Heathcote, Way, and Slade have focused on the child development aspects of informal drama, emphasizing psychological growth and particularly the development of a particular system of values. Hornbrook sees in recent drama teaching the propagation of ideological views and a covert conformism fostered by a fruitless distinction between drama and theatre. Part of a drama curriculum must be knowledge, skills, and understandings about drama as a discipline. The kind of undirected re-exploration by students of the "televisual conventions" they know, doesn't lead to deeper understanding of the nature of drama/theatre. In closing, Hornbrook points out that music and dance educators commonly use a tripartite structure of composition, performance, and appreciation. He feels drama teaching will only grow stronger as it adopts this way of thinking about curriculum. This author has expanded on his point of view in *Education in Drama* (1991). Read this source for a different way of thinking about drama, in the context of comments about the same problem made by Robinson (1980).

McNamee, G. D., McLane, J. B., Cooper, P. M., & Kerwin, S. M. (1985). Cognition and effect in early literacy development. *Early Childhood Development and Care, 20,* 229–244.

The article provides useful research support for having children dramatize stories they compose. In ten different urban classrooms, nearly 200 mostly minority three-, four- and five-year-olds were involved in composing stories that teachers recorded. The experimental classes dramatized their stories, while the control groups did not. Over a period of twelve weeks the children's stories were gathered. Stories were coded for *structure*, for *dialogue* during dictation, and for *content*. At the end, the experimental students: (1) composed stories of greater complexity and coherence, (2) were more aware of the writing process, and (3) participated in composing at a more sophisticated level. The authors conclude: "Dramatization of stories enhances the storytelling of preschool children, and thus influences their literacy development" (p. 243).

Rice, D. R., & Sisk, P. F. (1980). Teaching elementary science through creative dramatics. *School Science and Mathematics, 80,* 61–64.

Approaches to learning in most schools rely almost entirely on logical and analytical thinking. Research suggests this approach develops only the left hemisphere of the mind, the verbal, analytical, and propositional specialist, and neglects the right hemisphere, the spatial and imaginal specialist. Yet the right hemisphere can simultaneously process and remember more information than the left. In addition, the learning and memory of linguistic materials processed and stored in the left hemisphere can be significantly increased using approaches that facilitate both the verbal and the imaginal.

Creative drama provides a balance between the two cerebral hemispheres. Use of drama is predicated on the idea that material is not really learned until it influences the individual's consciousness in both thought processes and feelings. The authors show how creative drama can be used to teach the concept of phototropism in science more effectively than analytical processes generally taken. Not only can dramatics produce such positive effects as stimulating the imagination, but it also can be used to translate material laws of science because the child relates intellect content to his or her own feelings.

Schattner, R. (1967). *Creative dramatics for handicapped children.* New York: John Day.

Formal drama is different from creative drama. Nonetheless, some teachers are interested in doing play production with children. Despite its title, this book is about more formal play making. The author describes plays and musical revues developed with handicapped children as examples of what they can do with music, dance, song, speech, and poetry. The plays emphasize active participation in a developmental and group experience. The methods used in dramatic production are outlined, and suggestions are given for introducing and organizing a play with attention to the significant role of the teacher and the rehabilitative value of the experience for the children. Although terminology in educating exceptional children has changed since this book was written, the drama material remains of interest.

Smith, E. C. (Ed.). (1972). Drama and the schools: A symposium. *Elementary English, 49*, 299–306.

This article consists of three papers by different authors, representing an overall, broad view of drama and education. One author provides broad goals for a "theatre in education" program, including aesthetic, pedagogical, and psychological values. The theatre can bring enjoyment, expression, and the actual aesthetic experience. Pedagogical benefits include four classes of information learned from plays, namely, the content of plays, conventions of the theatre, cultural learning, and ethics. Psychologically, the child can learn behavior from plays. Another author identifies five developmental behavior patterns that should result from dramatic activities for children. Impression behavior results from lessons based on the five senses. Expression behavior includes control of voice and body. Communicative behavior shares thoughts or feelings. Social behavior includes role playing in order to identify with other people. Creative behavior is shown by fluency, flexibility, originality, and elaboration. In education, the professional theatre company can provide plays, workshops, and inservice training. A third author lists fifteen attitudes shared by the educator and the theatre professional. For example, there are illuminating similarities between the teacher–student relationship and the actor–audience relationship.

Williamson, P. A., & Silvern, S. B. (1986, October). Eliciting creative dramatic play. *Childhood Education*, pp. 2–5.

This describes in detail procedures used in one teacher's second/third-grade classroom, in which children are regularly encouraged to dramatize stories they have heard read aloud or read themselves. The rationale for this is that "they are no longer just hearing words, they are re-creating events" (p. 4). The authors give very practical comments (i.e., the wisdom of beginning small, with a few of the most advanced children, allows the novice teacher to master the techniques of leading such informal drama more easily than attempting it all at once with an entire group). The comments about moving from a very directive to a more nondirective stance will also be useful for beginners. After children understand the procedures involved, they can move from familiar stories that are easier to dramatize, into unfamiliar ones that require more skill.

RELATED CHILDREN'S BOOKS

Bond, Felicia. *The Halloween Performance*. New York: Harper & Row, 1983.
Although the book you are reading is about informal, classroom-based drama, children's writers have done many very funny accounts of more formal play giving. This picture book by Bond is one example. Young Roger mouse is the hit of this small play, shown in simple language and engaging, full-color pictures.

Butterworth, Nick, and Mick Inkpen. *The Nativity Play*. New York: A Dell Picture Yearling Book, 1991.
Harking back to a simpler era when it was permissible to do religious plays in schools, the authors show young Tracy, who is to be an angel, and Sam, to be a shepherd. There are no major problems here, just a wry look at how everyone's nativity play was done. Sam, "with enough striped towels he'll look just like . . . " (a real shepherd). The wise man "with the bath salts" (frankincense). There are minor problems: One of the shepherds is in the bathroom when he should be on stage; the door the wisemen are to enter through sticks shut, and the three-boy camel has trouble walking up the stairs to the stage. Despite these minor inconveniences, everybody has a good time enacting this well-known story. The pleasantly pastel watercolors show the children and adults with good humor.

Byars, Betsy. *The Cybil War*. New York: Viking Press, 1981.
"Being Ms. Indigestion" is a very funny chapter in which Young Simon fears that he will be cast as the Swiss cheese in the nutrition play. "The thought of himself in a yellow box full of holes made him miserable" (p. 3).

Cohen, Miriam. *Starring First Grade*. New York: Greenwillow, 1985.
An equally funny story features human characters enmeshed in giving a play, which the play giving nearly results in best friends Jim and Danny becoming enemies! In the end, Jim, in his part as the river, saves the day.

Goffstein, Brooke. *An Actor*. New York: Harper & Row, 1987.
On a serious note, in a book for all ages, the author distills into almost cryptic language the tasks a performer must accomplish, for example, "I will relax, emptying my mind of everyday thoughts."

Holms, Barbara Ware. *Charlotte Shakespeare and Annie the Great.* New York: Harper & Row, 1989.

Consistently funny throughout, this features the sixth-grade playwright and her best friend, a shy and talented kid thrust into being the lead in the play. When Annie overcomes her shyness, and the other kids begin to ignore what Charlotte has to say about her own play, she must deal with not being the center of attraction.

Jane, Pamela. *Just Plain Penny.* Boston: Houghton Mifflin, 1990.

In this book for intermediate grade readers, Penny livens up her summer by writing and putting on a play. The kids in the cast have ideas of their own about the characters they play, and in the process melodramatic Penny discovers the difference between real and invented drama.

McCully, Emily Arnold. *The Evil Spell.* New York: Harper & Row, 1990.

Young animal characters are used by this author to deal humorously with the serious problem of stage fright. Edwin bear's family theatre troupe does all the jobs from designing sets to operating the lighting. But Edwin yearns for a star part until he discovers that there are pitfalls to being the center of attraction. His family helps him conquer his stage fright, ending in a performance that "was magical."

McCully, Emily Arnold. *Speak Up, Blanche!* New York: HarperCollins, 1991.

A family of bears run the Farm Theatre, writing the plays, acting in them, selling tickets, and all the other tasks associated with a performance. A former actress, Eva the sheep, returns with her granddaughter, Blanche, who is "stagestruck." The problem is that shy Blanche never speaks above a whisper, and, despite the bears' good-natured efforts, they cannot help her out of her shyness. Unfortunately, they overlook her only talent, exemplified by her omnipresent sketchbook. When she finally gets angry enough over their ignoring her talent, Blanche asserts herself, and the bears discover to their delight that they have a talented scene designer in their midst. Now the actors will have sets worthy of the plays they perform. The watercolor wash paintings are defined by a thin black ink line.

CHAPTER 2

The "What" of Spontaneous Drama

In ancient Greek tragedies, a character called the Prologue appeared on stage before the play began, to describe briefly the action to come. The purpose was to capture the audience's attention, informing them of what was to follow. In a way, the purpose of Chapter 1 was the same. Now that you have been introduced to informal classroom drama, the purpose of this chapter is to detail more completely some aspects of drama you will need to know in order to lead drama sessions with your students. We'll begin with the components of the drama session.

COMPONENTS OF SPONTANEOUS DRAMA

The Material

To motivate the drama session, the leader should select material that appeals to children's senses.

A. The teacher may use part of a story or a poem. Read such prose selections as "Rats on the Roof," by James Marshall (1991). In using prose selections, be aware of the need to condense and simplify, for most of them are too long to be used in their original form. Pare the story down to the "bare bones" of the plot to bring it to manageable length for playing. Or the teacher might use a poem, perhaps such as the following:

SOME ONE

Some one came knocking
    At my wee, small door;
Some one came knocking
    I'm sure-sure-sure;
I listened, I opened,
    I looked to left and right,
But nought there was a-stirring
    In the still dark night;
Only the busy beetle
    Tap-tapping in the wall,
Only from the forest
    The screech-owl's call,
Only the cricket whistling
    While the dew-drops fall,
So I know not who came knocking.
    At all, at all, at all. (Frank, 1982, p. 11)

B. The leader may use a visual stimulus of some nature, for example, art reproductions (Walt Kuhn's *White Clown*), objects (a mask borrowed from a historical society or a piece of Mexican sculpture), or photographs, such as the one shown in Figure 2.1, taken from Leavitt and Sohn's (1985) book.
C. The teacher may use the sense of touch, for example, having children interpret, through movement, the surface textures of a piece of wood, corduroy, glass, corrugated cardboard, or tweed.
D. The sense of smell could be used by giving the children paper cups filled with such unfamiliar spices as cumin, savory, and chervil, and letting them smell these and pantomime their thoughts about the spices. Naturally, actual odors are preferable to imagined ones, and children easily create impromptu scenes built around imagined characters' reactions to olfactory stimulation.
E. Even the sense of taste, perhaps the least utilized avenue of learning, may be used to evoke a dramatic response among children. By using such a simple taste as that of a lemon, for example, teachers can give children an opportunity to react. Other suggestions about this sense are given by VanTassel and Greimann (1973, pp. 46–68).
F. The children's choice of topic, plot, characters, or type of conflict may be used. Experienced drama leaders, knowledgeable about their group's strengths and weaknesses, interests, and previous background, often can use a group's thinking as a material (Hodgson, 1981, p. 242). Through

FIGURE 2.1. *Look, Think and Write*, by Hart Day Leavitt and David A. Sohn (1985), is a modestly priced paperback full of black and white photographs like this one that provide motivation for character interpretation.

judicious questioning, such a leader—without using the types of materials listed above—can help a group fashion a drama. This technique is best delayed, however, until a leader feels very confident

These, then, are the *sources* of material to which the teacher may turn in preparing drama sessions. But what should teachers do with these basic sources?

The Discussion-Questioning Segment

After exposing children to the motivation, and indeed sometimes *as* this is going on, discussion occurs. This kind of exchange is spontaneous, unplanned, but directed by the leader through questioning.

Lead off with such questions as the following (keyed to the examples given in the preceding section):

A. Do you have any clues in the poem as to who the caller might have been? Do we know anything about the owner of the house? How could this have ended differently—for instance, if the caller had waited?
B. What are some words we could use to describe the expression on the boy's face (in Figure 2.1)? Does the picture give you some indications of what the situation is? What do the boy's clothes tell you about him? Do you get the feeling he may be from another country? Or do you think the picture may be old?
C. What does the surface of the material feel like? Is it regular? If not, do the irregularities form a predictable pattern? By using your body in recurring up-and-down movements, could you represent the contrast between the two levels of the corduroy?
D. What do they smell like? Are they pleasant? If so, why? In what sorts of places might you encounter an odor like this? What types of people could be there? What things could they be doing?
E. Who might be tasting this? Where could they be? Why might they be alone? What could have happened before this to lead the person to want to taste the lemon? What could happen after he or she tastes the lemon?
F. What have you been thinking since our last session that might make a good drama? Do you have a topic we could work on that we haven't used yet? Can you think of an intriguing character we could build a scene around? Are there some things that happened last session that we could redevelop differently today?

Remember that these are simply sample questions designed not to be followed prescriptively by a teacher interested in emulating what is described here but rather only as *examples*. The world is crammed with motivations. The only problem is to open yourself to the motivation and develop the ability to ask sensitive questions about it, questions that will in turn help children to open up! A particularly effective sample of teacher-generated questions about a motivation is provided by Goodridge (1970, p. 32).

Similarly, there is no *one* right answer to the questions. You will notice that although this book is full of questions, no answers are provided. This is because the teacher's primary concern is to elicit from children many responses of much variety, to get at the diversity of ideas available when working with children.

The Actual Playing of an Idea

This stage varies greatly, depending on the children's age, the amount of experience they have had with drama and their leader has had in directing it, where the lesson happens in the sequence, and the students' creativity.

Often teachers begin this segment of the lesson with preliminary "warm-up" activities. Sometimes these are simply chosen from among the many lists available and are not particularly related to the lesson. At other times they are more closely related to the main playing of the session. The decision of how closely these are related to the actual lesson material is up to the teacher. By using warm-up activities, according to one expert, "teachers will find a greater security in pre-improvisational activities than they would be able to experience if they plunged immediately into improvisation" (Shuman, 1978, p. 49).

Sometimes children will respond with movement, either representative or abstract. At other times they will pantomime (see Figure 2.2) and, with gestures and facial expressions, convey without words a thought or idea (Fisher & Terry, 1990). At still other times boys and girls will be moved to add dialogue to their playing to supplement the more basic bodily communication.

FIGURE 2.2. These students are doing a mirroring exercise, which increases concentration and observation skills. A key to success in this preliminary "warm-up" activity is to insist it be done very slowly.

The above variations are not to be thought of as stages, for if they are progressive at all, it is only in a very rough way. Although it does seem that dialogue is among the last of the dramatic elements to appear, groups and individuals will make use of one or several of these possibilities at different times, depending on both the type of motivation used in a particular session and their response to it at a certain moment.

Evaluation

There are basically two different types of evaluation in creative drama: concurrent and terminal.

Concurrent Evaluation. This kind of evaluation includes teacher evaluation and group evaluation. As the teacher observes children working, he or she notes which children are successful in capturing an idea and conveying it, and further encourages the group and individuals by commenting positively as the group works. You may make such general comments as, "My, I see so many dogs, and they *are* being very different," or "I can really feel the heaviness in your bodies—it comes across well." In contrast, you may wish to make such specific comments as, "What an effective snake Billy is being," or "Mary's frog is moving so well."

Group evaluation occurs when the teacher senses a need to consolidate something particularly effective, wants to help the group shift direction, or simply feels the class needs a change of pace. Draw the children together, usually in close physical proximity, to encourage their participation in this transitory quiet period, as they briefly share their reactions to what has been going on. In such activities, children are using language for reflecting on what they have done. Sometimes teachers start the discussion with a very specific question: "What could we do with our legs to make them seem more like a horse's legs?" At other times leaders ask more general questions: "What did you like about what you were doing?" This phase of the session is short—rarely more than a few minutes—but it both helps children return to thinking more analytically about what they have been doing and helps change directions or make transitions to related but different activities.

Terminal Evaluation. Terminal evaluation occurs at the end of each session. On paper this looks like a logical and fairly easy thing to accomplish, but in actual practice it is not so. You may find it takes quite a while to arrive at the ability to lead this evaluation, which should be a summing up both of what has been accomplished and of what remains to be accomplished. Children and leader together discuss

1. What they did that was particularly effective
2. What was honestly attempted but did not, for one reason or another, turn out to be effective
3. What skills, ideas, thoughts, and feelings remain to be worked on during the next session

It must be emphasized that this is not the teacher evaluating the children, but the teacher and children evaluating *together* how the session went.

In both kinds of evaluation, the leader has a short- and long-term purpose. The short-term purpose is to help children focus their thinking on the specific action that was taking place, so they can evaluate it. The long-term purpose is to help them understand evaluation as a necessary part of spontaneous drama. As teachers achieve this second purpose, the boys and girls can assume more and more responsibility for their own evaluation, internalizing the procedure and making external encouragement to evaluate less necessary. Children can be brought to the point of evaluating their work by themselves as they participate in an improvisation, but it takes time and expert guidance to develop this rather sophisticated skill.

Sometimes teachers are mistakenly concerned that evaluation will stifle children's expressive abilities. Yet drama without evaluation is little more than unconsidered play. Winifred Ward (1933), the woman most responsible for introducing drama into the elementary curriculum, commented on evaluation many years ago. Her comments ring true today, despite the passage of years and changes in drama methodology.

> The criticism which follows the playing of every scene is one of the most valuable parts of the entire process of dramatization. It induces clear, logical thinking, careful character analysis, and . . . shows the teacher the exact degree of development that her class has reached. It is often severe but always good-natured; and the pupils, far from dreading criticism of their work, welcome it with eagerness. (p. 43)

A Moment to Reflect

Teachers find it helpful to arrange for a few minutes following the session to make notes for future use. Perhaps the children can work independently for a time, or the drama period might precede the children's scheduled time with one of the content specialists, like the art or music teacher. The leader will profit by having a short time to review what occurred in the session and to make some notes about what he or she wishes to try next time. Because sessions may go in directions other than planned, it is desirable to have this time to check plans against outcomes, to assess what was done and what should be tried again next time. Given the pressures faced by most classroom teachers, it is important to jot these few notes. By the time the next session comes, aspects of drama that seemed to need attention at the close of the previous session will have faded from memory, diminishing the program's effectiveness.

This, then, begins our definition of drama. It is children responding to a motivation, sometimes simply in rhythmic movement, at other times in more complex but informal playing of a theme or story. While they experience dramatics, children grow socially, emotionally, rhythmically, and intellectually. In addition, children also develop increased competency in oral language. There are four components of the drama sessions: (1) the material, (2) the discussion, (3) the playing of the ideas, and (4) the evaluation. In thinking about these ideas and in actual work with children, however, the leader must keep in mind the basic premise that drama is drawing out ideas, thoughts, emotions, and reactions from within the child. It is freeing the creative impulse children possess.

QUALITIES OF SPONTANEOUS DRAMA EXPERIENCES

Like any many-sided process in which people are involved, a simple definition of drama is impossible. To continue this process of defining, some unique *qualities* of this type of drama will be considered here. These were mentioned briefly in Chapter 1 and will be expanded upon here.

Inclusive

Perhaps one of the most distinguishing qualities of informal drama, setting it apart from other theatre activities, is its inclusiveness. Opportunity is provided for all children to participate, and a premium is placed not on the potential Barrymore or Bernhart, but rather on the ability to take an idea and react spontaneously to it. This ability is one most, if not all, children can develop.

The key word in the preceding paragraph is *opportunity*, for it is crucial that, even with very young children, drama be an opportunity, not a requirement. Teachers first make a genuine attempt to involve all children in the group, allowing timid or unresponsive students to play inanimate objects, if this gives them security. We have encountered such students frequently—from the kindergartner who preferred to be a blade of grass when the rest of us were slithering along on our snake stomachs, to the two college juniors who didn't relate to our poem about animals and preferred to be the dam in the river. We were doing Mary Austin's "The Sandhill Crane" (Sutherland, 1976), and this seemed like an original idea of their part, so they were encouraged to use it.

Although leaders work diligently to involve all children, sometimes this doesn't succeed. Since we are attempting to release creative potential and *not* simply add another compulsory subject to the curriculum, it is perfectly acceptable if a child wants to retire to a corner with a book rather than participate. Usually the eavesdropping begins quickly enough, and seeing others enjoying their involvement, the child rejoins the group. Sometimes teachers must bide their time, continuing to try to involve all students, since all can both contribute to the activity and learn from it.

Ongoing

The dramatics leader has a plan for the session. Among less experienced teachers this should be rather carefully written out to detail materials, motivation, procedures, and evaluational techniques. With more experience, this may be simply an idea of the general direction for the lesson. In both cases, however, the leader remembers that there are other sessions coming later. Although a session should not be devoid of purpose, it is by no means a failure if the exact purpose is not reached in that particular session. Provided that something of benefit occurred in the session, the teacher can be content and work with the original idea again later. Perhaps an example will clarify this.

Suppose a leader is working with the idea of mood, using the story of *Little Red Riding Hood* by Trina Schart Hyman (1983) (see Figure 2.3). The main purpose might be to help children sense the mystery of the forest and how the trees, growing closely together, allow only dimly filtered light to sift through to the narrow, rocky path beneath. Suppose, however, that in attempting to play this with children, they become fascinated with the idea of Little Red Riding Hood's character. One group became concerned with how she could be so gullible, so oblivious to obvious danger signals. So the class developed a characterization of a slightly more perspicacious Little Red Riding Hood. The devious wolf had a much more difficult job in our adapted version of the folktale, when Little Red Riding Hood took on some of the sophistication natural to the space-age children who were improvising.

The leader should not be dismayed when such deviations from the plan occur. While it is true that I intended to work on mood, it is also true that, because there is no specified material to be "covered," I could plan another session on mood later. Children too often experience curricula established by state commissions, by textbook writers, by local curriculum guides, and

FIGURE 2.3. In enacting Trina S. Hyman's (1983) retelling of the old Grimm tale, *Little Red Riding Hood*, we get interesting contrasts between the movement of an old grandmother, the little child, the wolf, and the brave huntsman. The story provides many opportunities for individual and group mimes.

by subject matter authorities—all of which specify a quantity of materials (*X*) that must be covered in a quantity of time (*Y*).

The drama program is not contained within the boundaries of *X* and *Y*. The leader can, next session perhaps, choose another story. For example, he or she can use Bernadette Watts's *Goldilocks and the Three Bears* (1984), also set in a forest, for work on mood. The leader is not bound by considerations of "finishing" something by a given time. Teachers tailor the dramatics program as they go and do not rush on to something else, fearing what the teacher next year will expect children to have learned.

Teachers need to be flexible enough to follow leads from the children. The teacher may not have anticipated such ideas in planning the session. The sensitive leader notices, however, how often this occurs. If children regularly go in directions other than those planned and accomplish purposes other than those identified, some re-examination of planning may be in order. Then consider such questions as

1. Do I have a purpose firmly enough in mind that I could describe it to someone? Or could I write it out?
2. Have I been careful enough in selecting materials to achieve my purpose? (While it is true that most materials are multipurpose, it is also true that some are better than others for particular purposes.)
3. Have I been taking enough time to communicate my purpose to the children?

Sensitive leaders are flexible enough to change directions, or purpose, during the session. However, such leaders are also aware enough to re-evaluate their own planning and teaching techniques if changes happen with regularity.

Recurring

There are certain basic recurring ideas, strands, or organizing elements that pervade drama making at any level. These are *mood, plot, conflict, characterization, rhythm, unity,* and *dialogue.* Because they recur, college students, even though they may have been in drama programs for some time, are as concerned with them as kindergarten children. Two examples, using characterization, may help. Once, while working with a group of kindergarten children, I used Grace Hallock's poem about snakes.

SNAKES AND SNAILS

Through the grasses tall and slim
All about the water's rim,

> Lie the slimy secret trails
> Of the water-snakes and snails. (Sheldon, 1966, p. 331)

We delighted in moving through the mind-created swamp grasses as threatening snakes. However, this particular group of kindergartners was ready to progress beyond simple movement to more complex characterizations, so we stopped and talked about snakes. Some questions we considered were

- Are all snakes alike?
- If not, how are they different?
- How would a heavy, fat, old rattler, steeped in the sun, move?
- How might the rattler be different from a lithe, young grass snake?
- If you were hungry, how would you move differently than if you were full of a foolish mouse dinner?

These and other questions stimulated children to think of differences, and we were on our way to a simple understanding of characterizations. If children were interested in working on this, a related poem that would be useful is "The Black Snake" by Patricia Hubbell, included in a collection of animal poems, *To the Zoo* by Lee Bennett Hopkins (1992). Large and small animals and birds are described by poets using many different styles, all illustrated in beautifully varied watercolors by John Wallner. This could lead into another language arts activity not specifically related to drama, if the teacher chose to use Seymour Simon's *Snakes* (1992) to enhance children's factual understanding. Simon writes in his usual crisp, concise style, accompanied by full-color, full-page photographs, showing a wide variety of snakes, including the emerald tree boa, island vine snake, ball python, and eyelash viper, among many others. Children will be engrossed with the factual information presented, that is, snakes are not slimy, and they can eat prey so large that it takes them hours to complete swallowing.

In one sixth-grade class we used the nonsense rhyme about the old lady so silly she swallowed a whole menagerie (Westcott, 1980). It's excellent for work on characterization. The verse begins:

> I know an old lady who swallowed a fly,
> I don't know why she swallowed a fly,
> Perhaps she'll die.

> I know an old lady who swallowed a spider
> That wiggled and jiggled and tickled inside her.
> She swallowed the spider to catch the fly,
> I don't know why she swallowed the fly,
> Perhaps she'll die.

The poem goes on in its absurd fashion, as the old woman swallows bigger and bigger creatures until the last verse:

> I know an old lady who swallowed a horse,
> She died, of course!

Ordinarily, we would consider sixth graders too sophisticated for such a poem, but in this case it proved effective stimulus for character extension. I read the poem, we laughed over it, and then we sang a version of it that the children had learned in their music class. As a warm-up exercise, we discussed and then pantomimed what she was doing before the song began. Then we began our main work and explored verbally some questions.

- What is the old lady really like?
- Was she always as silly as she is now?
- If not, what experiences might have made her the way she is?
- What kinds of problems could she have? How might she react to these problems?

After a discussion of her peculiarities, we divided into pairs of small groups. One of the groups was to invent a problem for the hungry old lady, and the other small group was to create her response to the problem, establishing their conception of her character. The questioning and improvising challenged the children to think more deeply about the woman, to expand and develop their characterization of her. In the poem she is a two-dimensional character, a silhouette set against a series of bizarre behaviors. We attempted to examine her characteristics, thoughts and attitudes, reasons for the behaviors, and responses to problems and people. In the process, we created several different versions of the old lady and could compare and contrast them. In addition, this drama session provided many opportunities for creating other characters who were involved with the old lady and her problem.[1] As a follow-up on another day we talked about how the pictures are different in the version by Dick Bantock (1989) and in one by Glen Rounds (1990).

Process

There is a danger in unnecessarily raising the dichotomy of process versus content. Yet it seems important to point out that drama is a process for

---

[1]To begin a set of experiences with this story, you might use the film "I Know an Old Lady Who Swallowed a Fly," produced originally by the National Film Board of Canada, a producer widely honored for the quality of its films. This film (6 minutes, color) is available from International Film Bureau, 332 S. Michigan Avenue, Chicago, IL 60604–4382.

elementary school children rather than a content area with specific grade or level expectations.

While it is true that for college students and teachers there is content about drama to be learned, this is less important in drama used with elementary school children. Drama is primarily a process used with many materials to evoke responses from children.

Children certainly do learn about such things as mood, plot, conflict, characterization, rhythm, and unity, but they learn about these drama techniques with any material. For example, it does not matter whether the leader uses *Snow White* by Paul Heins (1974) or *Hansel and Gretel* by Lisbeth Zwerger (1979) to develop ideas about characterization, or Jan Brett's *Beauty and the Beast* (1989) or Errol LeCain's *The Snow Queen* (1979) for mood development. If none of these interests the leader and the group, he or she may choose an entirely different story motivation—perhaps one seldom or never used before by a drama leader in developing ideas about characterization or mood.

Thus it is possible for children from two different elementary school drama programs to emerge with equally highly developed drama abilities, but without having worked with the same motivational materials.

DRAMA AND LANGUAGE GROWTH

Children who have regular drama experiences gain facility and expressiveness in many areas of language. An early experimental study by William E. Blank (1954) points out clearly some language learnings enhanced by dramatics. Blank studied three aspects of children's development: voice qualities (including articulation and tone flexibility), personality factors, and vocabulary. Using two groups of school children, one that met weekly during the school year for creative drama and one that did not, Blank administered pre- and posttests in the three areas of concern. In vocabulary and in the voice qualities he measured, Blank's experimental group showed a significant improvement over the control group. Drama had been effective in stimulating growth in voice quality and size of vocabulary.

It seems, then, that one approach to justifying creative dramatics as an integral, rather than a peripheral, part of an elementary language arts program is the possibilities it offers for growth in language. What particular aspects of language growth does drama encourage?

Vocabulary Growth

As Blank found experimentally—and drama leaders have known intuitively for some time—one aspect of language growth that drama encourages is vocabulary development (Wagner, 1979). Teachers must be concerned with this because of the crucial relationship between vocabulary development and success in school. By vocabulary development we do not mean, however, the learning of specific lists of words. We have ample evidence this is not effective. What we need to pursue is that passionate involvement with words, and the wonder at what they can do, which makes coming across an unknown word a challenge rather than a bore. Not nearly enough children leave elementary school caught up in the adventure of words.

The delight in words as objects to be explored, played with, and reveled in, which is manifested in young children, is seldom seen in adults. Somewhere along the way too many lose this sense of the wonder of words.

What is your curiosity quotient about words? Take these examples:

Have you ever felt rubicund?
Have you ever seen dehiscence?
Have you ever had a papeterie?

How many of them do you know? Do they intrigue you enough that you would like to know more about them?

How are we to get this involvement with words so that we develop adults whose curiosity is piqued by unfamiliar ones? Certainly not, as mentioned earlier, by drilling children on lists. But drama can provide one way. Much literature used as motivation for drama will result in exposure to new and unfamiliar words. Ward (1957) says that in using literature to stimulate dramatics, "the children will take hold of as much of the original language as they are able for the sound of it is fascinating to them" (p. 187).

In using drama to further vocabulary growth, the leader is concerned not with specific words to be memorized, but rather with a captivating exposure to words that will sensitize children to their "lure and lore." Several excellent examples of this are contained in the book *Push Back the Desks*, written by an experienced elementary school teacher, Albert Cullum (1967). In one example he describes his work in a kindergarten classroom.

> From my meager linen closet I sacrificed a good white sheet to make a dramatic entrance. As a roaming language arts teacher I was able to indulge in such activity. . . .
>
> There I was in the middle of the kindergarten covered with my last good sheet, in which two holes had been cut out for my eyes. I saw twenty-two pairs of eyes looking at me.
>
> "I am a friendly apparition," I slowly stated. "What's that?" asked five-year-old Tony.
>
> They all started to talk at once, of course, so I asked them to sit in a circle, and I sat in the center. I proceeded to whirl about in a flashing dervish manner and explained to them that for Halloween I was going to be a very

friendly apparition. "What do I look like?" Finally Anette guessed that I was dressed as a ghost. They then took turns wearing the large sheet and . . . flew through the kindergarten air as friendly apparitions. It was so simple for them to accept apparition as a good kindergarten word. (pp. 60–61)

This is simple dramatization—the very beginning steps—but even at this stage children take delight in responding to words.

Cullum (1967) also describes his work with older children and writes of using Shakespeare, who "may be for scholars to debate and discuss . . . but he is also for Corky, a fifth-grader who died beautifully as Julius Caesar. There are murderers galore in the elementary school ready to help Macbeth kill Banquo; many a fifth- and sixth-grade girl can readily whip up a moment of insanity as Ophelia" (p. 81).

It is one thing to let children respond with fervor to words (and it does build sensitivity to words), but do these words remain with a child? Cullum (1967) describes results achieved with kindergarten children.

It was exciting to see them go home during the school year as twenty-two eerie apparitions . . . well-trained pachyderms . . . [or] proud, snorting stallions. . . . They carried their big words home to astounded parents, grandparents, and older brothers and sisters. They were proud of their new words. Together we had added sixty new words to their speaking vocabulary. At the end of the year I devised a test to see how well they had retained their big words. Without any review, over ninety percent of the class scored one hundred. The words were still alive. (p. 65)

Though now out of print, the book remains a fresh and convincing description of drama work. It is probably still available in libraries.

In summary, what the drama leader accomplishes is to share words with children. As Lewis (1968) says so well, "the pupils are off their guard . . . and it is then that something is not learned, but absorbed through the intuitive channel" (p. 325).

In addition to this subconscious assimilation, there are other words that become part of a child's speaking vocabulary because they are closely related to creative drama. Some drama leaders use the term *sincerity*—an honest response to the motivation—which other leaders refer to as "staying in character." Leaders regularly use such terms as *environment* and *symbol*, even with young children. We talk of the *conflict* we are developing in an improvisation and discuss the *resolution* of that conflict.

Paralanguage

Another area of language growth through dramatics is paralanguage—pitch, stress, and juncture. Teachers work to help children understand pitch, the high or low sound; stress, the accent in a word; and juncture, the stops or pauses between words. Children grow to a *conscious* knowledge of how they can use this expressive overlay of language. Probably all children, except those with severe emotional and/or learning problems, *subconsciously* assimilate the basic features of paralanguage along with the other early language learning that experts unanimously tell us takes place largely before the age of six (Pflaum, 1986). Most children come to school, undoubtedly, as fully in control of paralanguage as they are of the more basic verbal symbols of language. Beyond their basic mastery, however, the school provides children with scant opportunity for conscious study and manipulation of these three elements to convey ideas more expressively.

If we listen carefully to their comments, we become aware of children's intuitive understanding of this aspect of language. One teacher of second graders was being especially precise in giving a set of directions, pausing between words. When she finished, one of the children commented, "Teacher, there are holes in your talking." Another time, in evaluating a drama session, a fourth grader commented that another child, playing the role of Grandfather Bear (a character added to an improvisation) talked with an "under-the-ground" voice. Both comments indicate boys' and girls' intuitive understanding of paralanguage. But such understanding needs to be brought to a conscious level.

Why should children learn about these language features? Linguists and other language scholars agree that they are critical factors in communication. For instance, psychologists Mehrabian and Ferris (1967) estimate that of the total impact of the message, 7% is accomplished by basic verbal symbols, while 38% is conveyed by vocal overlays of pitch, stress, and juncture—paralanguage. In addition, they estimate that 55% of the message is determined by the accompanying facial expressions called *kinesics*, which we will consider later. Apparently, only a small portion of the message is transmitted by the basic verbal symbols.

If these extra-verbal factors are so crucial in communication, then children should learn about them in order to become more effective in using language.

Examination of basic language textbooks reveals that little is done to make children aware of how they can achieve desired effects by manipulating pitch, stress, and juncture. While much is included about the correct use of *went* and *gone*, and *seen* and *saw*, little is concerned with helping children experiment with these three elements of paralanguage to become more effective speakers of English (Stewig, 1979).

What we are concerned with here is the conscious control of paralanguage to create desired effects. By motivating children to improvise dialogue for a variety of characters, dramatics helps raise to a conscious level the idea that different people speak differently.

Sometimes these learnings come up incidentally as they are related to story motivation. It is possible to have excellent sessions experimenting with voices for a particular story. In using Janet Stevens's *The Three Billy Goats Gruff* (1987) (see Figure 2.4) with young children, for example, a leader may explore such questions as

- What do you think a troll sounds like?
- Do all trolls sound the same? How does a river troll (as the one in the story is described) sound different from a forest troll? How would a cave troll sound different?
- How does a father troll sound when he is content after a filling dinner of succulent goat?
- How does a mother troll sound when she is nagging her lethargic husband to get a tender goat for dinner?

Children find such questions as these delightful. They provide an opportunity to create story line (plot) spontaneously. More important, such questions allow children to explore paralanguage, to play with and speculate upon the speech of this created troll family, and to imaginatively create trolls with their own voices. Ziskind (1976, pp. 85–96) offers other suggestions for working with this story.

At times, we stimulate paralanguage learnings purposely, as when we confront children with pictures of people and ask them to create voices and manipulate pitch, stress, and juncture to make the characters come alive. Since a picture provides only visual clues, the child is challenged to create a person using the three elements of paralanguage to augment the basic verbal symbols.

Sometimes we work with just a sentence in isolation to explore the variety of effects possible in a minimal combination of words. Given a sentence used by one of the characters in an improvisation, children can experiment to see what different connotations can be expressed by altering the stress on words. Sixth graders enjoy working with such sentences as, "My, that's a pretty green dress you have on today." A myriad of interpretations are possible.

My, *that's* a pretty green dress you have on today. (Interpretation: I like that one, but the one on the rack leaves me cold.)

My, that's a *pretty* green dress you have on today. (Interpretation: You sure wore a homely green one yesterday.)

My, that's a *pretty green* dress you have on today. (Interpretation: If it were any more green, I don't think I could stand it!)

My, that's a pretty green *dress* you have on today. (Interpretation: But you're wearing an ugly fuchsia scarf.)

My, that's a pretty green dress *you* have on today. (Interpretation: The girl beside you is wearing an outlandish turquoise dress.)

FIGURE 2.4. The contrast in animal movement makes the story of *The Three Billy Goats Gruff* particularly fine for dramatization. Help children plan movements to show differences between the three differently sized goats and the aggressive troll, here shown in an illustration by Janet Stevens (1987).

My, that's a pretty green dress you have on *today*. (Interpretation: So, at last, you've worn a pretty dress.)

Sometimes, drama teachers work with more abstract sounds than the recognizable words and paralanguage we have been discussing. Recently, we watched an experienced dramatics leader explore the abstract sounds made by the Furies that Pandora released from the box (Lisl Weil, 1986). Improvising on the basic idea, fourth-, fifth-, and sixth-grade children decided that threatening movement was not enough, so they explored such questions as

- Would each of the Furies make the same sound?
- How could the sound differ? In pitch? In constancy? In duration?
- What sound would Hope make while trying to get out the box? After it was released by Pandora?
- How would the sound made by the Furies change when they heard the sounds made by Hope?

The class worked with this idea and changed volumes, breaks, durations, inflections, and other elements to create a composition of abstract verbal sound, devoid of recognizable English words, but nonetheless conveying the conflict between the Furies and Hope. It was an exciting experience: Children, stimulated by contact with a literary form and encouraged to create using a basic idea, were learning how expressive their voices could be, even apart from conventional verbal symbols. Rather sophisticated learnings for an elementary school!

In these examples, we have seen how boys and girls can learn consciously some ideas about paralanguage that were previously known subconsciously. These ideas remain unconsidered by far too many adults. Who has not had the experience of hearing someone say, "Good morning," when the real message conveyed by paralanguage was, "All this is too much bother, and you're the cause of it!" Adults use paralanguage each day. If we can teach children to manipulate the three elements consciously, we will be teaching them to use one of the most expressive devices of a marvelously flexible language as they increase their ability to communicate.

Kinesics

Another aspect of language that children explore in dramatics is *kinesics*. Lefevre (1970) defines the term to include "all bodily gestures, nudges, nods, finger, hand and arm signals, shrugs, and facial gestures such as winks, smiles, sneers and leers—the whole gamut of expressive actions, so important in . . . interpretation and in the small events of daily life" (pp. 274–275).

Despite this, and the universal use we make of this aspect of language, kinesics is seldom a matter of much concern to the authors of elementary language series. There are, however, some useful trade books that deal with this topic (*Your Silent Language*, by Elizabeth McGough, 1974; *You Don't Say: How People Communicate Without Speech*, by Vernon Pizer, 1978). Dramatics can make up for this lack, as children examine characters in depth and work to convey their understandings through the use of extralinguistic features.

A group of fourth- and fifth-grade children recently worked with the old folktale entitled "The Stone in the Road" by Winifred Ward (1952), concentrating especially on the villagers' reaction to finding the stone in the otherwise meticulously maintained kingdom. Their leader talked with them about nonverbal means they could use to develop characterizations of the villagers. The differences in the shrugs, hand and arm movements, frowns and gestures, and other kinesics made obvious to an observer the character of the soldier, scholar, carpenter, and other inhabitants. In the evaluation following the session, children enjoyed comparing the way one child's characterization differed from another's. As they did this, the students evaluated which kinesics conveyed ideas they wanted to communicate, which needed to be modified to be more effective, and which needed more practice.

Hennings (1977) recommends conscious study of kinesics and spatial relationships. Elementary teachers who lead spontaneous drama sessions with children can begin developing an understanding and appreciation of these communication factors. Her book, now out of print but probably still available in libraries, is well worth locating, for the many useful ideas it includes.

Spontaneous Oral Composition

An even more encompassing goal than the specific ones mentioned earlier is that of encouraging growth in the child's ability in spontaneous oral composition, that is, impromptu or extemporaneous invention. We work for this goal when as drama leaders we work with plot development. Ward (1957) says that giving children experiences in "thinking on their feet" and expressing ideas fearlessly is an important concern of creative dramatics. She further notes: "When older children are asked what . . . [drama] is worth to them besides being so enjoyable, they often think first of this objective because they feel so strongly the need both for the poise which comes from being articulate and the power it gives them among their fellows" (p. 8).

One of the ways Ward (1957) suggests getting at this ability is to allow a child to give a lead sentence, for example, "The boy was uncertain about what to do now." Without allowing the child who contributed the sentence to explain it, she selects volunteers to build an impromptu scene around the lead sentence. This idea, the use of starter sentences (also called conflict lines), is further explained in Chapter 4.

Another successful way to stimulate oral composition is to use a piece of literature and present an additional problem related to it. For example:

- What would have happened if the goat couldn't get across the bridge?
- How else could Midas have solved his problem?
- What would have happened if the slipper had fit Cinderella's sister?
- Who might have come to the aid of the gingerbread boy as he rode across the river on the fox's back?
- Who else besides the knave might have stolen the queen's tarts?

Children respond easily to this type of problem and develop oral proficiency in the process.

Recently, we used this approach with third-grade children; the motivation was the Mother Hubbard rhyme that Torrance (1962, pp. 245–246) suggests as a test of creativity. The rhyme reads:

> Old Mother Hubbard went to her cupboard,
> to get her poor dog a bone.
> When she got there, the cupboard was bare,
> and so the poor dog had none. (Tomie dePaola, 1981)

The question posed to the children was, instead of simply letting the poor dog go hungry, what *else* might Old Mother Hubbard have done? Among the more inventive responses suggested, which lent themselves to playing in drama, were these:

She went to the butcher and asked for a job. He needed help, so he hired her to cut meat from the bones. At the end of the day, she got to keep the bones.

She went to the police station and got their help tracking down the thief who had stolen all the bones.

She planted a garden in which she grew many vegetables. The extra ones she sold at a stand and used the money to buy bones for her dog.

She went out begging from door to door, asking for a penny at each house. The townspeople were embarrassed to give her just a penny, so they gave her more. When she was done collecting, she had so much money she built a mansion and bought all the bones she wanted.

Since she didn't have bones, she made up some porridge, and it was so good the dog ate that instead.

As a follow-up to this experience of generating additional ideas about a story, we used John Yeoman and Quentin Blake's *Old Mother Hubbard's Dog Dresses Up* (1990) and other books in this series. It is, in picture book format, an imaginative extension of the basic poem into many other possibilities, as the dog has a variety of adventures.

Sometimes, instead of presenting a problem to children, we simply describe two people in a situation and let students create both story line and dialogue. The results are not always predictable. Children learn through their improvisation, but the revelation of perceptions for the teacher listening to the improvising may not be encouraging. We recently worked with third graders who used words, paralanguage, kinesics, and movement to create a story line about adults and children. Although the stimulus had been neutral, all of the adults were cast in repressive, controlling roles. However, the exercise was useful as it provided a way for the children to play out their feelings of powerlessness in a socially acceptable mode.

It was similarly interesting to listen to college juniors as they paired off to create spontaneous dialogue between a principal and a teacher. Their use of the elements of communication was creative, but the hidden attitudes revealed toward principals as authority figures would chill the heart of the most determined public school administrator.

Children *can* learn to become proficient in spontaneous oral composition, although this skill is slow to develop and difficult to measure. Despite the fact that oral language is a basic skill, growth in it is too seldom measured, probably because gathering and analyzing oral samples is cumbersome. Teachers who use drama with boys and girls rely more often on their intuitive awareness of oral growth. Does this growing oral ability affect a child's written expression? Does the oral facility gained mirror corresponding growth in composition? A tantalizing question—waiting for an interested researcher! Like oral growth, improvement in composition skill takes place slowly over an extended time. Analyzing written samples is a complex process and so this other basic language skill also is too seldom measured. Drama leaders infrequently have concrete evidence, of the kind provided by standardized tests, of the language growth drama encourages.

SOME USES FOR DRAMATICS IN OTHER SUBJECT AREAS

Now that we have considered at length the specific language uses of spontaneous drama, we will consider briefly other uses of drama, because dramatics is not limited to the language program. A perceptive teacher is able to see many subject areas in which to use drama. One inventive leader interested in social studies helped intermediate children to understand themselves better by working with the idea of fear, interpreting an explorer's feelings as he set foot on the white-grained edge of an unfamiliar continent. A more recent social studies problem explored through drama is described by Blair-Clough and Wheeler (1979), who recount how they turned the reality of a nuclear reactor incident into a positive learning experience. Other uses of drama in social studies are provided by Dumas (1970), in history by Murphy (1976), and in citizenship education by Juliebo (1989).

Another teacher helped children evolve sensitive rhythmic patterns based on the concept of number bases in mathematics. His group, divided into different bases, interwove, moved, split, and regrouped and then enjoyed working with the concept on paper after they had interpreted it rhythmically. Ehrlich (1974, p. 105) gives other suggestions for relating drama to mathematics content.

One music teacher interested in drama helped kindergarten children respond simply to the ebullience of a Sousa march and later led sixth graders in a sensitive response to the brooding and evocative counter rhythm in Ravel's *Bolero*. Two museum educators have described how to use drama to deepen children's responses to the visual arts, like the sculpture of George Segal (Hayes & Schindel, 1992). Doing drama in a museum is also described by Mitchell (1985).

In science, a second-grade leader used the life cycle of flowering plants to explore dramatic improvisation. He enriched the topic considerably by helping the children understand the subtle difference between larkspur and hollyhock, fuchsia and dandelion, and how to interpret what these flowers' responses might be to outside influences. The hollyhock and the larkspur responded to the wind's effect, for example, and the children understood and played the differing effects of the sun on the shade-loving fuchsia and the sun-loving dandelion. Cottrell (1984, pp. 179–180) gives additional suggestions for dramatizing science materials. Science is just one of five categories of experiences suggested by Fox (1987) in her book of methodically laid out lesson plans, which beginners in drama teaching find useful. Her lesson on solids, liquids, and gasses (pp. 82–83) is particularly well-developed.

Teachers have found opportunities to integrate drama into the school program in other areas, but these examples should make the point. While there are many applications of this art in a whole language curriculum, the ones we will focus on most are those integral to the language arts. Readers interested in other uses for dramatics in elementary school will find periodical articles on this topic listed in Chapter 6.

SUMMARY

In this chapter we have attempted to

1. Detail the diverse activities included in spontaneous drama so you may have a clearer idea of the nature of the activities this book is encouraging you to try with your children
2. Identify the many types of language growth that may take place as a result of using drama as part of your language arts program

The problem remaining now is procedural: Given a group of thirty children, how do *you*—a teacher in a self-contained classroom of average size—"do" drama? Though your experience may be limited, that doesn't mean your class can't have the benefits of regular drama experiences. If you are convinced of its values, Chapter 3 should help you learn some ways you can lead drama sessions with your boys and girls.

RELATED READING

Kase-Polisini, J. (1989). *Drama as a meaning maker*. New York: University Press of America.

A collection of articles for the determined reader, this is a wide-ranging look at not only drama, but such other things as the brain and how humans structure language. Each of the chapters—originally speeches presented at an invitational conference—is followed by a response from a drama expert. Elizabeth M. Quinn has, for example, given some very useful comments on why movement experiences are essential to the development of self-concept. Kim Morin commented on recent research that points out that imaginative play is not necessarily natural to children but "flows out of an environment that supports it" (p. 167), suggesting that we need to think about how to structure classroom environments in ways that facilitate such play, leading into drama. Marci Woodruff's comments on the importance of exploring "different ways to see, organize, react and learn life itself" (p. 179) are potentially useful to all drama leaders. Cecily O'Neill reminds readers of the importance of children transcending themselves in drama, learning in the process new ways of seeing the world. These and other of the sections will be helpful to the diligent reader.

Lewis, S. (1974). Creative drama in the treatment of emotionally disturbed children from six years of age to pre-adolescence. *Australian Occupational Therapy Journal, 21*, 8–22.

Lewis presents suggestions for implementing a therapeutic creative drama program. Some causes of emotional disturbances in children, general methods of treatment, and the value of creative drama are discussed.

Mazor, R. (1978). Drama as experience. *Language Arts, 55*, 328–333.

This article illustrates how one inner-city elementary school used improvisation to promote positive attitudes toward others. The school's student population comprised several ethnic groups that were hostile toward one another, their environment, and themselves. A drama teacher created situations in which the different ethnic groups participated. The common experiences presented problems whose resolutions demanded group coordination and sensitivity. These activities allowed students not only to confront the problems but to effect change, exert control, and experience feelings of self-worth.

Noble, G., Egan, P., & McDowell, S. (1977). Changing the self-concepts of seven-year-old deprived urban children by creative drama or videofeedback. *Social Behavior and Personality, 5*, 55–64.

Urban seven-year-old children were expected to describe more adequately their current self and self projected into the future, both verbally and nonverbally, after systematic training in creative drama (Study 1) and after videofeedback of themselves in action (Study 2). In each study ten children were randomly assigned to both experimental and control groups. Pre- and posttest self-drawings and verbal statements describing "I am" and "In 10 years I will be" were collected. Students in creative drama were significantly more aware of individual differences both for current and future self. The videofeedback experiment showed that drama students were significantly more conscious of individual differences (current self) and physical characteristics (both now and persisting in the future). References to other research about special populations and drama can be found in a summary by Campbell (1981).

Petrilli, S. (1986, Summer). Training creative drama teachers with television. *Youth Theatre Journal, 1*(1), 12–14.

This article reports on efforts to provide inservice education for teachers without previous background who are interested in doing drama. The taped classes focus on using drama with other classroom subjects; the tapes feature sixth graders, but a related workbook, describing how procedures could be adapted to other levels, was also developed. For further information on the course, which includes six, one-hour tapes, write: Gary Fisk, Communication Services, Center for Extended Learning, Governors State University, University Park, IL 60466 (708) 534–4094.

CHAPTER 3

The "How" of Creative Drama

To separate the "what" of a complex subject from the "how" of that subject is often futile and frustrating. One reason for attempting the task is to point out more clearly factors that influence the success one expects to have. To that end we will in this chapter explore how one "does" drama with children.

CHARACTERISTICS OF THE LEADER

One of the most crucial factors in drama is the leader. What are the requirements of a successful leader? Are classroom teachers likely to be good drama leaders, or should children work with someone especially trained in improvisation techniques?

Efforts to characterize the "typical" elementary school teacher usually fail, simply because of the diversity of people who teach. To characterize the successful creative dramatics leader is also difficult. Given the array of personalities who work with children, is everyone likely to be successful with drama? Probably not. What kinds of people are likely to succeed as drama leaders? Several other authors, including Heathcote (1980), have given their opinions on this question. A teacher thinking about launching a program would do well to read these authors. For our purposes here, we will discuss four characteristics that we feel are basic to a successful drama leader. These are certainly nothing new—we hope all classroom teachers possess them—but they are especially important to the teacher when he or she is leading spontaneous dramatics.

Flexibility

The willingness to abandon a previous plan when something more worthwhile comes up during a session is an important trait of the drama leader. An actual example may demonstrate why this is important.

While visiting a student teacher recently, one of us watched a group of second graders improvising about Christmas. The leader had created some situations, one of which involved a young sister who was sick on Christmas Eve. The children working with this idea attacked their challenge with dispatch, but this resulted in rather poor playing. The sister was unceremoniously picked up and lugged laboriously down the imaginary stairs. No attempt was made either to pick up the invalid gently or to deposit her carefully on the sofa once she was moved to the living room.

Basically, the idea was potentially profitable, but it failed—primarily because the student teacher was more interested in "acting-out" than in a valid improvisation. To make the lesson a success he would have had to abandon plans to hurry along to three other improvisations and, instead, turn the group's attention to such questions as

- Are there any special things we do to carry someone who is sick?
- How could we pick her up in order not to make her sicker?
- How would we arrange her on the sofa once we had carried her to it?

This changes the whole thrust of the lesson, from one of improvising superficially on several ideas created previously by the teacher to one of more spontaneous and yet more thoughtful response to questions evolving at the time. Such a change is admittedly difficult to make, especially when the leader is inexperienced. To effect such profitable changes, a teacher must listen intently and continuously for the children's ideas throughout the lesson.

Another student teacher, with less singleness of purpose, noted that children, in trimming a tree, were simply picking an endless succession of imaginary ornaments out of one hand and putting them on branches with the other. He saw that the children never unwrapped the ornaments, put hangers on them, went to a box or other sources for more ornaments, or moved a branch to find room for another ornament.

This was a discrepancy in the improvisation; although he, too, had other groups that had not yet taken part, the student teacher took time to talk with his students. He asked the students to think about all the components of the act of hanging an ornament on a tree, and they practiced these mimes together. After this simultaneous playing, the children were ready to do their improvisation again, and there was a noticeable improvement in believability.

Being flexible enough to do drama with children is a characteristic not everyone possesses innately. If a teacher did possess this characteristic, it might have been suppressed, either during student teaching or full-time teaching. The encouraging thing, however, is that this characteristic can be developed.

Ability to Listen

This leads to a related characteristic—the drama teacher's ability to listen. As teachers, we expect children to listen to us, but frequently the reciprocal nature of listening is ignored. We expound; children listen. Studies have indicated this is what children in elementary schools do most frequently throughout the school day (Anderson & Lapp, 1988). In dramatics sessions, however, teachers must listen as intently as they hope the children do. Without this listening, teachers will never hear the many comments, often fragmentary or not directed specifically to him or her, that can result in a much richer experience for children.

This does not mean changing plans willy-nilly, for this type of program would not help children learn in each area of drama. There are times when teachers hear a comment of the nature described above and simply make a mental note of it—a referent to return to later. Perhaps because of the involvement level of the children, the closeness to reaching the desired goal for the day, or the unrelatedness of the comment, the leader decides to ignore a perfectly valid comment. This is a sophisticated sifting of possibilities, the continual reordering of priorities that a drama leader does during a session. When such an ability is developed, the session takes on a flexibility leading to some valid learning experiences for children. Without such ability, the sessions may develop into the rather wooden "playlets" so often confused with dramatics. The remedy: Concentrate on the ability to listen.

This ability is related to the flexibility mentioned earlier but may be difficult to develop. Some people drawn to teaching are convergent, rule following, and noninnovative. Teacher education programs often appear to attract such individuals, people who would be too inhibited to get down on the floor with a group of children and be a snake right along with them. Few teacher education programs have a strong listening component to encourage future teachers' ability in this area. Finally, teaching in public schools—where the emphasis is on teachers talking while children listen— may interfere with teachers' listening.

Ability to Ask Stimulating Questions

Another characteristic, also related to flexibility, is the ability to ask stimulating questions. Why should the teacher need to be a questioner? Throughout this book, you will see the emphasis on the teacher's need to be a skilled questioner. To ask the right kind of questions is difficult for many teachers. Research on the types of questions teachers ask is not encouraging (see summary of research in Klein, 1988). This may be because few teachers ask questions to which they really don't know the answers. As Craig and Edwards (1992) point out, teachers must be genuinely curious when asking questions; otherwise the drama will remain superficial.

Because the art of the questioning is difficult to develop, teachers need to practice asking questions and to ask many of them before this skill is well-developed. The skilled drama leader does not ask such closed questions as: Who is Billy's friend? What happened when the father came home from work? Why couldn't Betty find the answer to her problem? These kinds of questions, as MacDonald (1986) points out, "imply that there is a single, correct response" (p. 5). Rather, the teacher should ask such provocative, stimulating questions as

- What other things could bears who had no porridge do?
- What would have happened if Cinderella's foot hadn't fit the glass slipper?
- What would have happened if Little Red Riding Hood had gotten lost in the forest and never arrived at Grandmother's house? (see Figure 3.1)

One way to learn the art of questioning is to listen carefully to children—their ability in asking questions is enviable, especially when they are young. A third-grade child, part of a class studying the Eric Metaxas version of the King Midas story (1992), thoughtfully asked how Midas could still move after the touch was bestowed: "Wouldn't his clothes turn to gold because they touched his body?" The teacher, inept at handling such intelligent and provocative thinking, had not anticipated this one and so ignored his unique question.

Certainly, this was the time to stop the lesson and encourage children to discuss their ideas about the child's question. The teacher could have let the children explore this unusual idea, suggest they compare several versions of the story to see if other versions offered any clues, or discuss with them the similarity between the Achilles' heel myth[1]—an example of a localized physical quality—and the Midas myth. Listen to the questions your children ask—then try asking similarly exciting ones.

You will be mostly on your own in practicing the art of questioning, for most school materials offer little encouragement. Questions in basal reading

---

[1]This myth is included with many others in *Gods Men and Monsters* by Michael Gibson (1982). An excellent source of the myths, the book includes watercolor illustrations that are very effectively done with a delicate ink line that provides much detail.

FIGURE 3.1. Beatrice Schenk de Regniers's *Red Riding Hood* (1990) is another version of the old tale recommended in Chapter 2. You could have children compare and contrast these watercolor and ink line illustrations by Edward Gorey with those by Trina Schart Hyman.

materials, for example, are too frequently banal and literal. There are, however, some books devoted solely to questioning. The inexpensive paperback by Sanders (1966), though old, remains very helpful.

Another suggestion, related specifically to questions in drama, might be of help. Select a poem you enjoy from one of the poetry anthologies like Sutherland and Livingston (1984). It is probably simpler to begin using a poem because of its shorter length. Ask some motivational questions about it related to the images in the poem or about images only suggested by the poem. After you have created some questions, analyze them. Ask yourself:

1. Do they go beyond the literal level?
2. Do they capitalize on the material that is included?
3. Are they open-ended, so children can do more than one thing in responding to them?
4. Might the questions stimulate children to ask more questions themselves?
5. Do they utilize "cues" in the poem that are not expanded upon by the poet?

To illustrate this, we took the following poem by Virginia Brasier and wrote some questions that could be asked to motivate children in drama. As you read the poem, think about the kinds of questions you might ask about it.

WIND WEATHER

The wind's an old woman in front of the rain
Picking up papers and laying them again;
Muttering, fussing, and slamming a door
That only comes back to be slammed at some more.

The wind's an old woman indignantly trying
To gather her goods from the rain's hasty prying.
She frightens the trees till they circle and flail.
But the sensible cows turn their back to her wail.
Yet, when the rain starts its imperative fall
The old-woman-wind doesn't mind it at all.
She chuckles and puffs, unconcerned as you please
At the terrible scare she has given the trees.

(cited in Huber, 1965, p. 120)

Here are some questions about this poem. What others can you come up with?

* In what ways is the wind like an old woman? What things might be similar in their actions?
* How do different people react to being in the wind before a rain? Does your reaction depend on your age? Or on what you are doing? What else might affect your reaction?
* The poem mentions gathering "goods" before a rain. What might

that mean? How have you prepared before a rain? How might other
people prepare? Could you show us?
* What kinds of motions might trees in the wind make? How would it
depend on the kind of tree? Type and age? How might this be different at different seasons of the year?

To build a unit centering on different kinds of wind and people's reactions
to it, you might use the set of five poems by Christina Rossetti and James
Reeves, among others, in *The Random House Book of Poetry for Children*
by Jack Prelutsky (1983) or might use "Fall Wind" by Aileen Fisher and
"Days That the Wind Takes Over" by Karla Kuskin in Lee Bennett Hopkins's
The Sky Is Full of Song (1987). Each of these poems examines very different
kinds and conditions of winds.

One further word about questioning is necessary. After you have asked
questions to encourage different answers and allow for different bodily
movements in response, you must treat these responses in an open-ended
fashion. Even skilled drama leaders must avoid the tendency, so fatal to a
vigorous discussion, to accept the first or best idea offered, thereby losing
other ideas of potential interest. Only by skillful reasking of the basic question, or by the framing of related questions, can one hope to derive the
widest possible range of responses.

Commitment

One other characteristic, or quality, is very important. Indeed, perhaps it is
the *most* important attribute. Do you *believe* in the values of drama?

Teachers are confronted daily with requirements to teach something—
by the school board, by state laws, by the principal, by interested pressure
groups. Fewer pressures exist to include dramatics, and teachers are free to
omit this from the program. A bit of sage advice is to do so unless, and *only*
unless, you completely believe in this art form as a valid means of learning.
Perhaps no other instructional area in the curriculum can "fall apart" as
quickly as when a teacher who is not completely committed to it tries to do
creative drama with children.

The teacher must be convinced about the importance of helping children learn about themselves, others, and their world through dramatics
before attempting to use this art form with children. Certainly, the language
arts program will continue, and no one will fault the less adventuresome
teacher for *not* doing drama with children. If you do not truly believe in
spontaneous dramatics, no quantity of glossy professional gimmicks will
cover up this basic attitude. Once children discover that your attitude toward
informal drama is not sincere, their attitudes will be affected, for children
sense attitudes easily. However, if the leader *does* believe in drama, almost

any amount of technical ineptness in selecting, motivating, and questioning can be overcome.

Therefore, before attempting to do drama with children, analyze your own attitudes. The following questions may help:

1. Do I really believe children can learn as much from themselves and from other children as from books?
2. Do I really believe art forms are important to children? Am I willing to allocate a chunk of "prime time" during a crowded school day to these art forms? A convincing statement about this is provided by Williams (1991).
3. Do I really believe that art forms children create have intrinsic validity, or do I feel that a child's more important role is as a consumer of the arts?
4. Am I willing to take an idea and work with it, capitalizing on children's contributions and following where the lesson leads? Or must I have an end in mind (and reach it) for each lesson?
5. Do I believe that all learning can be measured, and therefore will I be unhappy if I cannot objectively determine *what kind* and *how much* learning has taken place?
6. Can I tolerate seeming chaos (as is bound to exist for the first few sessions) in order to reach my goals of student participation and responsiveness?
7. Am I comfortable enough with myself so that I can participate with children until it is time to withdraw? Could I improvise the hop of the old father frog if the children need my participation as demonstration of my belief? How much will my dignity suffer if I do this? Is my dignity more important to me than my children?
8. Can I express myself articulately enough about what I believe to be able to "sell" my ideas to parents, co-workers, and administrative superiors?

This emphasis on the importance of belief in drama is not intended to minimize the need to study, read, work with children, and then reflect, to learn about and refine specific skills necessary to be an effective leader. It is rather to reinforce the idea that belief in, or commitment to, the goals of drama is a major factor in the ultimate success of the drama leader.

MOTIVATIONS FOR DRAMA

Selection of Materials

Once the teacher has decided to try improvised drama with children, the immediate problem is selecting materials. A key to success is making sure both the materials and the motivation provide for active participation and not simply passive discussion. We choose a particular material to get children involved in *doing* something. Each motivation must further enhance the involvement potential of the material.

While it is perhaps true that any material *can* be used to motivate drama by a leader adept in adapting and using it, it is also true that it will be easier to use material that is not simply descriptive. The following poem by Langston Hughes, while a wonderfully evocative piece that would be read beautifully by a choral speaking choir, is of less use in motivating drama than something with more active images.

APRIL RAIN SONG

Let the rain kiss you.
Let the rain beat upon your head with silver liquid drops.
Let the rain sing you a lullaby.
The rain makes still pools on the sidewalk.
The rain makes running pools in the gutter.
The rain plays a little sleep-song on our roof at night
And I love the rain. (cited in de Regniers, 1988, p. 20)

To use the poem for its language qualities, a teacher would need to work with children to develop ideas suggested by the poem, but not included there. Using the film "Rainshower"[2] in conjunction with this would help establish the mood. The teacher's questioning skill would be necessary to make this material useful for drama. The poem does provide "cues" for further questioning that could be developed by the perceptive teacher. The following questions expand these cues:

- What could you do in one of the still pools on the sidewalk? How might you get around a wide, but shallow, pool? What happens when you walk out of a shallow pool? How could you splash through one of these pools? What might happen if there was a hole in one of your rubbers when you walked through the shallow pool? (Joyce, 1980, p. 9, presents a similar line of questioning in a helpful book about dance.)
- How could you jump over the running pool in the gutter? What things might happen if someone rode a bicycle through the gutter

---

[2]This film (15 minutes, color) is helpful in setting the mood for dramatic playing. It records the progress of a storm from the first few drops hitting a dry farmyard to the torrent pounding on a city street. Available from Churchill Films, 12210 Nebraska Ave., Los Angeles, CA 90025.

> while you were walking along? What things might be floating along
> the pool?
> • How would you react if you woke up at night to hear the "little
>   sleep-song" on your roof? What might you do?

If children respond positively to this poem, you could lead them to other poetry by this pioneer black poet. Three of his poems are included by anthologist Lee Bennett Hopkins in *Ring Out, Wild Bells* (1992), and the subject and tone of these could be compared and contrasted. Thus, the leader might use the poem as a point of departure, but by itself it is too much a "mood" piece to be of maximum effectiveness in drama.

By contrast, the delightfully alliterative poem by Rhoda Bacmeister (1984) provides several images of children enjoying, perhaps surreptitiously, the joys of rain.

GALOSHES

Susie's galoshes
Make splashes and sploshes
And slooshes and sloshes
As Susie steps slowly
Along in the slush.

They stamp and they tramp
On the ice and concrete,
They get stuck in the muck and the mud;
But Susie likes much best to hear

The slippery slush
As it slooshes and sloshes,
And splishes and sploshes,
All round her galoshes! (cited in Cole, 1984, p. 28)

Like "April Rain Song," this provides word pictures, and children can revel in the beauty of language. However, it also provides—better than does Hughes's poem—concrete images for children to interpret. The images are limited, but the effective leader will help children move beyond them. This is one of over 100 poems by well-known older poets like A. A. Milne as well as contemporary poets like Myra Cohn Livingston included in *A New Treasury of Children's Poetry* (1984). These works have been selected and introduced by Joanna Cole and illustrated with small brown watercolor sketches by Judith Gwyn Brown.

Thus, the teacher always asks what children will *do* as a result of the stimulus, not what will they *talk* about. Skilled leaders can adapt anything as motivation but, to begin, choosing poems or stories that give children something to do is a better idea.

One way to accomplish this is by selecting a piece of literature and examining what kinds of verbs are present. Ask yourself these questions:

1. How many verbs are included? Are they active or passive?
2. Are they verbs *I* would be comfortable enacting?[3]
3. Are they verbs likely to suggest other active verbs children can use?

If your poem or story does not stand up well under such questioning, perhaps—especially if you are a beginner—you would be wise to set it aside for future use and search for a more "active" motivation.

Treatment of Material

After selecting a material, how does a leader go about building a spontaneous drama session? New leaders share a common mistake: They frequently use too *much* material rather than too little. An example of a very simple motivation is included here to demonstrate how even very slight ideas, if handled imaginatively, can stimulate valid improvising.

THE KING OF HEARTS

The queen of hearts,
    she made some tarts,
all on a summer's day.

The knave of hearts,
    he stole the tarts,
and took them clean away.

The king of hearts,
    called for the tarts,
and beat the knave full sore.

The knave of hearts,
    brought back the tarts,
and vowed he'd steal no more.

---

[3]This is probably one of the best tests of material: Can I do it myself? If you cannot do it, e.g., if you would feel silly drifting down like a snowflake or swaying in the breeze like a buttercup, perhaps you should propose another motivation.

Behind the uncomplicated lines of this rhyme lie many possibilities for discussion leading to playing. As one approach, begin by asking children if they do something especially well, something of which they are very proud. Discuss with children:

- What is it you do well? When do you do it? With and/or for whom?
- Did it take a long time to learn how to do this? What type of practice did you need?
- How do you feel when you have done this? Can you describe your feeling of accomplishment?

Having established interest in things well done, the leader could then link the children's specialties with the queen's specialty, making tarts. At this point begin questioning to get children to build on the basic, unexpanded idea in the rhyme.

- Where had she learned to make these tarts?
- Is this the only thing she can cook well, or has she other specialties as well?
- Why is she making them this particular day? (A child might suggest, for example, that she is making them because it is the king's birthday. This simple idea, or others, could lead to varied improvisations. If a different suggestion is made, the improvisation would follow in that direction.)

The rhyme, though short, allows much opportunity for characterization. Thinking about the queen, teacher and children might discuss

- What is she like? Is she clever? Is she friendly?
- What does she look like? Are there any other physical characteristics important about her?
- What kind of relationship does she have with the king? Is she domineering, sweet, reticent, overbearing, mild, or what? (One child suggested the queen was very crafty—with her skills she could get the king to agree to anything she wanted.)

The character of the king is a fruitful one for exploration.

- What is he like? Is he a pleasant person?
- What has he done before we meet him that has made him the way he is? Is this his first wife?
- What is his relationship to the queen? (One possibility might be that he is a gruff, crotchety king, who simply melts when his sweet, young queen approaches him.)

Children could also improvise on the knave's character. In one class, children suggested the knave was the king's royal chef and explored these questions.

- How secure is he in his job? Is he afraid he might lose his job? If so, why?
- How does he behave to the other kitchen help, for example, the salad person, the pastry maker?
- How does the knave like being interrupted by the queen?

In this situation, some sort of crisis could be developed. Exploring with children the effect the queen has on the smooth running of the kitchen can lead to some interesting conflict development.

- What might go wrong while the queen makes her tarts? (Perhaps some ingredient was missing, or a proper tart-making tool had been misplaced.)
- What if the queen got flustered working in a strange kitchen and did something wrong in the recipe?
- What could happen if we discover that once the queen gets into the kitchen she really can't cook at all, that her reputation is a fabrication of her own making? How would she get out of her dilemma?

Other elements of the rhyme lead to plot and conflict development.

- Who else might have wanted to steal the tarts? Why?
- Where could they go so they would not be discovered?
- What might the queen do when she discovered that the tarts were gone?

Any number of possibilities might develop. Two are suggested, simply as ideas, not necessarily to be used as is.

1. The knave has stolen the tarts because he is anxious to make the queen lose favor with the king. Perhaps he is jealous because this beautiful young queen is influential, and the king no longer listens to the knave as he did before he married the queen.
2. Perhaps the knave is anxious to establish himself as an important person in the eyes of the people of the kingdom. There is to be a county fair soon, and he wants to enter the tarts as his own in the cooking contest, to win the prize, and to receive the glory.

The above is a general outline of some possibilities that exist within a short piece of literature. As follow-up to using this with children, they might enjoy hearing B. G. Hennessy's *The Missing Tarts* (1989), which involves the queen in meeting and questioning many folk literature characters like Jack and Jill, Old Mother Hubbard, and others. The humorous watercolor illustrations are by Tracey Campbell Pearson (see Figure 3.2).

After choosing an appropriate selection, thinking about it, formulating questions related to it, and practicing reading or telling it, the teacher is ready to use it. While actually "doing" drama with children, the teacher-leader has a rather carefully defined role to play.

THE LEADER'S ROLE IN THE DRAMA SESSION

The danger in identifying stages is that it may give the impression that the stages can be divided; this is not so. We have separated the role into two stages for easier examination of the leader's two different functions in drama sessions.

FIGURE 3.2. Tracey Campbell Pearson's illustrations in B. G. Hennessy's reworking of the old rhyme, *The Missing Tarts* (1989), show a variety of actions both large (like running) and small (like cutting pastry) that can be incorporated into an improvised drama based on the poem.

Stage One: Teacher Participation

The inevitable question, and one difficult to answer, is, how much does the teacher participate? This cannot be answered without considering the context of a particular teacher and a particular group of children.

The advantage of participation is immediately evident. Children, seeing the leader actually taking part, will participate with more enthusiasm. If the leader is really bending and moving to the rhythm of the music, or stalking stealthily through the alley as the cat searching for food in Miska Miles's *Nobody's Cat* (1969), the children can enter wholeheartedly into the action. The tacit thought is, "He is doing it—so can I." By participating, the teacher is capitalizing on a child's desire to emulate the actions of a respected teacher. The teacher is at that point acting the role of "cooperator" in the dramatic encounter, as Barnfield (1968, p. 20) calls it. That impulse, however, leads to a consideration of the drawback to teacher participation—the child's subconscious attempts to imitate, not just the *spirit*, but the *letter* of the teacher's actions.

Children, particularly those who are unsure of themselves in creative drama, may subconsciously seek approval by copying, movement for movement, the teacher's improvisation. Instead of getting their fresh ideas, the leader may only get a mirror image of his or her own ideas. This is furthest from our goal, as what we are searching for and rewarding is the child's spontaneous response to the stimulus. What, then, is the teacher-leader to do?

The teacher can remember that the only point in participation is to encourage children, to show by concrete action that this is an important learning activity. Therefore, as soon as this goal is achieved, the teacher withdraws from active participation and moves, instead, to verbal encouragement. This takes no less ability but does indeed remove the model, so that overly hesitant children, who find dependence hard to avoid, must move to more reliance on their own thoughts.

When does this occur? The apparent answer must be, at different times and with different speeds for different groups. With some drama groups it may happen before the end of the first session—and fortunate is the leader with so spontaneous a group of child improvisors. With other groups it may take much longer, and even after establishing this hard-won independence, the leader may later sense the children's hesitancy, wanting him or her to take part again. This is acceptable, but keep in mind the real purpose of participation—to encourage the children.

It seems almost inevitable that the leader will want to participate, if for no other reason than that it demonstrates his or her conviction that the activity is significant. It is crucial, however, to be aware of the need to withdraw from the action to a position of sideline support as soon as you sense growing independence on the children's part.

Stage Two: Verbal Reinforcement

The second function is verbal—through questions and comments, the leader spurs children on, encourages the less sure, and points out strong ideas. This is often called *side coaching*. To encourage children, say such things as

- I am really getting the feel of a jungle with all those crawling things wiggling and twisting around.
- Such a lot of slippery fish I see, with their tails brushing from side to side—that stream is very full.

To encourage children who are less sure, make such comments as these.

- Now I can see the idea you have, Pam. It's coming through very nicely.
- Good, Bob, that stretching goes with our music so well.

To point out strong ideas you might say:

- I can see Carol's cat is arching her back so slowly. It looks like it has just awakened.
- Did you see how Joe kept his arms and legs stiff? His toy soldier was very convincing.

The teacher's purpose in side coaching is to further encourage children. Don't be concerned if suddenly all the students become stiff-legged toy soldiers; soon, other ideas of their own will emerge.

The commentary should always be balanced. Some comments, or words of commendation, are for the individual child who needs private encouragement unimportant to the group. Then some comments are aimed at a particular child, pointing out what he or she is doing well, but also influencing the group. Finally, other comments are directed purposefully to the group in general, simply to convey approval, rather than to point out specific ideas to be emulated.

Notice that in the above comments we used specific children's names. Leaders vary in their reaction to this. Certainly, further along in the series of drama sessions (for instance, when one is developing facets of character), it can destroy the session to call Carol, at work creating the old woman loaded down with parcels and waiting for a subway, by her right name. However, when the group is doing more fragmentary and less sustained impressions, personalization and supportive comments cannot be anything but helpful, especially for younger children.

Both leader participation and verbal reinforcement have a single purpose: building such a sense of security that children feel totally free to say or do whatever seems appropriate to them in the context of the improvisation.

Another Alternative: Teaching in Role

The two kinds of teacher involvement, participating and providing verbal reinforcement, are related to the kind of story drama this book describes. Another alternative, teaching in role, is an approach most forcefully advocated by an English educator, Dorothy Heathcote. In it, the leader does not introduce drama, preparing the children for story material by doing introductory warm-up experiences (Hall, 1973). Rather, the leader develops from children the theme to be used and participates as one of the major characters in the drama, in order to lead and direct the playing. A helpful interpretation of this approach is offered by Wagner (1976), an articulate disciple of Heathcote's approach. Brownlie and Gilchrist (1989) point out how this technique helps children understand point of view. A complete book, *Role Drama* by Tarlington and Verriour (1991), exemplifies teaching in role by presenting literature-based, as well as other, dramas in which what the leader is to do is quite specifically spelled out. Throughout, the authors talk directly to the teacher-reader, using phrases like "At this point, you may wish to. . . . " The book reports what the authors have done with children and would be helpful to other teachers interested in, but apprehensive about, teaching in role.

GAINING FREEDOM OF RESPONSE

As stated earlier, the leader's intense belief in this art form as beneficial is necessary to encourage children's honest responses. Getting such an honest response from students may be difficult, especially if you are trying to begin dramatics with an older group for the first time.

One startling characteristic adults notice often about young boys and girls is their frankness. Most kindergarten children are characterized by a forthrightness seldom encountered elsewhere. The children both ask questions and state their opinions with disconcerting candor. Similarly, their imagination or dramatic sense is, at an early age, relatively unfettered. Their creativity is matched in vigor only by their eagerness to use it (Chaparro, 1979).

Somehow, before children leave a typical elementary school, much of this creativity, this spontaneity, is either lost or repressed. Why? Several psychologists have advanced answers: These may include the changing nature of the curriculum in the middle grades, or perhaps less interest in creativity on the part of teachers of those grades.

For our purposes it is sufficient to note the problem and then say simply that the leader may have a difficult time getting children to react spontaneously to a motivation. Often students have been conditioned to look to the teacher for the idea and, after following the lead, to look for reinforcement that something has been done correctly.

To the drama teacher this is anathema. We are interested in getting children to respond openly. To get this freedom, we may have to accept for some time attempts that are not open, free responses, but rather a young child's attempt to figure out what we want. At such times we are careful not to criticize a particular child's obviously false behavior and are simply content to ask again—in a group or, perhaps, individually—"Is that what you *really* feel?"

We recently worked with a beginning teacher of third grade who demonstrated in his handling of an informal play-giving situation obvious insensitivity to the possibilities in that dramatic situation. Each reading group had devised a way of sharing with the rest of the class the story they were studying. One group had chosen to "do" a play based on the story. When they stood in front of the class, the players, some of whom tried to hide behind others, giggled and shoved each other in embarrassment and read their parts poorly, with little expression. Once they began, the children, with one exception, stood frozen to the spot; even minimal movement, for example, answering the door, was absent. A song, to be sung by six children, was mumbled in an uninteresting monotone, although the words were set to a melody every school child knows. All in all, it was a total waste of the children's time! There were myriad possibilities in this informal dramatic situation, but there was time to do the play only once, as spelling was next on the schedule.

Certainly, the teacher needed to consider the following:

1. Since there was no continuing drama program in the room, the children needed supervised help in practicing their scene. The children were not used to such activities, and although they voluntarily chose to share their story this way, they needed help doing it.
2. As the children were not used to dramatizing for an audience, provision might have been made for the group to present their play to one reading group at a time, rather than to all the children. For most children small audiences are less formidable than class-size groups.
3. Some provision needed to be made for *evaluation*. Probably in this case,

such evaluation needed to be done when the teacher had time to speak privately with the group. That some evaluation was going on among the children is shown by the next paragraph.

Perhaps the most interesting happening was the comment of a young boy sitting next to one of the adults. In a silly attempt to make small talk, the adult said to him, "Did you enjoy the play?" His candor was evident. "No—it wasn't very interesting." He then proceeded to make three suggestions that would have, indeed, improved the improvised drama—the child would have made a better leader at that point than the actual teacher had! He had been concentrating on the dramatic qualities of the idea and in a noncritical way had identified some possibilities the self-conscious "performers" had ignored.

Somehow we too frequently condition children and their teachers to expect particular types of activities in elementary schools. As a result, freer and less structured experiences, in which children can experiment with ideas in informal, oral situations, seem silly, if not impossible. The self-conscious children in this example, given the opportunity to develop their own ideas, instead made stilted and lifeless use of the author's ideas. They were too inhibited to add anything of themselves because they were not ready to dramatize for an audience, although the situation had much potential.

John Holt (1969) described this utter dependence, and children's disbelief when confronted with the need to exercise independence and make choices. Although he was not talking about drama, the following illustration makes the point well. He described a situation in which he gave children a choice of what they were to read and told them he did not intend to either quiz them or make them give book reports. "The children sat stunned and silent. Was this a teacher talking? One girl . . . who proved to be one of the most lively and intelligent children I have ever known, looked at me steadily for a long time after I had finished. Then, still looking at me, she said slowly and solemnly, 'Mr. Holt, do you really mean that?'" (p. 86).[4] Is there any wonder that, confronted with a class so conditioned to expect a particular type of situation in school, some of us feel that it is imperative we offer children an opportunity to express themselves through drama?

-----

[4]Holt's experience teaching at a variety of levels made him an acute observer and trenchant commentator on the ills, many of them still critical over two decades after his book was written, of American schools. Many of his comments are startling (those on the need to abolish compulsory attendance laws); some are merely common sense we have ignored (comments on the problems besetting reading programs)—a refreshingly contentious book that makes us think about continuing problems.

HOW DOES ONE BEGIN WITH CHILDREN?

The problem of how to present dramatics differs according to the age group with which one is working. In the early primary grades, a *direct approach* is quite possible. Simply begin the activity; there is no need to talk about it. You can start with rhythmic activities to music or, after reading a poem to children, they can show how the action took place. For boys and girls at this level, activity is pleasurable for its own sake, and resistance will be minimal.

In the intermediate grades and above an *analytical approach* is undoubtedly necessary; that is, the teacher needs to talk with children about what he or she is going to do with them and why. Allow them much opportunity to discuss the idea, think about it, and react to it before beginning.

Some leaders have found that much work with rhythmic movement is a good lead into dramatics, no matter what the level. Graham, Holt/Hale, and Parker (1987) give many positive ways to loosen up children, help them understand what their bodies can convey, and remove inhibitions. Though these authors remain concerned with movement primarily for its own sake, drama leaders would find the book helpful in beginning work with children.

Drama leaders also find the Barnfield (1968) book full of suggestions about ways to begin, even though it was published some time ago. This book is particularly encouraging for those doing drama with older children because he reports on work done with boys between ten and fourteen years of age. In addition to suggestions for introducing this activity for the first time, he also includes some stimulating loosening-up exercises for relaxing the body (and consequently the mind) at the beginning of each session. Sklar (1991) gives other preparatory exercises, including both breathing and body work.

A description of how one of us begins an actual session in spontaneous drama with older children might be of interest. I often use the material in Chapter 1 on "The Sandhill Crane," and when the students enter, the room is dark except for the light from a slide of a crane showing on the screen. We talk briefly about the crane, including the fact that the wingspread is nine feet from one tip to the other. Then, sitting on the floor, we stretch our arms until we feel the tingle that comes to the ends of our fingertips when we reach as far as we can. We then begin to move our upper torsos around, while remaining seated. We stretch as far in all directions as we can, retaining the feeling of the wide wingspread. Commenting continuously on the tingle, and the size of their "wings," I encourage the students to get up and move around, to see what problems being that size entails. As they move and interrelate in the space, the mood begins to establish itself. When we sit down on our imagined nests some minutes later, the children have changed—if not into cranes, at least into beings more able to forget themselves and work with the ideas presented. Only after this introductory movement session of perhaps five minutes do we begin to consider other aspects of the poem and to work out what happens in it. The introduction has worked well with intermediate age students, who are very unused to expressing their thoughts with their bodies in a classroom.

The foregoing is certainly not intended to be a prescription for exactly how to begin drama with children. Intelligent decision making about the kinds of drama experiences a particular group needs can be done only when a leader is able to look analytically at the group. The teacher tries to determine what the students have done, what he or she hopes they will eventually be able to do, and what types of activities may help them achieve these goals. These determinations are always made within the context of the teacher's strengths and weaknesses. Since we know neither you nor your group, all we can do is encourage you to read this, and anything else you can find, and then diagnose the drama needs of your group.

ESSENTIAL DRAMA ELEMENTS

Both in choosing materials for classroom drama and in working with children, the leader keeps in mind the elements necessary to good drama. These were introduced in Chapter 1; three of them will be discussed further here.

Conflict

The element that most often makes stories and plays interesting is some sort of conflict. The most beautiful sets, convincing dialogue, or effectively written descriptions rarely hold even an attentive audience for long. The playwright or author needs to establish some conflict, and this is also essential in spontaneous drama sessions.

Children enter into conflict with gusto, for, as Maurice Sendak says, "being defenseless is a primary attribute of childhood" (Hentoff, 1966). Children enjoy acting out their feelings of defenselessness through the acceptable vehicle of drama sessions concerned with conflict.

Three types of conflict have been identified by drama writers, and examples of all three are found in stories for children. First, there is the conflict of person versus person. An example of this type is the conflict in *The Fisherman and His Wife* (Stewig, 1988) (see Figure 3.3).

A second type is the conflict of person versus fate, that is, nature, the supernatural, or something larger than the self. An example is the old Italian

FIGURE 3.3. Margot Tomes's illustrations in John Warren Stewig's *The Fisherman and His Wife* (1988) depict the tale of the wife's increasing greed in a rich variety of brown and related tones. By the end of dramatizing this retelling of an old Grimm tale, students will have had many opportunities to develop dialogue.

folktale, "March and the Shepherd." In this tale the wily shepherd contends against the stronger force, the month, but finally loses (Galvino, 1981).

In the third type of conflict—person versus self—some internal flaw propels the character toward disaster. An example of this type is found in a longer work appropriate for middle school students, *Circles in a Forest* by Dalene Matthee (1984). Saul Barnard, an introspective woodcutter in South Africa, must come to terms with this sort of conflict before he can deal with other conflicts.

Characterization

The problem of making people or animals real is a continuing one. The leader's goal in dramatization is to help the child develop an honest interpretation of the character. Keep several things in mind in trying to achieve this goal.

Characters should share these three qualities.

1. *They are active, not passive.* In Dr. Seuss's *The 500 Hats of Bartholomew Cubbins* (1938), Bartholomew is actively involved through most of the story in escaping from his perplexing problems. The king is equally active in attempting to punish what he sees as Bartholomew's insolence.

2. *They are clearly defined.* An example of this is the array of children and adults Helen Cresswell has created for a series of books about the Bagthorpe family, the latest of which is *Bagthorpes Abroad* (1984). In the opening scene, an irreverent one in which the children are doctoring their largely unfavorable school reports, we meet once again the three youngest children.

> William and Rosie were walking computers and good on the science side, and Tess's languages, especially her French, were better even than her teacher's ... [Jack] did not have a single good subject. (p. 3)

They are, other abilities apart, uncommonly clever at making use of the large empty space on the cards where the headmaster hasn't commented!

3. *They are logically motivated.* Even within a fantasy, characters can act and behave logically—they need not exhibit realistic behavior to be believable. An example is Bobby Bell, the slightly disheveled hero in Val Willis's *The Surprise in the Wardrobe* (1990). It's easy to understand his motivation in this delightful fantasy, as clearly different from the motivation of his surprise (the witch) and the motivations of his teacher, Miss Potts, and prissy Jenny Wood.

In addition to selecting materials that include appropriate characterizations, the leader works during the session to increase the children's concentration on the characters by asking them questions. Three types of concentration are critical.

1. *Intellectual*—are you thinking like the person would think?
2. *Emotional*—are you feeling like the person would feel?
3. *Physical*—are you moving, standing, or sitting like the person would?

Barnfield (1968) describes his approach in getting children to *become* characters rather than "act" them, an important distinction.

> Let them start their scene and let it run for a minute. Now stop them and ask one of them what his name is. He may look puzzled, then give you his own name. "No," you will say, "Who are you in this scene?" He probably hasn't thought. Ask another, and another, and you will find that their imagination has

been very general in its working. Now, explain to them, "I want you to think who you are: how old or young, man or woman, school boy or school girl, when your next birthday is and what age you will be then. Are you poor or fairly well off? What kind of clothes are you wearing—What are you carrying? . . . Are you with anyone? . . . " With all these suggestions . . . let them have another try at their . . . scene. (pp. 98–99)

Dialogue

Some drama leaders believe dialogue is, logically enough, one of the last elements to develop (Blackie, Bullough, & Nash, 1972). A child first develops a mental image as a result of the motivation, then this image stimulates actions, and only later does it evoke dialogue. Betty Jane Wagner (1983) comments:

Oddly enough, nothing seems to help children believe in a drama more effectively than to stop talking and start moving to the cadence of a group task. If language comes too soon, it sounds thin and chattery. Nonverbal knowing comes before the language of conviction. (p. 157)

Anyone who has worked with children is aware of their verbal self-consciousness in many situations where other children are listening. Both Canadian and British drama leaders attempt to solve this problem by making use of *simultaneous speech*, either individually or in small groups, to break down children's reticence at hearing their own voices.

This effective procedure, which will seem like chaos in the beginning, is simple to initiate. Begin with single child dialogue. The children position themselves in the room; the leader provides a situation that requires a verbal response; and each child creates spontaneous dialogue of his or her own, saying it aloud and ignoring all the other children.

For example, use the character of the mother rabbit in Beatrix Potter's story about Peter Rabbit (1988) and set the stage for children to improvise the warnings she might have given to her children before sending them out to play. Each child becomes the mother rabbit, and each makes up a warning, ignoring the rest of the children in the room. Other literature-based, dialogue possibilities could include

Theodore explaining to his mother why he must keep a particular toy (Ellen Stoll Walsh, 1981)
Pearl telling her parents about her newfound friend (William Steig, 1976)
Eleanor Owl and her assistant, Mr. Paws, discussing the strange happenings in the hotel (James Marshall, 1977)

Dialogues are not limited to a literature base, however. Students could create dialogue for

> A child explaining to the teacher why the assigned homework isn't done
> A vacuum cleaner salesperson trying to convince a homeowner to let the person in to give a demonstration
> A political worker trying to convince someone to sign nomination papers for a candidate
> A child trying to convince a parent to change vacation plans
> A salesclerk trying to convince a reluctant customer to make a purchase

Both Canadian and British drama leaders report informally that greatly increased oral fluency results from these sessions, but in this, as in most other aspects of drama, empirical research is limited.

Another approach that works equally well is to divide the children into small groups (of not more than four) and have them create dialogue spontaneously from some motivation. Working in this intimate group and thus concentrating intently on what others in their group are saying, children forget the presence of others in the room and concentrate on improvising their dialogue.

One can, if desired, progress from individual monologues to small-group dialogues and continually increase the size of the group, gradually lessening children's self-consciousness in speaking with others and making the creation of spontaneous dialogue seem easy.

REDOING THE IMPROVISATION

One of the recurring themes in this book is that to any motivation there will be, if encouraged, a variety of responses from the children. Stimulated by an idea, and challenged by the leader's skillful questioning, children will be eager to share their responses. The leader does not choose which of these he or she thinks is "best" but, rather, will frequently allow different groups of children to show their response to an idea, or let the total group respond several times to the same motivation. We do this for several reasons.

1. *To give all children a chance to participate.* In Annabel Williams-Ellis's Gingerbread Boy story (1986), for instance, the basic characters are few. Though children will undoubtedly be able to suggest other peripheral characters that can be added to the story, the total number will probably

be less than the number of children in the group, thus necessitating dramatizing the story more than once.

2. *To work on different dramatic aspects possible in a motivation.* In Beatrice Schenk de Regniers's version of *Jack and the Beanstalk* (1985), one could work on characterization, plot extension and development, or mood. The story probably should be done more than once in order to concentrate on these different aspects.

3. *To "set" an improvisation, when children have expressed a desire to do it for another group of children.* This term is used to describe doing a number of improvisations on the same theme, and selecting the better ideas and rejecting the poorer ones. The purpose is to build a dramatic piece to be learned, which will still retain the freshness of the original spontaneous idea. Remember that this does not happen at the beginning of a sequence of drama experiences, when we are interested in encouraging diversity of response. After children have worked in drama for some time, however, they may want to "set" the improvisation, so it can be done for another group of children.

Thus, there may be several occasions when children will work more than once with the same motivational idea. Each time this happens the improvisation is at least slightly different from what went before, a quality encouraged by the leader. This quality can be illustrated by drawing a parallel between variety in drama and in a piece of music. Listen, for example, to Rachmaninoff's *Rhapsody on a Theme of Paganini* (Seraphim S-60091). In this piece the composer has taken a short melodic idea and given it back to the listener in twenty-two variations, each different enough so that the listener follows from one to the other with increasing interest. Given a basic idea, the composer shows us the infinite variety possible.

Similarly, if the teacher is effective, each time a group works with an idea the results will be different. Although leaders are by no means interested in doing anything twenty-two times, groups often need to play the idea more than once; each time the idea will turn out to be slightly different. The teacher capitalizes on this and encourages such differences, as part of developing the children's creativity.

EVALUATING THE SESSION

The final aspect of a drama session is at least as crucial as the other steps, for it involves assessing what happened during the session.

Using the term *evaluation* necessitates careful definition. Often, simple grading of past performance has been called evaluation. In some instances, it means that the teacher discusses the children's work with them, as opposed to writing an evaluation. In drama, however, evaluation means a very different type of activity, the major feature of which is its *truly* cooperative nature.

The teacher does two types of evaluation. One, the supportive comments, given during the playing, are spontaneous and point out the effective aspects of what children have been doing. This is called *concurrent evaluation* and was described in Chapter 2.

The other type, also described in Chapter 2, is called *terminal evaluation* and is done at the end of the session. As the period draws to a close, the leader will bring the children back together, perhaps having them sit in a circle near him or her, as proximity is helpful. Then they discuss what went on during the session. The teacher remembers always to draw ideas from the children and is careful not to offer too much, so the children don't try to guess what they "should" say. The teacher *leads* the discussion after the children have improvised, but does not *manipulate* it—a crucial distinction.

The leader asks questions that, as O'Neill (1988) points out, will help children reflect on and evaluate the experience. For example:

- Which were the best parts of our improvisation? What things helped make the story clear? Could people follow what was happening?
- What parts could be improved? How could we convey our idea more clearly?
- Which characters were most believable? What aspects made them believable?
- How did the dialogue help make the story live? What made it interesting? Was there enough dialogue, but not so much that it got to be mainly talk?
- How could we make it better next time? What are some things we did today that we will want to do again next time?

There is a natural pitfall involved in this procedure—teachers subconsciously communicate their own ideas without identifying them as such. In the first question (above), for example, what the leader sees as "best" about the day's work might be quite different from what the children view as "best," perhaps because he or she misunderstood the intent of what they were trying to accomplish. At this stage in the session the teacher must listen as intently as during the actual dramatizing. You may learn something about children's ideas related to the motivation or what they were trying to do, which could be of help during the next session. All of this emphasis on careful listening to children, and on accepting their efforts, does not suggest a bland acquiescence in mediocrity, insincerity, or superficial praise of everything children do.

Always avoid praising unjustly, for children will know when they have done something that is good. The teacher who, for whatever reason, intellectually or artistically deceives the children by excessive or inappropriate praise inevitably loses the group. Knowing that the teacher accepts anything, regardless of its quality, children lose their interest and thus their desire to participate. The teacher must come to grips with inadequate efforts. Avoid both excessive praise and censorious evaluation by seeking to establish a healthy rapport with children. This rapport allows leader and students to investigate together what has been done, what was done well, and what needs to be done better.

We cannot resist sharing with you again our feeling that a few minutes away from the children after the session is crucial. Drama is not sedentary—the teacher (if effective) has concentrated intently and been active physically. Therefore, you need a few minutes not only to regather your forces, but also to reflect on what happened. A crucial purpose of this brief respite is to jot a few notes that will help you give continuity to the sessions as a *sequence* of drama experiences. Because it is almost inevitable that a few days will elapse before the next session, brief notes jotted down about the day's session will help you remember what you want to do next. In the interval—spent helping with such diverse problems as the addition of equal addends and the expansion of air molecules—the memory of the previous drama session will become hazy or nonexistent. Looking back at these minimal notes will refresh your memory of what the group did, what it needs to do again, and what it did not get done. These few indications surely do not take the place of a sequential drama plan, but they serve to augment it, bridging the gap between plan and reality. Brown (1992) comments on the usefulness of this sort of group assessment; Kase-Polisini (1989) gives other helpful evaluation suggestions. In a drama guide offering suggestions from preschool through twelfth grade, Last (1990) provides a "Scale for Assessing Personal Growth" in drama, which could help preschool and elementary teachers determine how their students are progressing.

PHYSICAL ENVIRONMENT PROBLEMS: WHAT TO DO?

The teacher faces myriad problems in attempting to do drama in the classroom. Let's consider here the physical problems of the number of pupils, the amount of space, and scheduling.

Number of Students

Recommendations of optimum group sizes for drama vary, but it is apparent that few classroom teachers normally operate with classes this small. It is a rare and gifted leader, and seldom a beginning one, who can be totally effective with thirty children. Therefore, your first job is to reduce your thirty children to a smaller number for efficient playing. How can you accomplish this?

1. Let those students you are not working with go to a corner of the room and do something else.

   The key here is *seclusion*. Perhaps a folding screen, movable shelves, or a piano on rollers could provide a secluded corner. A second key to success is to have these children doing something pleasurable. Engrossed in a compelling story *they* chose to read, their attention is less likely to wander than if they are doing make-up math lessons. After the first group has its turn, switch groups.

2. Find another place to send the children.

   Could you work out flexible scheduling for art, music, and physical education classes? Perhaps half of your children, plus half of the teacher's next door, could go together for art. This would give the art teacher a full class, but give each of you only half a class.

   Is there a way children could help around the school? Could one group regularly read stories to younger children, or perhaps help with spelling drill in another room? Making such an arrangement with another teacher not only helps the children but allows the teacher to individualize. Another possibility is making an arrangement for the librarian to use part of your group as helpers. Perhaps the school office could use some helpers on a regular basis. Any or all of these techniques reduces the size of the group remaining in your room to one small enough to work with.

3. Enlist some additional workers.

   Working under your direction, a parent can become a second leader. One short planning session per week, after he or she has watched you work with the children, can inform the helper of what to do that particular week. Half the class can go to the gym, cafeteria, or other convenient space and work with the parent volunteer while you work with the rest. Or enlist the help of teacher aides, if your school employs such auxiliary personnel. In considering this suggestion and the next one, you need to check on state laws regarding responsibility for children. These laws vary greatly concerning the use of paraprofessional help.

   Another possible source of auxiliary personnel is a college or university in the area. People operating programs in creative drama at this level are frequently hard pressed for placement opportunities for students enrolled in their courses. They would usually be delighted to put one of their students in your classroom. Programs vary, but it is a rare college that would not be pleased to provide college students with more actual contact hours with children, and all benefit from such a setup. Don't wait for the college instructor to come to you—initiate the contact yourself, and you are sure to be pleased with the response.

Amount of Space

The second and often discouraging problem is one of space.

1. If you are going to use your classroom, children will need practice clearing the desks or tables from the middle of the room. Plan ahead where each should go so that you will get the largest amount of open space. Children should practice clearing the area and restoring it *several times*, to get the best movement of desks in the least amount of time with a minimum of confusion and noise. This can be done, as any teacher who has tried to overcome physical problems can tell you. But it does *not* "happen" automatically and can easily dissolve in chaos, unless you plan the process before you try it.
2. There may be an unused space somewhere in the building that you could use. Get the gym teacher's schedule to find out when that space is available. Ask when the cafeteria workers finish so you could use that space. Is there an art or music room unused for some part of the week? If there is a stage in the school use it, though that sort of formal space isn't necessary (Cheifetz, 1971). Look around—sometimes the most unsuspected spaces will do for a while! These are not ideal, but it is our—and we hope by now, your—feeling that good drama experiences can take place in poor locations. Once you have the drama program launched and children are spreading the word about it, you may be able to come up with a better space.

The problem of too little space is serious, but too much space is not good either. Often teachers move their class into a gymnasium, and chaos results. This is because in such a large space, children can move so far away from the leader that it is impossible to rechannel their energies without shouting. It is important to gradually give students more space in which to work, and for the leader to be aware of how he or she uses space. Heathcote (1970), in talking about teachers' self-awareness, introduces the concepts of teacher "thresholds." This is the idea that each teacher has his or her own limits in regard to many aspects of teaching: size of group, amount of noise, and other factors. She is definite in saying that many teachers need to have children in close proximity to work effectively with them.

If you do plan to use such a large space as a gym, decide beforehand which part of it you will use and how you will differentiate the space you will use from that which is off limits. For example, if the tile floor has a line design in it, decide which line is the boundary, or mark the outer limit with masking tape or with a row of chairs or tables.

Scheduling

The final problem often encountered is scheduling. The stereotype of the teacher handing out crayons and paper, and telling children to "draw what you want to" on Friday afternoons from 3:00 to 3:30 P.M. is, unfortunately, still too true. Most children cannot create then. Researchers agree that when people are either physically or mentally tired they tend to be less creative. Similarly, creative drama, being essentially an activity in which the child is expressing or "giving out," rather than impressing or "taking in," cannot wait until the child is physically and mentally exhausted. If the only time you can "spare" from a busy schedule is that last period of the day or week, perhaps you should re-examine the priorities.

1. Who is establishing for you what you should teach and when?
2. Is what the teacher in the next grade "expects" your children to have learned a legitimate expectation? If not, what should you be doing to change it?
3. Exactly what are your principal's expectations? How do you know? Has he or she said so, or do you "think" certain things are expected?
4. Do your children really "need" an hour of prime time in the middle of each morning devoted to reading? How do you know? Who should establish what children need? Can we determine these needs, especially subject matter ones, with certainty?

An interesting revelation to us was the comment made recently during a conversation with a school principal in Minnesota. In her school they are experimenting with behavioral modification techniques, and the tangible reward offered is a half-hour free period at the end of the day, during which children choose from several activities. Although this entailed shortening the academic school day—in essence, curtailing the amount of time for academic teaching—the principal reported that children did as well or better on the standardized achievement tests at the end of the first year of the experiment compared with the previous year when the teachers had the extra half hour each day to teach! Perhaps we waste more of children's time than we think we do. Time for drama can usually be found, provided you want to find the time.

DRAMA AND THE EXCEPTIONAL LEARNER

Although the Education for All Handicapped Children Act (P.L. 94–142) was enacted into law in 1975, some school systems were slow to comply with the mandate that handicapped students must be mainstreamed. Mainstreaming is a method of providing the most appropriate education for each child in the *least restrictive setting* possible. The implications of this law were that the normal classroom environment should include all types of handicapped students for as much of the school day as possible. Many professionals have viewed mainstreaming as the primary method by which schools can help exceptional children achieve normalization. Handicapped children who are integrated into general education classes for part or all of the day tend to feel less isolated from their nonhandicapped peers. The teacher in the regular classroom must set the tone as to how well the handicapped children are accepted by the other students, yet too often these teachers have not had the training necessary for dealing with exceptional students. Methods that have proven effective for dealing with this acceptance include using creative drama and role playing, puppetry, and social skills training, since they address some of the problems facing the integration of handicapped youngsters into regular classrooms.

Types of Exceptional Learners

Academically Gifted and Learning Disabled. Exceptional learners include both the learning disabled or slow learner and the gifted learner. In the past, students who learned at a pace slower than their peers were often retained and required to repeat a year or more in school. This practice is being used less frequently since research has shown that children who are held back are more likely to drop out of school later on. All children like to be part of the group, and when that membership is artificially severed many problems can result, especially in the area of socialization. Allowing disabled children to continue with their original peer group increases their chances of being accepted. Children can be very understanding and nurturing of others who are "different" if correct role modeling and a caring environment are provided. Drama is a ready-made vehicle for such an endeavor. Academically slow learners may find drama the perfect arena for developing other abilities. Whereas interacting with the printed page may be an ongoing frustration, participation in drama may release hidden talents in character development, role playing, use of body language, spontaneity, and the use of imagination, among other aspects of a creative drama activity.

Academically gifted children can pose similar problems on the opposite end of the learning spectrum. Due to their highly developed verbal skills and ability to learn swiftly, such students have often been allowed to skip a grade in school. Again, the situation requires joining a new group, this time an older one, and such a change can pose its own kind of obstacles to acceptance. A smaller physical stature and immaturity can be a handicap once a gifted student enters middle school. Instead, allowing gifted students to maintain group membership with age-equivalent peers enables them to share and excel in such areas as creativity, leadership, and organizational and imaginative skills. These are often the students who solve arguments, direct drama sessions, write plays and puppet show scripts, design scenery, create props, and even compose music.   .

Perhaps we should take note of the Japanese educational system. No student is ever retained or promoted, and all children are expected to support each other and build on each other's strengths. Their emphasis on group dynamics does indeed have some very positive features (White, 1987).

Mentally Retarded. Students in this category are generally a joy to teach (McCaslin, 1990). They love to work in groups and to be involved in simple games like "Pass the Face" and rhythm and movement activities. They can respond to simple directions like *smile*, *fall down*, *jump*. As they mature, more demanding forms of dramatic play, such as characterization and plot development, can be introduced. Simple story plots must be selected, of course. The essential element is to move slowly and provide much guidance. The children need to feel secure, important, and involved. Learning basic social interaction skills and seeing a drama project through to completion are important.

Physically Handicapped. Severely handicapped children are usually enrolled in a special school and will not be mainstreamed. However, children with mild forms of physical disabilities such as cerebral palsy, hemophilia, and so on can participate in creative drama, even if they are confined to wheelchairs or crutches. They can take part in a movement activity as much as their impairments allow, and often a normal child will assist a handicapped child to participate even more fully. Again, and it cannot be stressed enough, children *will* accept each other and work together, given the opportunity and positive guidance from the drama leader. The mutual joy shared when a drama session is well done is worth all the effort by the leader to make it happen. Even if children are in wheelchairs, their total being is involved in drama—socially, emotionally, mentally, *and* physically, even though the latter component may be limited.

Hearing Impaired. Children who can function with hearing aids will pose no insurmountable problem to participation in creative drama. However, those who are deaf and learning to sign or lip read need special consideration. Pantomime and puppetry would be obvious vehicles for success. Usually, deaf children understand body language extremely well, and this vehicle is especially appropriate for them. Puppetry offers an opportunity for interaction in mime as well, and the child can take on the persona of more than one character with ease by simply changing puppets.

Visually Impaired. Partially sighted children can enjoy most drama activities that nonvisually impaired children do, but an alert "buddy" can be assigned to stay near such children and help direct their movements as the need arises. These children generally have good oral language skills and will have no problem listening to directions or interacting verbally. Puppetry is a good vehicle for them since they stay in one confined area and manipulate puppets close to their own body space. Scripts can be recorded on cassettes to facilitate a smooth, nonthreatening performance. Taping is generally a good idea for all puppeteers. It removes a potential source of frustration if children do not have to turn pages and try to manipulate a puppet simultaneously.

English-as-a-Second-Language Students. Students who enter school with English as their second language often have difficulty. Many of the Asian and Hispanic children in schools today have to cope with first learning a new language in order to learn the academic skills taught. School systems generally provide special teachers to work exclusively with these students. The teachers totally immerse the children in English through the use of mime, pointing at items and naming them, oral repetition, and games of all kinds. Creative drama is an important part of the curriculum, since it affords children a multitude of opportunities to act out scenarios of everyday life or stories they learn. Drama helps present vignettes of a culture foreign to these children in a manner that is nonthreatening and that can be repeated as often as necessary.

Emotionally Disturbed. Boys and girls with emotional problems can range from those with totally aggressive behavior to those who are extremely withdrawn. The reasons for such behavior are varied and deepseated, but drama, under the direction of a firm but sensitive teacher, has a way of reaching such children. Again, the most severe cases are usually placed in institutions, not regular schools, and are treated by trained specialists who use special techniques such as drama therapy. The children in the regular school system, however, often benefit from creative drama since it allows them an opportunity to role play correct behavior, work on acceptable social interaction skills under the guidance of a teacher, and "walk in another character's shoes" for a while in the guise of drama. Besides, the release of pent up energy in warm-up activities and the drama class itself, plus the sharing time at the end of a drama session, can be truly beneficial for students who are coping with learning acceptable social behavior.

Puppetry

Puppetry is especially valuable for exceptional learners because it includes a multitude of affective and cognitive skills. Involved are design and construction, movement and speech, playwrighting and improvisation, performing and viewing, all of which can be used across the curriculum as an interdisciplinary art form. Puppetry allows children an easy means of communicating without fear of being "on display." A puppet, then, is a kind of alter ego that often liberates the puppeteer's spontaneity. On a therapeutic level, children can hide behind a puppet in order to safely reveal themselves through the puppet. On a more theatrical level, the puppeteer-actor transcends his or her individualistic and realistic posture to become part of a universal, symbolic means of expression. Teachers can work on both levels in using puppetry in classrooms (see Figure 3.4).

Stewart (1979) summarized several advantages of using puppetry.

1. Puppets have an indefinable power to attract attention and focus concentration.
2. Puppetry combines art/craft/drama in a more complete way than any other art form.
3. Puppetry at any level of intellectual development or technical competence can involve a range of disciplines, aesthetic principles, and craft skills designed to challenge (stimulate) the brightest and least adventurous member of any group.
4. The puppet as intermediary can serve as a safety device, allowing a child to explore ideas in the third person. Social interaction through puppets encourages risk taking and can often defuse potentially explosive situations.
5. The scale of puppetry enables a teacher to follow most of the processes of an elaborately staged drama project, but eliminates many of the action-space, storage-space, and cast problems.
6. Puppetry generates enthusiasm; with our children it is essential to illustrate that puppetry is no "kids' stuff." It is a challenging, creative, historically mysterious, technically sophisticated art form that can produce results, a performance that other people can enjoy and admire. (pp. 39–40)

While children are creating and producing their puppets, they forget themselves completely as they discuss what they are going to do. They develop more fully the skills of interaction, listening, negotiation, concentration, and sequential planning. Spontaneity and risk taking are also evident as they work their puppets and create the scenery, voice, characterization,

FIGURE 3.4. Having children make simple sock puppets and then use them to recreate a story is often a rewarding experience.

and sound effects that accompany their scripts. Cottrell (1987) feels that even "students who are communication-apprehensive or those with severe reading problems can tell the story with puppets while others narrate using a readers theatre format" (p. 167). The opportunities for learning in a puppet project are enormous because it incorporates art, crafts, and drama and is humanistic in scope.

The benefits to emotionally disturbed or other at-risk students are numerous. Hammill and Bartel (1975) present a theory and rationale supporting the use of puppetry.

> The puppets have specific meaning to each child and he or she is able to project his hate, anger, fears, and desires onto them in a neutral, fantasy-like manner. Many of these feelings ordinarily remain suppressed because expression of them in actual life situations is often too threatening to the child. (p. 137)

In like manner McCaslin (1990) believes in the therapeutic power of puppetry. She states that "through them, timid or withdrawn children can find release, whereas aggressive children learn to subordinate themselves to the personality of the characters they are presenting" (p. 151).

Puppetry, then, involves a multitude of skills, not only academic and artistic, but social as well. It provides for the involvement of all types and age levels of students. Not only do normal children receive the benefits of creating and performing with puppets; such an experience seems to be particularly effective with exceptional learners.

Social Skills Training

Social skills are those behaviors which allow an individual to successfully interact with others (Jensen, Sloane, & Young, 1988). The authors say that

> Achieving social competence is an essential part of growing up. Most people acquire social skills as part of their natural development, but others need assistance in developing the social skills necessary to successfully interact with others. A socially skilled person uses appropriate social behavior in a successful and positive manner during interpersonal interactions, and does so consistently over time and in the correct social context. All students can benefit from social skills instruction; students who are already socially competent may assist teachers in developing appropriate social behavior in other students who are not. (p. 276)

The "training" element in social skills training involves the instruction used to acquire those skills. The belief is that "teachers must not only make students aware of specific behaviors that are unacceptable, but must actually teach constructive behavioral alternatives as well" (McGinnis & Goldstein, 1984, p. 7).

A method called *structured learning* has been used for teaching such skills. This method is "a psychoeducational, behavioral approach for providing instruction in prosocial skills. It consists of (1) modeling, (2) role playing, (3) performance feedback, and (4) transfer of training" (McGinnis & Goldstein, 1984, p. 9). The authors have complied sixty prosocial skills and divided them into five basic skills groups: "(1) Classroom Survival Skills; (2) Friendship-Making Skills; (3) Skills for Dealing with Feelings; (4) Skill Alternatives to Aggression; and (5) Skills for Dealing with Stress" (p. 103).

There is no curricular scope or sequence involved in teaching these five skills, as when teaching a cumulative skill such as mathematics. However, the teacher must be perceptive and select an appropriate intervention for antisocial behaviors requiring immediate attention. In other words, the teacher must be flexible in meeting the needs of the children involved.

The underlying philosophy for social skills training is that early teaching of prosocial behavioral alternatives may enhance a child's personal development and aid in preventing more serious difficulties in adolescence and early adulthood. This is a valuable intervention for both handicapped (mainstreamed or not) and nonhandicapped children who demonstrate the kind of undesirable behaviors or skill deficits that result in personal unhappiness, interpersonal difficulty, or academic ineffectiveness.

The teaching strategies utilized in creative drama can easily be applied to social skills training. The modeling, role playing, and performance feedback are immediately applicable techniques. Carol Buege has used these methods with normal and emotionally disturbed students, and they work very well.

SELLING THE IDEA TO A SCHOOL SYSTEM

Now that we have discussed at some length the "how" of spontaneous drama, we have left only one brief topic—how do you convince your school system that drama is a good idea?

While you yourself may be convinced of the need to include dramatics, the social understandings that children gain from doing drama are too frequently not of interest to those planning and controlling curricula. Although schools in America give lip service to independence, self-expression, social self-confidence, and other "self-oriented" goals, there is evidence to suggest that these do not, in fact, figure largely in the planning of most curricula. We must admit such factors as these are difficult to measure. Apparently, one either accepts them as important and works from this philosophical position, or only gives lip service to the ideas and demonstrates that one's major interests lie elsewhere.

Successful teachers are aware that they *will* need to sell the idea of classroom drama and that conscious planning to do this will be necessary.

1. Talk about this idea with whoever will listen. This includes talking with other teachers informally in the teacher's room, with the principal, and even with parents encountered casually in the supermarket.
2. Present ideas in formal situations. Be willing to put forth the effort to prepare a talk about drama for the school board, for the administrators' meeting, or for the parent–teacher meeting. Such activities will help convince people of the benefits of drama.
3. Communicate with parents in writing. Some drama leaders send brief letters home periodically reporting on the drama sessions in order to keep parents informed.

Part of the job of "selling" drama experiences is taken care of by the children, whose enthusiastic comments about the program once it is underway will help inform adults of the benefits of such a program. But the teacher-leader can never rely exclusively on such informal and unplanned publicity. Rather, consciously analyze the people you are trying to convince of the value of a drama program. Identify what approach will appeal to them, what problems they may anticipate, and the arguments you may have to marshal to deal with these. It is by such conscious analysis and then by equally conscious efforts at publicizing the program that the enthusiastic teacher enlists the support needed to make drama a success.

SUMMARY

In this chapter we have investigated some important factors related to implementing a sequence of drama experiences. The teacher, being central to the success of such a program, needs to be flexible, to be a good question asker, to believe in the dramatic experience, and to be aware of the various stages in his or her participation. Some very specific suggestions were included about how to plan a session, including getting an honest response from children, selecting material, and developing conflict and character. Some attention was given to evaluating the sessions, to dealing with physical problems, and to "selling" the idea of drama to a school system. It is hoped that with this rather extensive chapter on the "how" of drama, you will be encouraged to forge ahead, if you are interested in beginning drama with children. The following chapter includes an examination of the specific language learnings that can occur as a result of drama experiences. This should give you some further ideas about how to convince people of the values of such a program.

RELATED READING

Burke, M. (1992). Who says? Why? Evaluation in classroom drama. *The Drama/Theatre Teacher, 4*(3), 10–13.
     The author sets her comments in a larger context than is customary: She remarks about how assessment is carried out in England, in Australia, and in America. The most critical question is, what *kind* of drama are we talking about evaluating? It is clear Burke feels the Australian approach to evaluating drama work is most effective. The teaching and evaluating of drama there look on drama as concerned with "the holistic development of the participant." Her comments contrast the criteria used in one Australian

drama document with the questions proposed in the section entitled Evaluating the Session, earlier in this chapter. The entire issue of this journal deals with evaluation of drama from preschool through college.

Koltai, J. (1974). You don't have to be an expert . . . some thoughts on the use of role-playing in the classroom. In L. Ollila, E. G. Summers, J. Downing, & P. Viel (Eds.), *Learning to read: Reading to learn* (pp. 138–147). Victoria: Vancouver Island I.R.A.

The author views role playing as one way of helping children see that their own private world actually overlaps the private worlds of many others. She is extremely supportive of teachers who would like to use role playing but are fearful of beginning. Koltai believes that skillful questioning to develop characterization is critical to success and describes ways to help a group select a problem that is personally relevant. She also describes how to develop a scene based on an issue. This chapter is useful for teachers who want to explore nonliterature-based drama motivations.

San Jose, C. (1971, March). A happening for parents' night. *Elementary English, 48,* 332–335.

This describes how one school dealt with the problem of preparing a program for parents. The teacher is often tempted to demonstrate competence through a polished product that requires an undue expenditure of time and energy totally unrelated to learning. As a solution, a third-grade class worked on a unit in social studies about Italy. They discussed the country, played music, danced to it, and collected objects from Italy. Meanwhile, the music teacher and author worked on creative drama to prepare the children for spontaneous acting. For the parents' night, a street scene in Italy was chosen. The children pantomimed ideas and danced to music. Teachers trying to establish the value of drama for parents and school administrators will find this helpful.

CHAPTER 4

Drama as a Language Art

How important is drama in elementary classrooms in the United States? Unlike British infant schools, where drama plays a more central role throughout the entire school, dramatics remains on the periphery of the curriculum in our schools (Dillon, 1981). Too many classroom teachers cannot find time to give more than fleeting attention to drama activities or cannot convince authorities of the value of such activities.

Drama is in the same tenuous position as the arts and foreign language instruction. All these are judged frills, indulged in as long as expenditures are minimal, but eliminated at the first signs of waning budgets. People responsible for planning programs add such subjects when it is convenient and eliminate them when it appears financially necessary, despite strong justification for arts as basic in the education of all children (Fowler, 1989).

REASONS FOR LACK OF EMPHASIS

Perhaps few teachers try drama with children because they receive so little support from two influential sources that determine the curriculum—the textbook and the curriculum guide. Despite recent changes that have taken place, at the impetus of teachers interested in the whole language movement, in many schools the main source of the curriculum remains the textbook. How do textbooks treat drama activities? Do they deal with such activities at all?

An early study by Brown (1967) focused on *all* oral activities, rather than only on creative drama. He found that "it is apparent that writing and grammar are emphasized more than speaking and listening" (p. 341). This emphasis is in spite of numerous studies that point out conclusively that such conscious teaching of grammar yields a very small return for the time expended. In newer language arts textbook series, revised content and emphases generally give greater priority to oral language; however, the question of how successful they have been in encouraging drama remains unanswered. In a recent survey of principals, "nearly half the respondents felt their adopted published materials were less than adequate in supporting the teachers who did drama" (Stewig, 1986, p. 16).

Another influential source on what is taught is the curriculum guide, and too few guides consider drama to be an important teaching method. Apparently the teacher gets little encouragement from either language arts textbooks or curriculum guides, the two major determinants of the curriculum, in efforts to establish a program of drama experiences.

The result of this lack of encouragement is that little time is devoted to drama in the elementary language arts curriculum. Haley-James (1981) reports a nationwide survey of 319 fourth-grade teachers. The majority (86%) spent thirty minutes a day teaching language arts. More than half (69%) devoted less than 5% of that time to informal classroom drama activities.

The reasons drama activities have been largely ignored are rather difficult to determine, especially in view of the cogent and convincing statements proponents have made about the psychological values of drama. There are numerous clear and concise statements of the social and emotional values gained by including drama in the elementary curriculum. A respected authority in the field, Geraldine Siks (1968), speaks specifically of five values. These include

1. Social development
2. Creative self-expression
3. Wholesome emotional development
4. Attitudes and appreciations
5. Development of inner security

Siks and other drama leaders for many years have been describing such psychological gains in detail. While it is not the intent to minimize such gains, we need to be aware that many critics of education believe such social-emotional needs are not a fundamental concern of educators. Silberman (1970) is one in a succession of educational critics who make us, through their acerbic but accurate accusations, re-examine what we believe. His comments, written some time ago, remain remarkably pertinent today.

One reason that drama has had only a minimal impact may be the experiences children typically undergo in drama. Most of these are long on creativity and self-expression, but short on the structure or sequence that allows for growth. In too many cases, any growth in drama may be attributed to simple maturity or individual talent, rather than to the effectiveness of the program itself, and the sequence of specific skills taught.

Two early attempts began the process of identifying drama skills. Oster

(1969) tried drama with her children, perhaps as you have tried, and was disappointed with the results. Because she could not find the help she wanted from authorities in the field, she worked to pinpoint a sequence of specific drama skills to teach children. These skills range from simple pantomime of common activities, like picking up a fork, to more elaborate techniques for faking physical conflict. After identifying these skills, Oster taught them systematically to provide a repertoire of skills children could use when appropriate. The article makes encouraging reading for a classroom teacher whose experiences with drama have been less rewarding than desired. More recently, Wagner (1990) has written about a suggested sequence of experiences that moves from simple to more complex. The article is enlivened by transcriptions of student oral dialogue and also samples of writing that grew out of the dramatizing. Although she begins with story drama, Wagner takes the sequence into more involved theme-based improvisations as well.

In addition to these attempts at outlining more specifically a sequence of steps that may ensure success with drama, another idea in education—behavioral objectives—has also been applied to creative drama. In an interesting attempt, Shaw (1968) specified with meticulous care the behavioral objectives that should be part of a drama program. Although people in the arts generally view this approach with skepticism (see, for example, statements by Richard Courtney in Booth & Martin-Smith, 1988), the insightful thoroughness with which this was done resulted in a useful resource for teachers.

Given the current minimal importance of drama, we would like to suggest another method by which such programs may be justified to doubting parents, supervisors, and principals. This is by exploring more fully the ways drama can be an integral part of a language arts program and a means of teaching about many facets of these arts in an exciting fashion.

DRAMA AND THE READING PROGRAM

It is most logical to begin by discussing how drama enriches the reading program because, as pointed out in Chapter 1, it is in this context that many teachers begin, by doing simple story dramatizations with children. Although this is only one facet of drama (Stewig, 1977), it is an easily accessible one and is, therefore, recommended to teachers who have never tried drama.

Spontaneous drama adds interest and vitality to a reading program, no matter which method of teaching is employed. In traditional programs, it is certainly true that some of the first stories in basal readers are ill-suited to dramatization, although Carlton and Moore (1968) report using them effectively. In more broadly based literacy programs many stories children will encounter are well-suited to drama. These might include a folktale or fairy story an individual child is reading, an information tradebook a class might use in some content area like social studies, or a story made up by children themselves in a language-experience approach program. In thinking about dramatizing literature, it is crucial to distinguish between two ideas and the terms describing them. The two terms are *interpretation* and *improvisation*. Although this distinction was introduced in Chapter 1, it will be described more fully here.

In doing story drama with children, one begins with interpretation of the story, that is, the teacher encourages children to choose characters and to portray, or act out, the character's role. In interpreting a story, the emphasis is on fidelity to the author's story line and on retaining the basic characterization. Naturally, each child's individuality will be apparent. If we have five different children who interpret the beast in Binette Schroeder's *Beauty and the Beast* (1987), each will be different. Nevertheless, in interpretation, the emphasis is not primarily on what the child can create, but rather on the ability to bring to life the author's words.

In doing a story improvisation, use the basic story as a departure point, and ask children questions that will encourage them to extend, expand, or in other ways go beyond the basic thematic material. Children may be encouraged to extend the plot forward or backward in time (Figure 4.1) or to expand the story, perhaps by adding a character (Figure 4.2) or enlarging the role played by one already in the story. To take a well-known example, let us consider the vain sisters in the story of Cinderella by Eleanor Farjeon (1981) or Padraic Colum (1968). Have you even thought about them? Probably not. Yet children gain new insights into their characters as a result of considering such questions as

- What things might have made them the way they were? Had they always acted that way? If not, when and why did their personalities change?
- In what ways were they different? (The story portrays them in silhouette, without much detail.) Are there differences about them we can infer from the story?
- Were they interested in anything beyond their finery? Had they any talents? What things might they have been good at doing? Did they have any friends? Who could have been interested in such selfish sisters? What evidence supports any interpretation?
- What could have happened if one of the sisters' feet had fit the slipper?

These are specific questions about only two characters. There are some more general questions that the leader keeps in mind as he or she encourages children to probe into characters in an effort to make them come to

Backward	Questions to consider	Forward
in time	**to extend the story**	**in time**
How had the mother died?	Actual time described in story:	What adventure might the Invisible Being and the girl go on?
Had the sisters always been cruel to the girl?	"Once, long ago, there was a village by the shores of Lake Ontario."	How did she use her courage and determination?
Why did the father ignore how the sisters treated her?	to	Was the Being's sister important to what happened after the marriage? How?
	"They lived in great gladness and were never parted."	

FIGURE 4.1. Plot extension based on a story: *The Rough-Face Girl*, by Rafe Martin (1992).

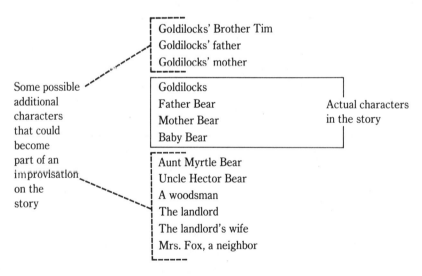

FIGURE 4.2. Character addition based on a story: *Goldilocks and the Three Bears*.

life. The physical, social, and psychological facets of the characters need to be considered. In discussing *physical aspects*, we are concerned with such questions as

- What age do we think the character might be? What evidence do we have about this?
- What is the character's health condition? An exuberant child will move differently than would Princess Lenore when she was ill (see James Thurber's 1943 or 1990 editions).
- What is the appearance of the character? Obviously Mr. Toad would move very differently than would Puss (Figure 4.3) in *Puss in Boots* by Gail E. Haley (1991).[1]

Related to *social aspects* of the character, we help children to think about such questions as

- What occupation does the character pursue? What effects might that have had on him?
- What kind of home life does the character have? How does he relate to others in his home? (Janice Lee Smith's series of stories about Adam Joshua [1984, and following] are particularly effective in depicting life today.)
- What kind of personal relationships does the character have outside the family? What clues do these relationships give us about the nature of the character?

Related to *psychological aspects* of the character, we may encourage children to think of the following questions:

- What do we know, or what can we infer, about the *feelings* of the character? Do we see shifts in the feelings of the character as the story progresses? How are these shifts manifested in behaviors?
- What do the character's actions and words tell us about his or her attitudes? Do we see changes in these as the story progresses? If we are improvising, can we infer how the character might feel, or what his or her attitudes might be in situations other than those described in the story?

By judicious questioning about any basic story, the teacher can lead children from simple interpretation into improvisation based on the story.

---

[1]The adventures of the irrepressible Mr. Toad in Kenneth Grahame's *The River Bank* (1983) make excellent material for improvisations. Stoic Mole and acceptant Ratty are good character contrasts, and the softly luminous ink drawings by John Burningham evoke a pastoral time and place unlike our own.

FIGURE 4.3. Illustrator Gail E. Haley is at the top of her form in *Puss in Boots* (1991), a book distinguished by vigorous pictures full of interesting detail depicting the period setting. The possibilities of walking in boots and cape like the cat, playing croquet with the king, or stalking like an ogre when in lion form will intrigue young children.

College juniors recently made up the following questions about favorite stories:

John Fowles's *Cinderella* (1974)
- What changes might have occurred if Cinderella had a fairy godfather instead of a fairy godmother?
- How could the prince have found Cinderella if the glass slipper had shattered on the steps?
- What if Cinderella had stepbrothers instead of stepsisters?

Harriet Pincus's *Little Red Riding Hood* (1989)
- What might have happened if the huntsman hadn't come to kill the wolf at the end of the story?
- What might have happened if Grandma had realized that the wolf was at the door and hadn't let him in?

Zena Sutherland's "Little Miss Muffett" (1990)[2]
- What could have happened if Little Miss Muffett had liked spiders?

Paul Galdone's *The Three Bears* (1972)
- What could have happened if Goldilocks had decided to stay in the forest with the bears?
- Suppose the porridge had been the right temperature and the bears did not have to go for a walk—what might have happened then?

Freya Littledale's *Snow White and the Seven Dwarfs* (1980)
- How could the queen have found out about Snow White if she had no magic mirror?
- Who might have taken in Snow White, if the dwarfs had not?
- How would the other dwarfs have acted if Snow White had married one of them?

Beatrice Schenk de Regniers's *Jack and the Beanstalk* (1985)
- What if a beautiful princess had lived at the top of the beanstalk instead of a giant?
- What if Jack wasn't able to chop the beanstalk down in time?
- What would Jack have done if the beanstalk had wilted after he reached the cloud where the giant lived?

Michael Gibson's "Midas, The Golden King" (1982)
- What if King Midas had touched his head and turned himself to gold?
- What would have happened if the man told Midas that he would no longer have the golden touch, but that he couldn't reverse those things that were already gold, including his daughter?

Yoshitaro Isaka's *Hansel and Gretel* (1971)
- What would have happened if the house had been made of squash and spinach?
- What would have happened if the witch had planned to starve them instead of push them into the oven?
- What would have happened if the bread crumbs had not been eaten by the birds?

Take a story with which you are familiar and try this approach. You'll be surprised at the possibilities that will become apparent as you think about it.

---

[2]After using this, read "Little Miss Tuckett" in Leonard S. Marcus and Amy Schwartz's *Mother Goose's Little Misfortunes* (1990) for comparison purposes.

If a teacher is able to lead children through interpreting stories to improvising on stories, such activities will greatly enrich the reading program. Support for including drama in the reading program is available: Research studies show improvement in reading skills as a result of drama. Henderson and Shanker (1978) found impressive increases in comprehension among second-grade black students from a low socioeconomic area. Burke (1980) found that positive changes took place in both attitudes and reading abilities of his seventh-grade students. Vawter and Vancil (1980) also comment on this. Related to the reading program is the literature program, the scope of which is broadened when drama becomes an integral part of the language arts curriculum.

DRAMA AND THE LITERATURE PROGRAM

For too long, according to writers on the topic, children's literature has been the neglected stepchild in the language arts curriculum. Recently, more teachers have been using more literature with children as whole language programs become widespread. One very useful way to encourage response to literature is to incorporate it as motivation for improvisation (Glazer, 1986, pp. 100–102, 201). Although drama leaders never limit themselves to literature only, knowing that movement and sensory motivations are important, using poetry and prose for this purpose ensures exposure to a larger quantity of literature than children ordinarily encounter. Many of the pieces the teacher reads to children during the fifteen or twenty minutes each day that make up the literature program can provide departure points for drama.

Probably few of us as adults feel that, as children, our exposure to poetry was as rich, varied, and pleasant as it could have been. Probably still fewer of us, as teachers, feel we are providing children with an exposure to poetry as stimulating, diversified, and challenging as we would like. One way to do this is to make more use of poetry in drama sessions. As we read widely, we find many poems of use. The most important quality in poetry is *action*; search for poems containing verbs appropriate for enacting. For example, in Sutherland and Livingston (1984) there are poems with such verbs as *canter* (in "The Centaur" by May Swenson); *frolicked* (in "Always Room for One More" by Sorche Nic Leodhas); *jostled* (in "The Rose on My Cake" by Karla Kuskin); and *galumphing* (in "Jabberwocky" by Lewis Carroll).

We also broaden children's exposure to prose by using stories (or parts of them) as motivation for improvisation. You might use the charming story of winsome Princess Lenore and her illness resulting from a surfeit of raspberry tarts as told in James Thurber's *Many Moons* (1943, 1990).[3] Or, as a contrast, use episodes from the life of the brash Harriet, a delightful terror, in *Harriet the Spy* by Louise Fitzhugh (1964) (see Figure 4.4).

Boys will be particularly taken with the endless possibilities in the adventures of Milo in Norton Juster's *The Phantom Tollbooth* (1961). Younger boys have enjoyed the adventures of Peter, as depicted by Ezra Jack Keats (1967, 1968).

In these, as in any stories you use, the *action* is the crucial element. All descriptive passages need to be rather ruthlessly eliminated to pare the story down to the basic skeleton of action so it can be played.

If you are uncertain about your ability to select and adapt prose for dramatization, find a copy of *World Tales for Creative Drama and Storytelling* by Fitzgerald (1962). In addition to providing stories already adapted for improvising, the book offers many suggestions about how to select and adapt stories yourself. More recently, Heinig (1992) has provided a helpful way of integrating drama into the reading/writing classroom through the use of old tales. She does not include the tales themselves, but rather annotates several different published versions of them, identifying ways they are similar and different. Her very complete plans for how to use the stories to achieve language benefits will interest teachers beginning to work in this way with children at various grade levels.

The stories you use need, of course, to be read in their entirety to children, either before or after their use as motivation for drama. This oral reading during the literature period allows children to savor the descriptive paragraphs that may be lost in the active involvement of improvising.

ORAL LANGUAGE DEVELOPMENT

Probably one of the strongest contributions that drama makes is to *oral language proficiency*. As pointed out in Chapter 1, oral language is pervasive in adult life, but the elementary language arts curriculum too often gives only minimal attention to further development of students' oral abilities. Yet Noble, Egan, and McDowell (1977) have shown that verbal fluency increased among primary age minority children as a result of systematic training in creative drama.

---

[3]A very useful language activity, not particularly related to drama per se, is to obtain the two editions of this tale and encourage children to compare and contrast the illustrations. The 1943 edition (still available from the publisher) features pastel illustrations by Louis Slobodkin, which won the Caldecott Medal. Children can observe many differences between these and the more vividly colored illustrations in the 1990 edition, by Marc Simont.

FIGURE 4.4. Pugnacious *Harriet the Spy*, shown in an illustration by the author, Louise Fitzhugh (1964), leads an active life. She gets into many scrapes because of her inquisitiveness, which makes the story interesting to dramatize.

There are several facets of oral language facility that drama encourages. The first is *spontaneous oral composition*. In drama situations, we frequently challenge children to create dialogue, to think orally on their feet, or to compose as they go. At times we give them situational clues, specifying (1) where they are, (2) who they are, and (3) what the problem is. For instance, the teacher might divide the children into groups of three and specify:

- You are yourself, coming home from school late and encountering your annoyed mother in the kitchen as she makes supper. Your little brother, who thinks it is funny, makes comments.

Children are then allowed time to create a dialogue resulting from the situation. After time to work on the spontaneous dialogues, the groups present them for the other children.

At other times, perhaps with older children, we structure the situation less completely. This is what Moffett and Wagner (1992) call the *"minimal situation."* We might say:

- Imagine you are a teacher and the other person is somebody's mother. Now, make something happen.

Sometimes, we may structure the situation to an even lesser degree, using a conflict line to motivate children. A *conflict line* is a single sentence that indicates some unspecified conflict children may develop in many different ways. Some examples might be:

I wonder why they're not here yet.
I couldn't believe Sally really said that.
That's not what we agreed to do.
Can you explain to me how this happened?
Can you see what that is up ahead?

Because conflict lines are so open-ended, and yet do give children some structure on which to build, the same line can be used by several different groups, with interesting results. In working with a class of thirty children, the leader might, for example, divide them into six smaller groups, each working with the same line. Comparing and contrasting the resulting improvisations would reveal wide differences in what the groups were able to create.

In such situations we help children work on the ability to create oral dialogue that is not written down and to project themselves into the person they are being, as they act or interact verbally in ways the person might.

Related to oral language proficiency is conscious understanding of such *paralinguistic* elements as pitch, stress, and juncture, introduced in Chapter

2. Sometimes we show children pictures of people and ask that they create voices for those people. We ask them to think about such questions as

- How would these people be likely to say a particular sentence?
- How might each of them use pitch, stress, and juncture to convey their ideas?

In this situation, as in so many others in drama, we are asking children to take a small bit of information and to build upon it.

Sometimes we simply ask children to take a sentence from their improvisation and manipulate it in as many subtle ways as possible. An alert leader will notice sentences in the children's dialogue that lend themselves to multiple interpretation. Encourage them to try out different ways of using paralanguage elements to change the meaning.

Notice the multiple meanings possible in even simple sentences.

Are you going home already? (Interpretation: I can't believe you've decided to go!)

Are *you* going home already? (Interpretation: You, as opposed to your friend.)

Are you *going* home already? (Interpretation: Going, as opposed to coming here.)

Are you going *home* already? (Interpretation: Home, as contrasted to going to some other place.)

Are you going home *already*? (Interpretation: It's too soon for you to be going.)

We can also help children understand the variety of dialects that are most obviously manifested in oral language, by using such stories as departure points in drama. When we use *Strawberry Girl* by Lois Lenski (1945), *Thee, Hannah* by Marguerite de Angeli (1940), and *Roosevelt Grady* by Louisa Shotwell (1963), we build both an understanding of and a tolerance for people whose oral speech patterns are unlike our own. This is especially crucial in a time when more and more children come to school speaking a dialect. Although we don't insist that children use the dialects while playing such a story, if this happens we encourage it as an additional language learning through drama. Mable Henry (1967) describes these learnings.

Did the character speak as they would have in the situation? Amazingly, children are more aware of speech patterns that indicate class and locale than we imagine, and the search for better words to incorporate into the dialogue sends them to the story itself; vocabulary and word recognition become concomitant gains. (pp. 56–57)

The anecdote that best illustrates her point is about a boy who was portraying King Midas: "In one group of seven-year-olds, King Midas said, 'Ok, y' c'n go.' He stopped dead and said aloud, to himself more than to the group, 'No, kings don't talk like that.' He then resumed his character and said imperiously, 'Very well, you are dismissed'" (pp. 6–7).

Authors continue to provide opportunities for children to listen to dialects that may be unlike their own, in stories full of possibilities for dramatizing. Recently, Ethel Footman Smothers, in *Down in the Piney Woods* (1992), introduced us to ten-year-old Annie Rye. This story of a young girl coming to terms with changes depicts a black sharecropping family in rural Georgia in the 1950s, while dealing with a very universal theme.

Related to these learnings about voice and words is the challenge drama offers to create sounds with the voice. The challenge of creating sounds, for instance, when we are using a poem about animals, helps children understand the beauty they can create and extends the expressive range of their voices. Children would be familiar with the sounds made by several of the animals in *Ring-a-Ring O'Roses* by Alan Marks (1991). Encouraging students to use their voices to make the sounds of the animals as they are dramatizing the poems is a good idea.

There are more abstract sounds with which children may experiment. They take delight, for example, in interpreting the less recognizable sounds made by the Furies, released when, in "Pandora's Box," she succumbs to temptation in the story by Alice Low (1985). These are neither human nor animal sounds and are unlike anything we have ever heard before because they are made by strange creatures outside our experience. As such they provide a definite challenge to children's inventiveness, and the results give children insights into the expressive qualities of their voices.

NONVERBAL ELEMENTS

Spontaneous drama allows us to discover elements related to oral language that are often ignored. Children can become aware of the importance of both kinesics and bodily movement as adjuncts to communication.

Kinesics

Kinesics accounts for about 55% of the total communicated message. By *kinesics* we mean those bodily movements made by arms, hands, shoulders, and the myriad subtle facial gestures by which we augment the basic message.

Everyone uses these additions to the basic flow of speech sounds, although often our use of them is subconscious. Only when the discrepancy between oral speech and the kinesics becomes apparent do we pause to notice this phenomenon. Unfortunately, we seldom proceed to the next step, the conscious manipulation of these kinesic elements to intensify or augment our words.

We challenge children to do this consciously when we ask them to think about, and show us, how characters might look or what kinesics they might use, in a particular situation. We might find a drama program involving children planning kinesics for the following:

> Alice, as the bewildering queen takes her arm.
> The two sisters at the moment the glass slipper slides onto Cinderella's foot.
> The wolf as he tries to talk his way into grandmother's house.
> The wicked queen as she offers the apple to Snow White.
> Dorothy, as she bids goodbye to her friends when she leaves Oz (L. Frank Baum, 1982).

Bodily Movement

A difference exists between kinesics and *bodily movement*; the latter is characterized as larger movements taking place in the context of the available space. Of interest to the general public because of such books as *Body Language* by Julius Fast (1970), this aspect of communication has been a concern of drama people for some time. Wall and Murray (1990) have written helpfully about four movement concepts for teachers interested in doing drama with children. These four are body concepts, effort concepts, spatial concepts, and relationship concepts. Several of the activities they suggest would be appropriate lesson warm-ups prior to moving into more sustained dramatization (see Figure 4.5).

Movement experiences often provide helpful introduction to a drama session. Such experiences

1. Provide a transition between more academic concerns and the freer drama class
2. Help encourage exploration of problems that children can solve through body movement
3. Focus on the specific content of the drama lesson itself

There are essentially two kinds of movement, nonlocomotor and locomotor (Pangrazi & Dauer, 1992). The first, *nonlocomotor*, presents children with a series of problems to solve within their own space. Standing beside their desks, as shown in Figure 4.5, children may be asked:

FIGURE 4.5. These students are doing a stretching exercise, one of many body awareness experiences that are an effective preparation for more involved story drama.

- How high can you stretch?
- Can you reach to the right, bend forward, and then twist in reverse?
- How many ways can you find to lift or push?
- Can you make up a sequence that combines a dodging, a swaying, and a sinking movement?

Other questions to encourage movement exploration are given by Complo (1974, pp. 14–31).

In contrast, in *locomotor* motion we ask boys and girls to move through space. The poem by Mary Austin, "The Sandhill Crane" (Sutherland, 1976, p. 38), is especially good for this purpose because of its variety of verbs. The poem speaks of the crane *stalking*, the little frogs *jumping*, the minnows *scuttling*, the chipmunks *stopping*, the gophers *hiding*, and the mice *whispering*.

We talk about these verbs and encourage children to interpret the words in movement. Next, we have them propose other animals that might be suggested by the line in the poem mentioning "field folk," and we add a variety of animals and movements until we have an entire menagerie to challenge our abilities. These animal movements are more appropriate for younger students, though Barton and Booth (1973) describe teenaged students responding with intense concentration to animal motivation.

We also work to interpret body movement of humans. The problem here, as elsewhere in drama, is to have children create without resorting to stereotypes. If a story includes a little old lady, we must help children move beyond the stereotype of a little old woman walking with a cane and having a bent back that impedes her movement. This is the first characteristic that often comes to many children's minds, and we try to help them see that like people of all ages, old people cannot realistically be stereotyped in one way.

We might use Mary Norton's *Bed-Knob and Broomstick* (1957) to encourage children to think about the ways body movement differs among people. The story provides some large contrasts—for instance, between the inquisitive young children and the fastidious, middle-aged Miss Price. It also provides some small contrasts (perhaps more difficult to achieve) between the body movements of the three children, all about the same age. A successful characterization of ebullient Paul, helpful Carey, and bossy Charles would entail some differences in physical movement.

In these examples, and indeed in many aspects of drama, we are working for *particularization* of ideas. In "The Sandhill Crane," the idea of "field folk" is not specific enough. We need to spell out what kinds of field folk are possible and then also detail the particular information about each one. If rabbit is suggested by a child, we need to pursue what kind of rabbit: old or young, male or female, active or feeble, wild or domestic?

Similarly, the little old woman needs to be particularized. Who is she? Is she a cranky old lady or a nice old lady? We can even explore how she *feels* about where she is going. As children begin to develop their own answers to these questions, improvisations take on character and depth.

Attempts to have children particularize movement are worthwhile, even though at times the best intentions of the leader may go awry. Once while working with a group of kindergarten children on the idea of different types of movement, it became apparent that I was not getting through to one little girl. We had talked about people movement, especially about how daddies move differently than mommies, and brothers differently than sisters. The little girl was adamant in insisting that in her family everybody walked the same way. A very helpful little boy sitting next to her poked her in the ribs with his elbow and looked at her in a disgusted fashion. "What's the matter," he asked, "ain't you got no crippled sisters at home?" At which we moved to another activity, despite my conviction that particularization of movement is crucial to drama!

Pantomime

Pantomime, an integral part of drama and a concern of the participants at any level of experience, is related to movement. Being able to communicate through one's body, thus avoiding reliance on spoken words of explanation, is a skill of much value in drama. Such pantomime may be a tiny fragment, perhaps as momentary as unscrewing the top on a salt shaker or lifting a glass to drink. Or it may be an involved sequence of separate pantomimed actions that flow together to tell a story, perhaps one of the many actions involved in getting ready for, going to, and returning home from a party. Hillman (1975) provides several suggestions for quite involved mimes.

Remember that pantomime is *skill*. Whether it is a kindergarten child pantomiming bouncing a ball or the master mimist Marcel Marceau, as shown in the book by George Mendoza (1970), in an involved story sequence, good pantomime is always the result of both thought and practice. This is the reason children's pantomime is often so generalized; it communicates poorly or not at all. To pantomime well, one must perform a series of steps, the first of which is to *particularize* in the mind the actions and objects to be portrayed.

If children are to pantomime opening a box, for example, they must answer certain questions in their minds before they begin.

- How large a box is it?
- Of what is it made?
- How does it open?
- On what is it sitting?
- What is inside of it?
- How is it fastened shut?

How the child answers these questions will affect how the hand, arm, and torso muscles move as he or she performs the pantomime. At first these questions need to be posed by the leader orally, to challenge the group to think about these problems. As children develop more mature drama skills, they will ask the questions of themselves.

To mime picking up a fork, the children need to think about such questions as

- Who is doing this? A child picks up a fork differently from an aging and arthritic grandfather.
- Of what material is it made? A plastic fork taken along to a picnic would have a different weight from a heavy silver one used at a banquet.
- For what is it being used? In trying to maneuver spaghetti to the mouth, the approach with the fork is considerably different from that in eating something solid like meat loaf.

In the examples above, the common denominator is the mental preparation involved in pantomiming the physical movement. The leader may try to establish this mental set by talking with children about such aspects of the pantomime. Or use a different approach and have children observe themselves closely as they use the real object. For some children, picking up a real pencil helps them as they watch how their arm and hand muscles move. Most of the physical actions we make are subconscious ones, and observing reality before attempting to recreate it in pantomime may help some children become better at mime.

After establishing the action or pantomime mentally, the child needs to practice it physically until he or she eliminates all actions that are unnecessary and strengthens those that communicate. This practice should vary in many ways.

1. Perform the action slower or faster.
2. Perform it with one hand (or foot) and then the other.
3. Do it closer to the body or farther away.
4. Do it in a large space or a small space.
5. Perform it with the body in a different position, for example, standing, sitting, and lying down.

Later, you may want to add such other variations as doing the movement or action with one other person, with two, or with a small group. No matter what the sequence of practice, the important thing is that children realize that in successful pantomime the actions need practice to be convincing.

After practicing the pantomime, children need opportunities to perform it to get others' reactions. Although informal drama does not emphasize an audience, the child interested in perfecting this skill can profit from some evaluation by other children.

After the pantomime is performed, the children may guess what it represents. The important thing to remember is that guessing for the sake of guessing is *not* the goal. If children can't guess what action a child is performing, try to identify with the group what parts of the pantomime did convey an idea and at what point the idea began to evade the mime and those watching.

It is wise to choose ideas for mime from among actions with which the children are familiar, such as actions they perform at home or at school (Feericks, 1980). After children have developed some facility in such topics, they can progress to being people other than themselves doing actions other than their own experiences.

As children become more adept at mime, the leader can direct them to simple story dramatization utilizing pantomime. Then the activity moves from a simple, disconnected pantomime to a more elaborate series of mimes strung together to tell a story. No matter how involved the drama experience becomes, it is always based on the skill of pantomime.

Emotion in Pantomime. In addition to thinking about *what* the pantomime shows, the children can be encouraged to think about how the character they are portraying *feels* about what is happening. This is important because, as McCaslin (1987) asserts, our feelings affect, in sometimes subtle ways, the manner in which we perform certain tasks. Putting a book down on a table is done one way when a character is happy, another way when the character is angry (see Figure 4.6). McCaslin's section entitled "Emotions in Pantomime" is very useful for teachers interested in exploring this aspect of mime.

FIGURE 4.6. It is often effective to have children express their characters' emotions in pantomime, so they don't become overly dependent on language to convey meaning.

Puppetry

In both pantomime and movement experiences, as well as in story dramatization and improvisation, a key factor is the physical involvement of the
child. Drama requires this active physical involvement. This is a major difference between drama and puppetry, which requires far less physical involvement. Although a valid art form, puppetry will receive only brief mention,
because most drama leaders do not consider it an integral part of dramatics.

There is no denying that puppets are useful adjuncts to the language
arts program (Petty, Petty, & Becking, 1981, pp. 135–139). Writers have
detailed the values of puppetry for children. Jenkins (1980, pp. 11–17), for
example, identified nearly two dozen such values, including, among others,
self-awareness, an avenue of expression without fear, and the development
of creative thinking. Methodical descriptions are available to help teachers
in step-by-step production of puppets. *The Complete Book of Puppet Theatre*
(Currell, 1987), for example, includes specific instructions, shown in both
line drawings and photographs, for making a variety of different kinds of
puppets, from simple glove ones to very elaborate marionettes. Flower and
Fortney (1983) give equally helpful step-by-step instructions. Puppets can
make subject matter come alive, and older children can study the many
different types of puppets.

Nevertheless, the unavoidable conclusion is that puppetry and drama
are two different things. In all types of drama, children use their bodies and
their voices to express ideas. They may use their bodies to respond to music,
to visual stimuli, or to a story, but in all cases they are communicating
physically, in addition to vocally. This is not to discourage teachers from
using puppetry, but simply to point out the necessity of viewing the two as
quite distinct forms of communication. Yet in one way drama and puppetry
are similar—both are effective in developing the child's speaking vocabulary

VOCABULARY DEVELOPMENT

Two types of vocabulary can be developed by drama experiences. The first
is vocabulary *intrinsic to the art of drama*, which is simply drama terms.
The teacher does not attempt consciously to teach these terms in an academic way, but rather uses them whenever appropriate because such terms
convey effectively what needs to be said. Thus, children are exposed to
such terms as *sincerity*. The opposite term is *break*, used when a child loses
concentration and steps out of character. Leaders regularly use such terms

as *environment* and *symbol*—even with young children—and children themselves can talk about *plot*, *climax*, and *characterization*.

In one creative drama session, first-, second-, and third-grade children were working with the story "How the Robin's Breast Became Red" included in *Perhaps and Perchance: Tales of Nature* by Laura E. Cathon and Thusnelda Schmidt (1962). In improvising on this tale, it is essential that children understand the bear in the story as a *symbol* of snow. In this session children used the word *ferocious* to describe the bear and *distracting* to describe the bird's actions. In the same session the leader talked of the father in the story *fashioning* some shelter and the bear *representing* something.

There is also the vocabulary *intrinsic to the motivation* being used. Much poetry is full of evocative words; these motivate children to movement and action and can, in addition, become part of their vocabulary. They learn about winter, which *filigrees* the snowflake, and about spring, which *bunts* a breeze, in *A Circle of Seasons* by Myra Cohn Livingston (1982). They are exposed to such words as *skittish* in "Foal," *brambly* in "Picking Berries," and *tufted timothy* in "Hay Song," from the book *On the Farm* by Lee Bennett Hopkins (1991).

Prose also provides a similar enrichment of vocabulary. When children work with the engrossing tales in *A Book of Witches* by Ruth Manning-Sanders (1966), they encounter the *clamor* of witches, *peevish* princes, *braying* donkeys, *snuffling* daughters, and a *lamenting* king, as they all go through dangers to *procure* the rewards (see Figure 4.7). Similarly, when children work out the action for the unusually fresh stories in Dorothy Gladys Spicer's *The Owl's Nest* (1968),[4] they deal with such words as *splendor*, *cunning*, *grope*, *stalwart*, and *ashen*.

However, there is a principle we remember—we do not belabor the teaching of these words in a structured, organized way throughout the drama session. Rather we work with the materials in which the words occur, discussing the words informally, using them to pique children's interest and to broaden their exposure to the wonderful legacy of vocabulary. Teachers may elect to do some conscious teaching of these words, but this is always done in periods separate from the drama session. In fact, Bordan (1970) has pointed out that teachers should consciously teach such drama-related words in the language arts program, to achieve the full potential of this interrelation between drama and vocabulary.

We sometimes find children making up vocabulary, creating their own

---

[4]These distinctive stories, from the northernmost province in the Netherlands, provide a valuable source of drama material. The quality of the stories makes it worth a search in libraries to find a copy.

FIGURE 4.7. How could children use their bodies to pantomime pulling themselves up into the tower room? This is only one of many interesting pantomime possibilities offered in Ruth Manning-Sanders's collection of stories, *A Book of Witches* (1966).

nonce words. Henry (1967) mentions children using *glusterous* and *lumining* to describe the crystal city in the poem "Behind the Waterfall." These are perfectly acceptable coinages, and by approving them the teacher encourages word play and fosters the idea that language is a changing vehicle for our thoughts.

DEVELOPMENT OF LISTENING SKILLS

There are two types of listening skills that may be developed through creative drama. The first can be called *basic listening*, defined as listening required for the action of the session to continue. Children must attend to what is going on, in order to say or do whatever comes next. Such listening is necessary in any kind of dramatic activity, whether the child is listening to music in order to respond rhythmically or doing an interpretation of a folktale.

Basic listening is simple listening for cues, necessary whether one is considering first graders working out the adventures of the Gruff family in *The Three Billy Goats Gruff*, by Janet Stevens (1987), or sixth graders working out part of the sequence in *Rescue Josh McGuire*, by Ben Mikaelsen (1991). The cue may be to some action or to words, but children must be actively engaged in listening in order for the session to continue. It is especially necessary when the group is improvising, because participants often do not know exactly where the improvisation is going.

The second type may be called *evaluative listening*, in which children listen to the verbal interaction taking place to evaluate it, and their ideas about how they might do the same dialogue more effectively. Frequently, the teacher divides the group to provide a chance for every child to participate. For example, when we use the story "Tom Tit Tot" by Kevin Crossley-Holland (1987), we are working with four characters. To involve all the children, divide the class into groups of four and allow each group to work out its version of one of the episodes in the story. After students have practiced their version, they take turns sharing it with the rest of the group. The teacher sets the stage for evaluative listening by discussing with the class the need to listen carefully, pointing out some special things to listen for, and reminding them they will have a chance to discuss what they hear after the playing is over. After the playing, the leader gathers the children together to discuss how the segment went, asking such questions as

- What was particularly effective about the voice of the small little black thing?
- How could you tell when he was in different moods? When he was teasing the daughter? When he was angry because she guessed his name?

- Are there ways *you* could use *your* voice to make the small little black thing sound different?

Children are then encouraged to work out variations, to experiment with doing the voice in ways they feel would be effective. Sometimes the leader may simply have the children remain seated as they experiment with the voices in the story, instead of playing out the scene physically. However it is done, its effectiveness depends on the children's *evaluative listening*. McIntyre (1974, pp. 17–23) gives other suggestions about developing children's listening through dramatics.

DRAMA AND CREATIVE WRITING

Drama both leads to and comes from creative writing. In either case, both the writing and the dramatizing benefit. We will first consider how drama *leads to* creative writing. A leader may motivate children to improvise on an idea, a story, or a picture. As part of the motivation, explain that at the close of the experience students will write down what has happened. With younger children this may be a simple recording of plot sequence, while with older children it may include a more sophisticated description of such ephemeral elements as tones of voice and facial expressions. After children have done this—rather directly with no emphasis on mechanics—a profitable discussion can ensue about differences between what individual children have written.

This is a good point at which to discuss discrepancies among observers' reports of a single event. It is also logical then to discuss the difference between writing basic description and writing about elusive aspects of an improvisation. Describing simple sequences, as what happened first, next, and last, is obviously easier than describing the mood of a scene or the feeling of a character. Such discussions lead logically, especially with older children, into considerations of the differences between the written skeletal outline of a play and the physical manifestations of this outline when brought to life by the actor's interpretations of the basic directions. Although in classroom drama we are not working toward formal play making as an objective, such discussions give children insights into the theatre and encourage and stimulate them to ask questions about aspects of drama that ordinarily would not be considered.

After giving boys and girls a chance to discuss such ideas as these, the leader might—in another session—want to reverse direction and have children *interpret* these various written accounts concerning the original improvisation. After providing time for children to write down what they observed in an improvisation, select several of the most divergent accounts and then divide the children into groups to play out these written accounts. Differences that became apparent could be discussed. The approach doesn't matter—the point is the rich variety available when working with writing down what has been observed.

Drama can also *come from* creative writing. The teacher, using whatever means seem to work especially well, may help children select something they have written to be dramatized. Because in whole language programs children write every day, there should be plenty of stories from which to choose. Invariably, children will want to know why their story was not chosen, which can lead to a discussion of the characteristics of good motivation for drama. Instead of telling children what these are, the leader more frequently tries to draw these characteristics from the children. Do so by having them examine the stories that were used, to see what features they have in common. If they were good motivation for drama, they will invariably share some of the following characteristics that make stories effective for playing:

1. Clearly defined, active characters, with whom children can identify
2. A logical form with an arresting beginning
3. A clear and uncluttered story line
4. A climax and a satisfying conclusion

This naturally is much more effective if children can discover these characteristics by comparing stories than if they are simply told them as fact by the leader.

Usually such examination and discussion of stories lead to another request: "Can I rewrite my story so we can use it?" The rewrite sessions that follow, as the teacher helps children to edit characterization, plot, and dialogue, can be very helpful—not only in producing more story motivations for drama but also in encouraging children to write stories of more intrinsic value as creative writing. The rewriting sessions on a particular story last as long as the teacher deems them profitable. Not every story comes to the stage of being usable for dramatization, nor should it. But because the teacher uses this procedure at regular intervals, the children know that if their story is not chosen one time, it will be chosen another time. This gives them the needed incentive to continue working and refining their skills of writing and dramatizing. These two skills interrelate very easily, and an enrichment of each activity results.

A wide variety of different types of writing in role during drama are suggested by Tarlington and Verriour (1991). Working from the tale *Rumplestiltskin* by Alison Sage (1991), the authors suggest writing as the queen, as the baby girl when she is twelve years old, and as the character Rumplestiltskin. Children have written in the forms of newspaper profiles, diary entries, letters, memoirs, and autobiography.

Other suggestions for relating drama and writing activities are given by Walker (1975), who describes group story-writing activities that have led into drama. After a transcription of how each dictation session went, the author includes the finished story, as well as suggestions for drama activities, including rudimentary costumes and props. She extends this to other areas of the curriculum like music, math, and history.

SUMMARY

Drama should be an integral part of the elementary curriculum because of the way it leads to knowledge about language and the development of language skills. A teacher interested in doing drama with children should be able to convince parents, supervisors, and principals of the validity of drama by emphasizing the contribution drama makes to the language arts curriculum, whether in a more traditional text-based or a more innovative whole language classroom. Drama can provide an approach to and enrich learning in the reading program, the literature program, and the areas of oral language development, nonverbal communication, vocabulary development, listening skills, and creative writing. Teachers interested in the benefits drama provides know children will grow in ways other than these, but may find it easier to proselytize for drama if they emphasize the richness it adds to the language arts.

RELATED READING

Brown, L. J. (1986). Developing thinking and problem-solving skills with children's books. *Childhood Education, 63*(2), 102–106.

In an article dealing with a variety of ways to involve children with literature, the author concludes with a section on using fictional characters for role play and creative drama. She asserts that this process helps students understand the feelings and attitudes of others. Brown recommends the use of folk- and fairy tales, and poses several questions (of the type suggested in this chapter) to help children think more deeply about the motivations of the characters involved. Her concluding argument is that children retain and assimilate more of what they listen to or read when involved in drama than they do when engaged in more passive activities.

Cunningham, P. (1981). Story dramatization. *The Reading Teacher, 34*(4), 466–467.

This brief article, recounting the author's experience in using old familiar stories as a base for dramatization, makes the point about why these are important to children. She identifies the listening benefits, as well as improved speaking skills and reading comprehension, that result when children work with such material. Cunningham contrasts the success she had with this sort of material, with her attempts at using stories from basal readers, with which children were less familiar. She concludes that children need to have heard the story or read it again and again for their dramatizations to be effective.

Harp, B. (1988). Is all of that drama taking valuable time away from reading? *The Reading Teacher, 41*(9), 928–930.

This is a very useful short article dealing with the dilemma often facing teachers interested in drama: how to justify it to doubting administrators. The author identifies several different reasons for including drama as part of the reading experiences of children: Probably the one most reading teachers will respond to most positively is the effect drama has on comprehension. The article includes a brief summary of research evidence on the outcomes of drama. This could be more simply worded and used as a brief explanation to send home to parents at the start of a drama program. You might read this article along with Daniel Tutolo's "Beginning Reading in Italy," in the same journal (January 1982), in which he ties drama in America with "giuoco" in the Italian culture, which does not have a clear distinction between work and play. Giuoco is play toward an educational end, often as a prelude to learning. Tutolo sees informal dramatics as an American parallel to giuoco.

Juliebo, M. F. (1988). Drama for purposeful reading and writing. *The Reading Teacher, 42*(2), 261.

A helpful article, despite its brevity, this suggests how role playing can promote risk taking and reduce anxiety when the teacher uses such material as the story of the Pied Piper. She helps them transcend the particulars of this story, by focusing on the concept of breaking promises, a central theme of the story. Children improvised a town council meeting, playing roles of villagers deciding what action to take or not take. Juliebo prepared the children to move deeper into these roles by giving them written descriptions of their roles, which they knew but other children did not. A second experience involved the children first in role playing being in the cave with the Piper, who wanted them to write letters to their parents, asking for their help. This led naturally into a writing experience. In a brief, two-day experience, the author integrated movement, oral language, and writing.

Silverman, J. (1981). Creative drama and the problem of focus. *Children's Theatre Review, 30*(3), 1–2.

The author discusses two experiences working with inner-city children and her frustration because the children's energies were diffuse, which led them in many individual directions. As a consequence, the children, who had many interesting ideas, seldom listened to the ideas of others. She found that using the games originated by Viola Spolin helped build a sense of group with common goals and values, something missing previously. As they moved into doing situations and characters, Silverman discovered that the groups were "malnourished," that is, they had images derived exclusively from television. To counteract this, the author used many of the traditional stories included in Ward's (1952) *Stories to Dramatize*, which provided material that sparked their imaginations and drew forth their best efforts. Combining the structure in the Spolin games with the structure in the stories allowed the author to move the children past the glib television images into significant interaction with literature.

CHAPTER 5

Dramatizing Across the Curriculum—Kindergarten Through Grade 3

Drama fits quite naturally into the school curriculum. Because it utilizes all the senses, it makes a desirable vehicle for internalizing concepts presented in the arts and content areas. When children are socially, emotionally, mentally, and physically involved in learning, the probability of learning and retaining important subject matter increases dramatically. This holistic learning process immerses children in the many facets of language, providing experiential learning that utilizes both sides of the brain (Cottrell, 1987). Not all children learn effectively through the more common "listen, read, and remember" method. For those students especially, drama can be a key to understanding.

DRAMA IN THE CONTENT AREAS

The content areas of social studies, science, mathematics, and the arts are certainly amenable to the use of drama. The teacher just needs to be creative and resourceful in deciding how to incorporate drama in a unit of study. Whole language classrooms, cooperative learning, and thematic units all lend themselves to dramatic exploration of the human condition. Literature, historical moments, the study of scientific reasoning, and the understanding of mathematical concepts offer opportunities for heightened perception when creative drama is added. In fact, good teachers have recognized the value of creative drama and have been using it for years in their classrooms.

Because drama has proved to be such a successful learning tool, it is finally being recognized for its educational value. For example, first-grade children may not recall what was written on page 62 of their social studies textbooks, but they *will* remember enacting a scene depicting community helpers in action when an imaginary 911 telephone call brings firefighters and paramedics to an accident scene. The textbook, combined with field trips to the fire station and hospital, and the creative dramatization in the classroom conjoin to stress the importance of having trained community helpers immediately accessible by merely dialing numbers. In today's world of working parents, it is critical that even very young children know how to get emergency assistance. They will definitely benefit by role playing a "911" situation. An immediate follow-up unit extension dealing with safety and first aid would also lend itself to dramatic interpretation. A teacher could divide the class into groups and ask them to dramatize the steps they think would be included in applying different first-aid procedures. Some students may have learned these practices at home or perhaps from a scout troop. Others may know little or nothing about doing the simplest first aid— applying a Bandaid. When the dramatizations are given, the teacher can determine which students have received some training in first aid. These pupils could be leaders in the forthcoming unit, responsible for demonstrating certain first-aid procedures. If a teacher wishes to check growth in understanding concepts in a unit, the preparatory dramatizations can be a beginning for assessment as well, a type of pre- and posttest evaluation, as it were.

HOW TO USE DRAMA FOR ACQUIRING CONTENT MATERIAL

Content material can be offered to students in several ways. As a *preparation* mechanism, drama can set the tone for a unit of study to follow. It focuses children's attention on the topic at hand and indicates to the teacher the background information they have already internalized. When used as a *presentation* device, creative drama can be a means for pupils to exhibit critical concepts being studied. The *consolidation* of content material is evident as students pull together a composite of concepts learned throughout a unit and then portray them through drama. *Extending* a unit of study forces the students to move from the known to the unknown, searching beyond what was studied in class, but using it as a basis for a predictable logical leap forward. Dramatic presentations can be either reality or fantasy. The final element of *assessment* is particularly useful so that teachers can see whether the children understood the main ideas of a unit. The boys and girls can be required to incorporate certain major concepts learned within a broader framework of drama. It is then the teacher's responsibility to ob-

serve and question the children on how they included the concepts, to assess
their level of understanding. A more detailed exploration of each of these
five elements follows.

Drama as a Preparation Tool

Drama can be a useful preparatory tool to introduce a unit. It is also one
way to find out what students have already internalized about a concept.
This assists a teacher in deciding where to begin with a particular group of
children. Since even the best textbooks do not "fit" all the children in every
classroom, the teacher must match the books and other materials available
to the learning level of a particular class. The previous suggestion of initiat-
ing a first-aid unit is one example of utilizing this idea. Another possibility is
to have the class share what they already know about the care, feeding,
and training of various kinds of domestic animals in preparation for a study
of pets. Not all children will have a pet at home, but usually enough either
have one at the present time, have had one in the past, or know a friend or
relative who has one, to be able to enter into an initial class discussion.
Once the different animals have been named and listed on a large class
chart, children can compare different methods for caring for a variety of
animals (see Figure 5.1).

	Type of Pet				
	Dog	Cat	Bird	Guinea Pig	Fish
Care	Grooming Exercise Vet check	Grooming Vet check	Clean cage	Clean cage Grooming	Clean aquarium
Feeding	Dog food Water	Cat food Water	Bird seed Water	Pellets Fresh vegetables	Fish flakes
Training	Can learn simple commands	Independent Won't learn commands	May speak Can learn simple tricks	Like to be handled and petted	None
Where stay	In house or own dog house	In house or may be let outside	Bird cage	Wire cage	Aquarium

FIGURE 5.1. Comparison chart for pets.

For example, have those children who have dogs form a group and create a dramatization showing the proper way to feed a dog, keep it clean and groomed, and teach it to obey commands such as "sit," "lie down," and "stay." They can show that dogs have feelings just as humans do, and what happens when praise, petting, rewards, and discipline are used deliberately for desired ends. Perhaps they could take turns creating scenes with the dog and the person. Young children can be very astute in their observations of the relationship between people and their pets. As the teacher asks leading questions, the students will eagerly focus on the task and be ready to respond by creating a drama to share with the class. Perhaps, in regard to dogs, the teacher might ask questions such as

- How does a dog learn to sit down and stay in one spot?
- What do you do to teach him other behaviors?
- How does your dog let you know when he wants to play?
- How would your dog make you aware that he's hungry or thirsty?
- Does your dog greet you at the door when you come home from school? Why or why not?
- Can he show you that he's happy to be with you?
- How does a dog know which are his toys and what he can't play with or chew on?

Children can share pertinent facts about all kinds of pets: dogs, cats, guinea pigs, birds, and even tropical fish in an aquarium. Similar questions can be directed to the specific care and feeding of other animals.

Teachers can assist younger students in designing their presentations. A short session with each group taken aside privately provides the children with a sense of direction and focuses their thinking as they plan together. They need to discuss

1. Who will play which parts
2. What type of care or behavior they are attempting to dramatize
3. How they will show it to the rest of the class (see Figure 5.2)

Once all groups have planned and practiced, they will take turns presenting to each other. Again, the teacher should lead the class through a discussion session after each portrayal to reinforce the concepts that were presented. Using the dog again as an example, the teacher may ask

- How did Jimmy use his voice, face, and body to show you he wanted to play with his master?
- When Susan was teaching her dog to sit, how did she show firmness and patience with her commands?

FIGURE 5.2. Exploring movement for a character before enacting the scene results in more imaginative playing.

- How could you tell from her voice and her actions that she was trying to be a good trainer?
- What did Allen do as a dog to show that he really enjoyed being scratched behind his ears?
- How many of you have found out that your dog also likes to be scratched behind his ears? What else does he like?
- Can your dog perform any "tricks"? What are they?

Once the class has shared and discussed their presentations, the teacher will have determined the depth of information students already possess and can build a unit of study based on their prior knowledge.

Drama as a Presentation Device

Creative drama can also be used as a presentation device. Suppose that a class has been studying several different versions of *The Three Little Pigs* as part of a literature unit. It would be interesting to have several groups use drama to present the different accounts to the class.

While Paul Galdone's version (1970) is an enduring favorite, four recent "different" versions provide delightful contrasts.

The Three Little Pigs. In *The Three Little Pigs and the Fox* by William Hooks (1989), the Appalachian setting, culture, dialogue, and charming illustrations stimulate the children's interest (see Figure 5.3). The third little pig, who leaves home after the first two pigs, is a girl. She turns out to be the heroine and rescues her two older brothers.

The second account, *The True Story of the Three Little Pigs, by A. Wolf*, by Jon Scieszka (1989) is told from the wolf's viewpoint. He asserts that the whole situation has been misconstrued. He's really been framed!

The third version, a satire in poetry form, "The Three Little Pigs" by Roald Dahl (1986), adds the character of Red Riding Hood and contains a startling ending: When the third little pig telephones Red Riding Hood for assistance, she does come and gets rid of the wolf, but manages to get the pig as well.

A final story, *The Fourth Little Pig* by Teresa Celsi (1992), is an extension of the original, as well as a beginning-to-read book. In this, the three pigs are too afraid to face the world after their frightening encounter with the wolf, and the fourth pig, their sister, challenges them to get on with their lives. She says:

> "You can't spend your whole life
> Just sitting and shaking.

FIGURE 5.3. William H. Hooks's *The Three Little Pigs and the Fox* has a marvelous Appalachian flavor, both in the language used by the author and in the illustrations in watercolor—full of small details to be studied—by S. D. Schindler. In this version, all three pigs escape, and even return to mother for Sunday dinner!

There are places to see
And things to be making."

"You can build a canoe
Or go out and buy fudge."
But despite her suggestions,
The boys would not budge. (p. 14)

The class could compare and contrast each of the different versions of *The Three Little Pigs* stories on a large chart (see Figure 5.4).

"Places to See." Wouldn't it be fun to have different groups of children improvise their interpretations of where good "places to see" are and what "things they could be making"? The teacher will have to assist these groups with some elementary improvisational techniques and help them with their planning. Improvisation is one of the more difficult drama skills, but with help children can do very well with their presentations. Young children are quite adept at playing make believe—but organizational skills and planning generally need adult guidance at this stage.

Begin by having children generate a list of "places to see." They might suggest such things as visiting a farm, attending a circus, climbing a mountain, or taking a trip to the zoo. Once different groups of children decide which "place" they would like to use for their scene, meet with each group separately and ask them to share what they think they would see and do there. For example, a group planning to "visit" a farm might brainstorm and share such ideas as exploring a barn, looking at and feeding all the different animals, watching (or assisting in) the milking process of a dairy farm, gathering eggs, picking ripe vegetables (and sampling them, of course), even mucking out stalls and spreading fresh hay for the horses. Once their ideas are listed, students and teacher need to explore how to dramatize scenes showing these activities. You can focus their thinking by asking such questions as

- How does one feed a flock of chickens and ducks?
- What do they eat?
- How do the chickens and ducks act when they know it's feeding time?
- Who can show us how they act?
- How do they sound?

For the scene to work, some children need to be the chickens and ducks and someone needs to be the farmer or the farmer's spouse. Continue to ask more questions.

- Who would like to play these parts?
- How does the farmer (or spouse) let the chickens and ducks know it's feeding time?
- What would he or she do and say?
- In what kind of container is the food carried?
- Is it heavy or is it light?
- How can you show that?

Title	Three Little Pigs (Disney)	Three Little Pigs and the Fox	The Fourth Little Pig	The True Story of the Three Little Pigs	The Three Little Pigs
Author	Walt Disney	William Hooks	Teresa Celsi	John Scieszka	Roald Dahl
Characters	3 Pigs Wolf	2 original Pigs 3rd sister Pig Fox	3 original Pigs Wolf mentioned	3 Pigs Wolf Newspaper writers Police	3 Pigs Wolf Little Red Riding Hood
Setting	Rural-general	Rural-Appalachia	Rural-general	Rural-general	Rural-general
Problem	Build houses Watch out for Wolf	Build houses Watch out for Wolf Visit Mama on Sunday	Wolf is gone, but Pigs afraid to go outdoors	Wolf feels/he's been unjustly accused	Third Pig calls on Red Riding Hood for help
Solution	Houses of and sticks do not work Brick house works Wolf defeated	Third Pig builds house of rocks, catches Fox, frees two brothers All visit Mama	Fourth Pig, a sister, gets Pigs out into the world again	Wolf tried and sent to jail	Red Riding Hood gets both Pig and Wolf
Point of View	Pigs	Pigs	Pigs	Wolf	Pigs

FIGURE 5.4. Comparison chart of versions of *The Three Little Pigs*.

Once you and the group have thoroughly explored the different facets of the children's special "place," the next step is to plan the sequence of short scenes, or vignettes, to give some cohesion to their dramatization. Someone can be selected to be the farmer, continuing to play the role in every scene as a guide, explaining the different activities as they occur. Much of the fun and learning that take place in drama is the interaction, planning, and refining of a scene or scenes.

The teacher makes sure that everyone has an opportunity to help plan the presentation, and all should share ideas and take turns doing so. Again, younger children will need assistance in acquiring these interaction skills, but as they mature and have more experience in creating dramatizations, less and less guidance is needed from the teacher.

"Things They Could Be Making." Perhaps half the class could be involved in dramatizing "places to see" from Teresa Celsi's *The Fourth Little Pig* (1992), while the other half creates improvisations on "things they could be making." The teacher would go through the same process of having the class contribute ideas of what the pigs could "be making." Possible suggestions might include creating a product at a factory, building a fort, creating a unique robot, or putting on a special birthday party. Have different groups from this half of the class select one of the suggestions listed and, again, meet with each group separately to guide the decision making, helping children decide who will play what parts and what actions they need to show.

The factory product is the perfect place to introduce young children to the ideas of an assembly line, a favorite drama activity for group involvement. Depending on what product the children chose, each child could create actions and sounds unique to a special step in the building process. By the time each "worker" has a turn being part of the assembly line, the special product "appears" in its complete form. Even though it isn't actually visible, the factory workers could describe it, "feel" it, and "watch" it in action accurately enough for the audience to see it in their minds' eyes as well.

Incorporating higher level thinking skills is much easier when stories in which the scenes are sequentially portrayed are visualized through live drama interpretation, instead of being simply read from books. This is especially valuable for beginning readers who are still struggling with the written word. Even the slowest students can begin to incorporate verbally the higher levels of Bloom's taxonomy of educational objectives when drama is part of learning. Different groups of children can portray different versions of the story. Enacting one story while observing other versions will help the boys and girls note the similarities and differences in each dramatization.

Drama for Consolidation

An example using drama to consolidate content material involves incorporating grammatical concepts often introduced in the younger grades. Nouns, verbs, adjectives, and adverbs are better understood when children physically act them out in the sequential order often found in basic sentences. For example, "The huge elephant playfully sprayed water on the little elephant" would be more meaningful and enjoyable if different students portrayed the different parts of speech of the sentence. Someone could enact the adjective *huge* by standing on a classroom chair and then puffing up and stretching as tall as possible. A second child would be the elephant leaning over with her "trunk" swaying back and forth, depicted by extending her arms and linking them together with her clasped hands. The adverb *playfully* could be shown by a student demonstrating a happy, gleeful face while his body cavorts in place using a skipping or hopping step. The verb *sprayed* is easily acted out when a pupil pretends to wave a garden hose and makes a loud SHHHing sound with her mouth. The adjective *little* could be shown by having a student crouch down, wrap his arms around himself, and be as small as he could possibly be. The second elephant "noun" would try to minimize her body size to become a miniature copy of the larger elephant.

The teacher could have word cards prepared ahead of time for all seven of the important words in the sentence: The *huge elephant playfully sprayed water* on the *little elephant*. Additional cards with the four parts of speech being studied also need to be ready for use when the class discusses the sentence "in action." The seven students dramatizing the sentence line up in order from left to right at the front of the room and play their parts in sequence when the teacher or another child points at them. After each part is presented and discussed, a member of the audience selects a word card from the teacher to match the actual word from the sentence. The whole procedure can then be repeated with other children selecting the correct part of speech to match the dramatization. If the class is ready to be introduced to the fact that adverbs are extremely versatile and can be found in several places in a sentence, the teacher could have the child portraying the word *playfully* move to the following additional positions:

> *Playfully* the huge elephant sprayed water on the little elephant.
> The huge elephant sprayed water *playfully* on the little elephant.
> The huge elephant sprayed water on the little elephant *playfully*.

Visual connections between words, parts of speech, and sentence structure help children understand the English language system. When these associations are enhanced through drama, they are more apt to be internalized. Eighty percent of what people learn is through visualization, and drama certainly is visual! If children are responding enthusiastically to this, you might lead into using *The Right Number of Elephants* by Jeff Sheppard (1990) as a basis for dramatization. With humorous pictures by Felicia Bond, this shows a number of improbable, but very act-able events, cast in the context of counting down.

Drama as an Extension Unit

After completing a health unit on the basic food groups, children might be interested in doing an extension unit on how grocery stores obtain the varieties of food found in different sections of the store. A food store manager or assistant might be willing to visit the classroom and explain where the meat, fresh fruits and vegetables, bakery goods, canned goods, and dairy products are obtained. For instance:

- How does the dairy know how much milk, butter, cheese, and ice cream a particular grocery store needs?
- How do the people at the dairy know when to bring these items?
- How does the dairy get paid for bringing these products to the store?
- What happens to milk that sits in the cooler too long, gets sour, and therefore cannot be sold?
- What does the "expiration" date mean on the milk carton?

Gail Gibbons's book, *The Milk Makers* (1985), is particularly useful in helping children understand the many people involved in getting milk to their tables. As usual, her clear, crisp illustrations are accompanied by labeled diagrams to enhance understanding. Similar discussions about products in other sections of the store can lead to a beginning understanding of how our modern food industry functions.

Once the basic concepts have been established, children could dramatize a scene such as the following:

> The store needs to initiate a new dairy order. An employee takes an inventory of current supplies and gives that information to a manager. The manager uses that information to write up a new order and then telephones (or faxes) it to the dairy. The new order is then transferred to employees who fill orders. The products are then loaded on a refrigerated truck and delivered. A store employee checks to be sure that the order has been filled correctly. Then the truck driver unloads the order and places it in the grocery store cooler. The truck driver gives a bill of sale to the proper grocery store personnel. As the fresh dairy products are needed on the floor of the store, stock clerks get them from the storage

cooler and place them in the store aisle coolers for sale. Customers select the items they wish to purchase, place them in their grocery carts, and pay for them at the checkout counters. Finally, the products are brought to people's homes and placed in refrigerators ready for use. The entire cycle then begins all over.

The class could create a sequence chart (Figure 5.5) depicting all the steps involved in getting dairy products from the dairy to the store and then to people's homes. Once all the steps have been recorded, students can select the different roles they would like to dramatize. The four corners of the classroom could be used as

1. The dairy
2. The grocery storage area
3. The grocery dairy aisle and checkout
4. Someone's home kitchen

The same procedure could be used to portray how products for the other departments of a grocery store are obtained.

While a dairy is usually a local industry, children should also be aware of products that come from distances. Coffee, bananas, tea, citrus fruits, and other products have to be transported long distances. The different methods for shipping these products could become a unit on modern transportation. Studying maps of the countries where certain products originate would be an additional learning experience. The classroom could become a microcosm of the world, and students could "deliver" products to a certain store from all over the world. Children could stretch strings on a world map from the points of origin of products to the city where the students live. Labels of product names located at points of origin will show the children how interdependent we have become. Again, the teacher might have the children dramatize these larger ideas. Importing bananas from a South American country to a specific United States grocery store would involve picking the (green) bananas, getting them to a port, loading them aboard a ship, getting the ship to a United States port, unloading the bananas to a distribution center, and then placing them in trucks for long distance travel to the cities for distribution to area grocery stores.

Any outgrowth of learning that reinforces or augments children's understanding of basic concepts can be considered an extension of the original unit. The problem usually lies in choosing which ideas to develop. Generally there are many more possibilities than there is time available. One good place to go for suggestions as well as materials is the school library media center. A center director can be invaluable in suggesting possible materials for any unit or extension of it. This person not only has a professional

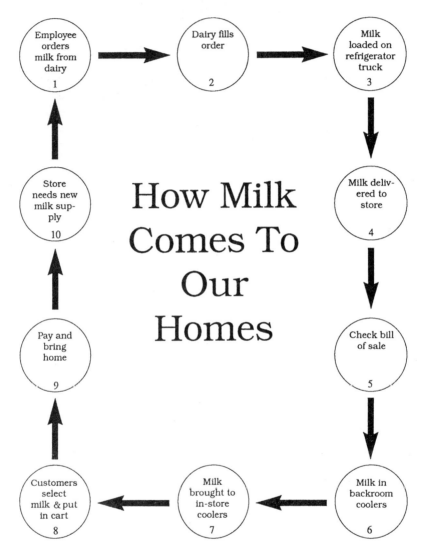

FIGURE 5.5. Business cycle for milk distribution.

working knowledge of what is available in a particular school, but often knows if other materials are available in the school system or elsewhere. It is vital to know this person well. Other ideas for extending units are found in teacher editions of textbooks, other teachers, and educational books and magazines. The ideas are out there; it's a matter of learning where to find them.

Drama for Assessment

The assessment of a student's learning is an ongoing process in whole language classrooms. Key concepts of units as well as basic skills mastered need to be recorded regularly throughout the year. Checklists of skills introduced and mastered as well as written comments from teachers are kept in individual students' folders for quarterly reports and use at parent–teacher conferences (Figure 5.6). While there are prepublished lists of such skills for different texts and grade levels, many school systems have designed their own skill charts to fit their particular student body and curriculum. A checklist of progress in writing could include the skill being assessed and the student's level of development at the time of assessment. The checklist might contain some or all of the items shown in Figure 5.6 and might include additional items. A teacher simply needs to make marks in the appropriate columns. Lack of a check mark indicates that a particular skill is not being developed or emphasized at that particular time. These checklists are very functional, easily changed, and efficient to use. They show progress at timed intervals and can be used with parents at conferences along with a portfolio of the child's work.

THE CONTENT AREAS

Social Studies

A wonderful holistic unit of study for beginning learners in the autumn focuses on John Chapman, or "Johnny Appleseed," as he has become familiarly called in the many legends that have arisen about his life. In developing this unit, we used books about Johnny Appleseed himself and some related books about apples. Resources we found useful were books by Aliki (1963), Patsy Becvar (1991), Gail Gibbons (1984), Gina Ingoglia (1992), Terry Jennings (1981), Hannah Johnson (1977), Theodore LeSieg (1961), Eva Moore (1964), Julian Scheer (1964), Millicent Selsam (1973), Shel Silverstein (1964), M. E. Sterling (n.d.), Shelly Thornton (1991), and Janet Udry (1956).

This may be the first time that some children encounter the idea of

ILLUSTRATIVE WHOLE LANGUAGE SKILL DEVELOPMENT CHECKLIST:			
SKILL AREA	LEVEL OF ACHIEVEMENT		
DATE:	BEGINNING	50% CORRECT	MASTERY
1. SPELLING			
Long vowels			
Short vowels			
Consonant blends			
Plural forms			
2. WRITING			
Complete sentences			
Begin capital letter			
End punctuation			
Dialogue quotations			
Paragraph structure			
3. GRAMMAR USAGE			
N-V agreement			
Pronoun usage			
4. STORY DEVELOPMENT			
Beginning, middle, & end to stories			
Descriptive language			
Plot development			
Character development			

FIGURE 5.6. Whole Language skill development checklist.

legend versus reality. After reading and sharing different versions of Chapman's life (see list at end of chapter), children can compare some things that really happened to him and then became embellished in legend. Although children at this level may not master the concept of the difference between legend and reality, introducing the concept lays the foundation for future development.

It would be appropriate for students to enact some scenes from various of these stories. The teacher, in the role of John Chapman, or "Johnny Appleseed," could involve different student groups in the roles of the settlers, Native Americans, and even the animals depicted in the various accounts of Chapman's life. When the teacher plays in role, it is easier to guide the children's actions and ensure that certain objectives are met and concepts are included. By the time the different groups have dramatized the different characters involved in Chapman's life, many fictitious apple trees will have been vigorously planted in the classroom.

John Chapman's birthday falls on September 26,[1] so why not have a class party with an "apple" birthday cake or cupcakes. You could also plan a field trip to an apple orchard so children can see the trees and purchase apples to bring back to the classroom. The next day they could make the cake or cupcakes or cook applesauce. There are many recipes available that include apples. One recipe, for "Charles's Apple Smack," is from a funny book about the adventures of three brothers, *The Little Pigs' First Cookbook*, by N. Cameron Watson (1987). The book includes recipes for throughout the day.

There are plenty of other classroom projects involving apples that could be done.

1. Hang apples from the ceiling on strings and let the children place their hands behind their backs and try to bite into one.
2. Invite a person from a local tree nursery to come and explain how to plant and care for trees.
3. Compare and contrast on a chart the differences in taste, color, size, and so on of a variety of different types of apples. This activity would involve higher level thinking skills, although even first graders can see the difference between a Yellow Delicious and a Wealthy apple.

Teachers interested in doing this with children would find the first section of *Fruit* by Gallimard Juenesse and Pascale de Bourgoing (1991), from the "A First Discovery Book" series, to be useful. The book uses clear acetate pages (showing the outside and inside of the fruits) between conventional paper pages, in dealing with a wide variety of apples. The close-up, very clear illustrations will help introduce the variety of apples to children who may never have thought of any except red ones.

Vocabulary and Writing. And wouldn't the children love a "taste" test? Just think of all the vocabulary words that could be introduced: tart,

---

[1]An invaluable resource is *Do You Know What Day Tomorrow Is?* by Hopkins and Arenstein (1990). This compendium of concise information about people, places, events, and fun facts will help you tie in observations of the serious and the humorous to units of study. The birth dates commemorated include those of real people like Johnny Appleseed and also scientists, artists, musicians, and writers, among others.

juicy, sweet, meaty, crunchy, sour, red, round, spherical, shiny, and so on. Making a class list of words children can contribute to would be helpful to the students in their attempts at beginning this activity.

Journals shaped like apples, with red construction paper covers, could involve the students in their first writing experiences of the year, using inventive spelling and creating original artwork. The concept of apple seeds becoming future apple trees can also be introduced as part of a scientific understanding of plants and the growth process. Children can write about this natural sequence of events in their journals, drawing pictures of the steps involved as a seed becomes a fruit-bearing tree.

Children would enjoy seeing the video of the Disney film about "Johnny Appleseed" (check your local school system audiovisual department), another presentation of the legend format of this story. Disney re-releases its films on a cyclical basis, so the film may not be available all the time. The song, "The Lord is Good to Me," from that movie is a catchy tune, short enough for first graders to learn easily. The rhyming couplets in the song's lyrics can introduce the boys and girls to poetry, and they could write their own four-line poems about apples and what they know and feel about them. To motivate children to write apple poems, read the five poems Arnold Adoff included about apples in *Eats. Poems* (1979). The advantage of using these poems, written in free verse, is that they exemplify for children that not all poetry depends on end rhyme.

Hands-on Mathematics. Math concepts can also be incorporated into this unit. The recipe for making applesauce, apple cake, or muffins involves measuring flour, sugar, apples, and other ingredients. A teacher might use apples to demonstrate the concept of halves (two halves make a whole) or quarters. Helpers, parents, aides, student teachers, or perhaps older students "borrowed" from an upper-grade teacher, can assist with the cutting, and later with spreading peanut butter on the pieces for a delicious wholesome treat. These people can also help with making the applesauce and cake.

Children can save the apple seeds found in their apples and paste them on individual premade graphs in the column headed "Number of Seeds Found in Apple." If the teacher wishes to further elaborate on this concept, the students can compile a total class graph of seeds. How many had an apple with six seeds? How many had eight? And so on until each child has had a turn to respond and contribute to the class total.

Many of these ideas could be reinforced through drama. Four students could form a huddle, suggesting a "whole" apple. They could split in "half" two by two, and in "quarters" singly. Physically representing mathematical concepts is necessary for developing the minds of young children, who think primarily in concrete terms. Why not add the component of their physical *selves* visually portraying these important ideas?

Art Project. Tree masks can be easily constructed from brown paper grocery sacks. All masks should have holes cut out so the wearer can see. Each of the four seasons can be represented with different decorations glued to the bag: green leaves for spring, blossoms for summer, red and orange leaves for fall, and bare branches for winter. This hands-on project helps boys and girls understand the correct sequence of the seasons, when groups of matching seasons take turns telling something about their particular season. For instance, the "fall" group could tell about the birds leaving, the color of their leaves changing, and the winds blowing off their dried leaves. This can be done either by individuals or as a total group with choral speaking. The latter suggestion, however, does take some extra planning and practice, but it makes a nice presentation.

Re-enacting the steps taken making an apple recipe reinforces sequencing skills. Of course, the singing of songs (Weissman, 1988) and reciting of poems are fun for the boys and girls, but the addition of body movements provides power and ownership of the words. The grocery sack tree masks just beg to be used in an improvisational role play, created by the children in groups.

The teacher who incorporates such learning opportunities has truly "immersed" students in whole language and drama skills during such a unit as described above. This is provided to show how the planning process works, not with the idea that you should try to implement the sample unit as described here. Rather, you and your children together can identify the starting point—a topic in which they are interested—and plan this way to develop a unit in which drama is integral. It takes thinking and planning ahead to provide such experiences, but it is worth the effort. Often two or more teachers at the same grade level collaborate in planning such units. Not only does this divide the planning process two or three ways, but more creative thinking results when ideas are generated in a teamed brainstorming session.

If children in your class seem to enjoy this experience, you could extend it by using *Miss Rumphius* by Barbara Cooney (1982), which won the American Book Award. It is a similar story, of the woman who made the world more beautiful by sowing lupines. There are a multitude of pantomime possibilities for enacting the stories; children could show young Alice painting pictures, working in a library, walking on the beach gathering shells, meeting the raja's wife, climbing tall mountains, and riding on a camel. The book is rich in dialogue possibilities as well, and children could incorporate both movement and voice in reinterpreting the story of the woman who traveled far and wide sowing beauty, as Johnny Appleseed did.

Science

Suppose a class of first or second graders is studying a life science unit on the plant kingdom. A correlating drama activity to consolidate the concepts being learned might be for the teacher initiate a guided dramatization with the students. To begin:

1. Students' desks need to be quickly and quietly pushed to the classroom perimeter. A simple but efficient method for doing this is to have the desks on the outside edges of the classroom be moved first. When those children have completed their task, the inner rows (or clusters) of desks can be added to the edges of the room. This method also cuts the noise level of moving furniture in half.
2. Direct the students to spread out so they each occupy their own personal space in which to move. To be sure that each student has enough space, ask them to stretch their arms out sideways as far as they can. They should not be touching anyone else. If they are, they need to adjust their positions. The children should also "test" again for enough space by spreading one arm out front and one behind their bodies to be sure they won't be bumping into anyone else that way either. Once this task has been accomplished, the students are ready for the teacher-directed drama session.

The following example is *not* to be read aloud, which would destroy the spontaneity and sound rather stilted. (If necessary, the teacher could use a wall chart of important vocabulary words that the class had been studying and glance at them to create a similar monologue to fit a particular class' unit of study.) This extemporaneous guiding of children through a drama lesson is called "side coaching." It allows the teacher the freedom to change, add, or delete ideas during the dramatization. For example, a teacher could guide the class through the entire process depicting plant growth by saying words similar to the following:

You are a little flower **seed** [unit vocabulary words in bold print] curled up under the ground. Let's see how tightly you can curl up on the floor with your eyes closed. Wrap your arms around your knees and hug yourself into a little ball until you feel like a seed. You *are* a seed. That's the way, boys and girls! You are so cold you're shivering and shaking. You're absolutely freezing! The cold is creeping into your skin. No matter how hard you hug yourself you cannot get warm. It's very dark and quiet under the frozen earth where you are. You can't see a thing. All you think about is how cold it is, and how cold you are. It's the middle of **winter** and you're **inert**, just lying there day after freezing day, waiting for **spring** to arrive.

Soon the sun shines for longer periods each day, and the **snows** of winter turn into the **rains** of spring. The frozen ground begins to thaw. You begin to feel a change in temperature. You're not shivering any more. The **soil** in which you lie is warmer now. Raindrops **permeate** the soil and you feel the delicious moist dampness all around you. You like this feeling; it makes you want to move just a little bit. You rock to the right, then to the left. Again, to the right, and to the left. That's it! The conditions are perfect for you, a seed, to **germinate** because the three key **ingredients** needed are now present: the soil in which you lie, the **sunlight** overhead in the sky, and **water** in the form of rain.

You're beginning to stir with the urge to stretch and grow, to reach slowly, ever so slowly, toward the sun overhead. You are starting to uncurl, to become **seedlings**, and slowly, ever so slowly, stretch upward. Your legs are **roots** digging deep down into the moist earth, and your arms are becoming **stems** and **leaves**. The sun feels delightfully warm as you emerge from the ground into the sunlight. **Rainshowers** sprinkle raindrops on you and they soak the earth. Your thirsty roots drink in the welcome water. **Buds** begin to form on the ends of your stems (clenched fists). Your **petals** open (fists unclench). What beautiful, colorful **flowers** you are becoming! At last you are fully grown **mature plants**, stretching on your tiptoes, feeling so joyful, so happy, in the glorious warm rays of the sun. You just smile and smile and bend gently as the breeze blows softly on you. Isn't it wonderful to be the flower that you are?

At this point have the children end the drama part of the activity and sit down in place. Ask them to imagine what kind of flower they are and what color they might be.

- Was anyone a rose?
- Why did you pick that particular flower?
- What was your fragrance like?
- Did you have thorns?
- What were they like?

- How did they feel?
- Were there any dandelions, or any other weeds?
- Tell us about yourself.
- What else did we have growing?
- How did the soil, sun, and rain affect you?

The teacher should be as imaginative as possible in conducting this session. The more the teacher gets into the role of coaching students through a drama session and accepting their efforts in a positive manner, the freer students will be in responding.

A class discussion following this session reinforces once again the key concepts and vocabulary terms of the unit. Allowing the children to share with one another what they did and how they felt as the seeds in the growing process helps them internalize what has been studied as actual fact in this life science unit. To expand children's awareness of how this theme, developed through drama, was interpreted differently through another medium, you could use the picture book *The Tiny Seed* by Eric Carle (1987). This lets children see that any message can be transmitted differently through different mediums. After that, make children aware of the variety in shape, size, and color of flowers. You might conclude by sharing *Alison's Zinnia* by Anita Lobel (1990). The oversized format allows generous space for Lobel's details, presented in brilliant full color. After using this alphabet book with children, have them create a group-dictated alphabet of their own, perhaps incorporating the tools necessary to grow flowers.

Mathematics

Understanding Ideas Physically. Younger students address mathematics concretely. To assist in establishing the concepts of addition and subtraction, which constitute the basis for all future numerical reasoning, it might be fun to dramatize different people visiting "Grandma's" house. She is warm and friendly, and people are always welcome. Besides, she doesn't let visitors leave without offering each person one of her delicious homemade cookies. The teacher could play the part of Grandma. Half the class, acting as neighbors, friends, relatives, the mail carrier, and so on, can visit Grandma and receive a cookie. This is a wonderful way to work on the concept of character for future longer and more involved dramatizations. In addition, it helps children acquire the appropriate behavior when visiting someone else's home.

The remaining students can be the observers and recorders who keep track of the cookies distributed (it's even more fun to have real cookies available) and add them up, subtracting the total from the original supply.

Some visitors might even bring Grandma some of their own "homemade" cookies as gifts to replenish her supply. This, of course, adds to the complexity of the math problem, so the teacher needs to be certain that the class is ready for this increased difficulty. The final total number of cookies tallied at the end of the scene could be put into groups of ten for counting purposes, or into groups of twelve to introduce the concept of dozens for older students.

Next the children can exchange responsibilities. Those who were recorders can become characters in the dramatization (and receive cookies too), and those who acted before can now be the recorders. All the while the mathematical concepts of addition and subtraction are being reinforced. After you've worked on this with children, you might read *The Doorbell Rang* by Pat Hutchins (1986) in which this perennially popular picture book author depicts, in cheerful, bright double-page spreads, the increasing array of multiethnic children who cope with a similar problem. Laura Joffe Numeroff's *If You Give a Mouse a Cookie* (1985) would be a fine follow-up to this experience, full of laughs but also many useful pantomime possibilities.

Understanding Money. Third-grade students often work with the concept of money and its use in society. The teacher might have the class enact several scenarios using and exchanging play money. Have the students "visit" a theme park like Disney World or "attend" a sporting event such as a ball game. They would be responsible for paying the entrance fee and seeing that they receive the correct amount of change. Additional expenditures such as food, souvenirs, and so on would also require exchanging money. Some students could play the roles of different employees at such an event, and other students could attend the event. Shopping for school clothes and supplies or ordering food at a restaurant provide other opportunities to work with numbers in real-world situations.

From Books to Drama. Many counting books provide ties into drama. For example, Peter Sis's *Going Up!* (1989) involves a surprising array of characters (e.g., a witch, a surgeon, a banana) on an elevator trip to the happy ending in young Mary's apartment. The ensuing birthday party could be the setting for imaginative enacting by young children. Or, with slightly older children, you might use *Each Orange Had 8 Slices* by Paul Giganti, Jr. (1992), with bold graphics by Donald Crews. This poses problems for children to solve, such as: The red flowers each had six pretty petals and two tiny black bugs; how many bugs were there in all? To answer the questions on each page, children have to perform mathematical operations and could be involved physically in grouping and regrouping in order to enact the answers. The possibilities are practically limitless, and children really enjoy learning about numbers in this realistic manner.

The Arts

Language, music, and art have a definite place in the elementary school curriculum. Language arts (and reading) are most often taught in the regular classroom, while music, art, and creative drama are usually handled by teachers especially trained in these fields. That is not to say that regular teachers should exclude music and art from their own classrooms. There are many songs and related musical experiences that blend in beautifully with a unit of study. The same is true of art and creative drama. As stated previously, learning is multisensory. Therefore, the greater the variety of experiences one can provide for students, the more holistic is their frame of reference for learning. If the premise of whole language instruction is to immerse children in language in as many ways as possible, music and art must be included as basic in the curriculum. One can, of course, use the expertise of the music and art teachers, if the school has them, for assistance in planning a unit, or ask them to coordinate their lessons with a unit in progress. They are often very accommodating this way, as some of them feel quite isolated from what is happening in the regular classroom. Even if your school doesn't have, for instance, a music teacher, you can nevertheless easily incorporate music and drama in your curriculum. You might, for example, use *Old MacDonald Had a Farm*, illustrated by Carol Jones (1989). Teach the children the song first, and then direct their attention to the pictures, which are actually a richer source of verbs for enacting than is the text. Encourage students to look carefully at Jones's detailed watercolor and ink drawings, to determine which actions are being shown. Half of the class could then dramatize the farmer's actions, while the other half sings the song.

Children's books today abound with wonderful stories for all age levels and interests. There is a plethora of books for teachers on how to select and use this wealth of literature effectively. To keep current with newly published books for children, one should also read periodicals such as

The Elementary School Journal
University of Chicago Press
Journals Division
P.O. Box 37005
Chicago, IL 60637

The Reading Teacher
International Reading Association
800 Barksdale Road
P.O. Box 8139
Newark, DE 19714-8139

Language Arts
1111 Kenyon Road
Urbana, IL 61801

School Library Journal
P.O. Box 1978
Marion, OH 43305-1978

Book Links and *Booklist*
Booklist Publications
American Library Association
50 E. Huron St.
Chicago, IL 60611

Instructor
Scholastic, Inc.
2931 East McCarty Street
Jefferson City, MO 65101

Whole Language Application. Let us select a typical story for primary children and use it as a basis for expansion into a whole language unit of study.

The Mitten is a story all children will love. It involves a boy who loses a mitten outdoors in the winter, and then various animals arrive and take shelter in it together. The mitten expands until it absolutely will not hold any more animals, and the result is quite amusing. For this unit we suggest using the versions by Jan Brett (1990), Margaret Lippert (1989), Johanna Poehlman (1991), and Alvin Tresselt (1964). After exploring and sharing several different versions of this tale, the teacher can create a class chart for the children comparing and contrasting all retellings by title, author, illustrator, mitten color/description, characters involved (including the boy and his grandmother), which animals came and the order of their appearance, the problem in each of the stories, whether the tale is real or fantasy, and what happened to the mitten (see Figure 5.7). This may be the first time beginning learners have been exposed to such charts, and the very act of creating them and filling in the information will be valuable.

Using creative drama to portray the different versions of the story would enhance children's understanding of plot, characterization, sequential development of events, and the concept of beginning, middle, and end to a story. It would also deepen the comprehension of the ideas on the two charts the class compiled together after sharing the different versions of the tale.

The simple dialogue between the animals offers an excellent opportunity to try different "voices," body movements, and facial expressions while dramatizing the story; all of those are critical elements in enacting a story successfully. The teacher could model this facet of drama by selecting a student from the class who has highly developed verbal skills and ask:

• How does a big bear sneeze?
• Would a bear's sneeze be different from a mouse's sneeze?
• How?
• Can you show us what that bear's sneeze is like?

Once the sneeze has been established, the next problem to solve is how the bear moves its body. Again, the teacher can demonstrate with the same child (or select a different one) and ask:

Title	The Mitten	The Mitten	The Mitten	The Mitten	The Mitten
Author	Jan Brett	Margaret Lippert	Macmillan Early Skills Program	Ukranian folktale	Alvin Tresselt
Illustrator				Johanna Poehlman	
Mitten color and description					
Characters involved (which animals came and the order of their appearance)					
Problem in story					
Realism or fantasy					
What happened to the Mitten					

FIGURE 5.7. Comparison chart of versions of *The Mitten*.

- How does a bear move?
- Does he walk delicately on his tiptoes or trudge with big, strong steps?
- Could you show us how a bear moves by walking from the door to my desk?

Contrasting small and large animals helps, too. After the bear's character and voice have been established, the teacher may have a student portray the same two characteristics for the mouse in the story.

As a reinforcement activity (and one that could be used for skill assessment), have the children make their own set of mittens and story characters out of paper bags. A large grocery sack with a very small one glued onto its side for a thumb could serve as the mitten "container." Let the students color and decorate it to give their own personal touch. More of the same very small paper sacks could become the eight animals in Jan Brett's version of *The Mitten* (1990) (see Figure 5.8). By stuffing and tying or taping the open edges of the bags together, the children will have a basic animal body shape. They can then cut, glue, and color the definitive animal features on their sacks. The snowshoe rabbit should have long ears and a cotton ball tail. The owl needs wings, tail feathers, small pointed ears, big eyes, a beak, and so on. If the teacher wants the children to remember the correct sequence of the animals as they entered the mitten, students could place the numbers 1 to 7 on each of their small "animal" sacks. All seven of the animals can be stored inside the larger "mitten" sack. This project could be used in dialogue with other students as well as taken home to share with parents. The teacher could also assess the children's ability to recall and retell the story events when they use their mitten bag of characters.

The Mitten is a perfect lead-in for a life science unit on winter animals. The idea that some animals hibernate while others must forage for food all winter is fascinating to children, as well as the concept that some animals change to thicker or different colored fur for winter survival. A field trip to a zoo, National Geographic videos, and books on animals would provide a wealth of information on the topic.

Two books, both coincidentally about wolves, would help children think about how animals adapt to winter. *The Call of the Wolves* by Jim Murphy (1989) describes how the wolf pack reacts to illegal hunters and a fierce arctic blizzard. Full-color, detailed paintings by Mark Alan Weatherby will help children unfamiliar with these animals understand them better. You might read this in conjunction with the *Moon of the Gray Wolves* by the eminent nature writer Jean Craighead George (1991). This is set in Toklat Pass in Alaska and is part of "The 13 Moons" series, a year-long look at North American animals and how they live. The crisp, lucid writing is accompanied by some detailed, full-page paintings by Sal Catalano. Again,

FIGURE 5.8. *The Mitten*, as illustrated here from Jan Brett's version (1990), includes both human and animal movement possibilities. Children can enact the young boy, Nicki, and his grandmother, Baba. In addition, there are both large (bear, fox) and small (mole, rabbit) animals.

drama activities would reinforce the concepts introduced. Poems, songs, journals, original stories, and art projects all add to the children's understanding of the differences in animals at different times of the year.

A whole language unit of study can be as diminutive or extensive as a teacher chooses. Again, teachers are the ones to make that professional decision for their particular classroom's needs. Children raised on farms who attend rural schools would not need an extensive unit on farm animals, whereas inner-city students would definitely benefit from one. Farm children would enjoy a field trip to a nearby large metropolitan area that maintains a zoo. Although these children understand and work with the domesticated animals on their own farms, zoo animals provide an entirely different dimension of the animal world.

EVALUATING A PROGRAM

The main difference between the traditional method of recording grades or percentages on tests, and holistic scoring is that each child progresses at an *individual* rate and no one "fails" a skill just because a certain time frame has expired. Often children just need more time to internalize a concept, and the holistic teacher's responsibility is to provide enough opportunities for each pupil to do so.

A portfolio of samples of each child's work can also be maintained. It usually contains such items as artwork, original stories and poems, reports, photographs of three-dimensional projects such as puppets or dioramas, and perhaps even an audiocassette of the child reading aloud, singing, or reciting a poem. These selected pieces of the child's work incorporate the progress of the *whole* child, not just grades on reading and math tests and an IQ score, as was previously done. This portfolio follows the child through all the grades and will provide a comprehensive overview of his or her development through twelfth grade. In some innovative schools, teachers have students present a large in-depth project to a group of teachers as a prerequisite for high school graduation.

Some schools are even developing their own criteria for recording skills that children are expected to master. For example, when recording student progress, teachers at the Konnoak Elementary School in Winston-Salem, North Carolina, use a simple whole language rating scale: 1–Not yet, 2–Sometimes, and 3–Consistently. Their intention is to look at individual development, not compare one student's scores with another's (Merina, 1992).

Creative drama skills can be evaluated much the same as other academic skills, when appropriate strategies and checklists are used. Six suggestions have been given by Barbara Salisbury (1986) to assist teachers with assessment.

1. Class discussion after creative drama sessions can be used for understanding, just as any other class discussion would be used. This chapter suggested holding such a discussion after leading students through the experience of enacting the part of germinating seeds.
2. Occasional use of audio- and videotape recordings is valuable for the students as well as the teacher to evaluate their progress.
3. Problem-solving projects such as the extension activity from *The Fourth Little Pig* exercise in this chapter, or even the factory assembly line activity, are examples one could use to evaluate how students reason together to design a class presentation.
4. Role playing, of course, demonstrates a student's ability to understand a character's part in a scene that the student helped to plan. The imaginary

visit to a dairy farm or the Johnny Appleseed dramatization from this chapter would be good illustrations of this skill.

5. Oral and written tests would be obvious choices to see whether students understand drama terminology such as *plot structure* and *character objectives*.

6. A final very usable tool is a criteria checklist. Salisbury's list focuses on theatre arts objectives and individual and group behaviors necessary for effective work. (pp. 246–247)

Buege used Salisbury's chart (Figure 5.9) in a research study and found it to be a very effective evaluation tool, especially when combined with videotaped drama sessions. A grading system using either check marks or a numerical rating scale would work, depending on teacher preference.

SUMMARY

More and more school systems across the country are recognizing the value of moving toward a whole language curriculum. Immersing children in language experiences throughout the day as they work in the content areas of social studies, science, mathematics, and the arts provides a multitude of opportunities for children to connect ideas and make sense of their world. Including creative drama enhances the effectiveness of this connection because all the senses are involved. The social, emotional, mental, and physical spheres all combine to increase the probability of learning and retaining important concepts.

RELATED READING

Cottrell, J. (1987). *Creative drama in the classroom: Grades 1–3*. Lincolnwood, IL: National Textbook.

This book, especially designed for children in the early grades, contains a wealth of useful ideas and examples of classroom-tested creative drama experiences based on sound child development theory. Providing much assistance to the teacher who wants to create a child-centered environment in which holistic and integrated learning can be fostered, this book gives teaching goals, student learning objectives, sample lesson plans, ways to assess student progress, and lists of resources.

The book discusses drama as an educational tool, how the teacher can be a drama leader, starting techniques, how to develop creative drama

On-going Drama Behaviors	S T U D E N T S									
CONCENTRATIONS										
follows directions										
sustains involvement in activity										
IMAGINATION										
contributes original ideas										
reacts spontaneously										
solves problems creatively										
incorporates imaginative detail										
COOPERATIVE INSTRUCTION										
contributes to group effort										
listens courteously to others										
takes turns										
assumes role of leaser										
assumes role of follower										
accepts group decisions										
NONVERBAL EXPRESSION										
uses appropriate gestures										
uses appropriate movement										
VERBAL EXPRESSION										
speaks clearly										
speaks expressively										
improvises dialogue										
EVALUATION AND CRITIAL ANALYSIS										
makes constructive contributions to discussion and evaluations										
incorporates improvelments into playing										
ATTITUDE										
cooperative, involved										
shy, inhibited										
disruptive, hostile										

Source: B. Salisbury, (1986), *Theatre arts in the elementary classroom.* New Orleans: Anchorage.

FIGURE 5.9. Salisbury's checklist of objectives and behaviors for effective drama in the classroom.

skills, integrating drama with content areas, and how to create workable plans. This is an excellent "how-to" source for teachers.

Heinig, R. B. (1988). *Creative drama for the classroom teacher* (3rd ed.). Englewood Cliffs, NJ: Prentice-Hall.

This is directed at the novice interested in teaching creative drama, who needs practical advice on how to begin. Well-written explanations accompany a number of activities, ranging from simple to more complex. Chapters are included on basic creative drama instruction, working in groups, simple drama activities and games, narrative pantomime, verbal activities and improvisation, story dramatization, and how to plan drama lessons and units. The book's focus is on material and methods for teaching drama rather than on discussing various theories. Heinig purposely relies heavily on children's literature, an excellent stimulus for original ideas. Numerous annotated references are included.

McCaslin, N. (1990). *Creative drama in the classroom* (5th ed.). White Plains, NY: Longman.

This text encompasses a lifetime of dedication to the field. The author stresses the importance of imagination, play, movement and rhythms, pantomime, improvisation, puppetry and mask making, plays, poetry, and other topics. Appendices, including one on pupil evaluation in creative drama, and a large bibliography provide valuable resources.

Whole language. *Oregon English, 11*(1), 4–7, 10–14, 23–25, 65–69.

The entire issue is dedicated to whole language, but of special interest are articles by Dorothy Watson, Andy Sommer, Duane Rebecca Spritzer, and Richard Ammon.

Watson gives a brief overview of the history of whole language, discusses where it is at present, and then looks forward to its future potential. Viewed from a curricular, cultural, social, and political perspective, she stresses the importance of students as a community of learners and lauds teachers who are risk takers, willing to do whatever is necessary to make whole language work for the children they teach.

Sommer's emphasis is on research being done in whole language and its implications for teachers. He emphasizes that whole language classrooms are child-centered rather than teacher-centered. The approach allows classroom teachers to establish a learning environment that fosters literacy in the lower grades and encourages lifelong learning. He states that "the whole language teacher must be able to combine oral expression, reading and writing in student-centered activities, while at the same time weaving in skill instruction appropriately matched to individuals" (p. 13).

Spritzer advocates integrating the language arts in the elementary classroom using fairy tales, fables, and traditional literature. Not only are fairy tales fascinating, but they contain themes that help children find meaning in life. These stories abound with conflicts between individuals or groups, conquering fears, facing loss and separation, using cleverness to defeat powerful oppressors, and the struggle for success through right behavior. Such stories link children to their culture and their past, and help them find meaning in life. Used with a whole language approach, fairy tales can help students develop prediction and critical thinking skills.

Ammon provides suggestions for evaluating the rate of children's progress in a whole language program. He proposes several ways for children to respond to reading material, among which are speaking, art, drama, and writing activities.

RELATED CHILDREN'S BOOKS

John Chapman ("Johnny Appleseed")

Aliki. *The Story of Johnny Appleseed.* New York: Trumpet Book Club, 1963.
Becvar, Patsy. *Who Was John Chapman?* Chicago: Nystrom, 1991.
Gibbons, Gail. *The Seasons of Arnold's Tree.* New York: Harcourt Brace Jovanovich, 1984.
Ingoglia, Gina. *Johnny Appleseed and the Planting of the West.* New York: Disney Press, 1992.
Jennings, Terry. *The Young Scientist Investigates Seeds and Seedlings.* Chicago: Children's Press, 1981, now o.p.
Johnson, Hannah. *From Apple Seed to Applesauce.* New York: Lothrop, Lee and Shepard, 1977.
LeSieg, Theodore. *Ten Apples Up on Top.* New York: Random House, 1961.
Moore, Eva. *Johnny Appleseed.* New York: Scholastic, 1964.
Scheer, Julian. *Rain Makes Applesauce.* New York: Holiday House, 1964.
Selsam, Millicent. *The Apple and Other Fruits.* New York: Morrow, 1973, now o.p.
Silverstein, Shel. *The Giving Tree.* New York: Harper & Row, 1964, now o.p.
Thornton, Shelley (Ill.). *The Star in the Apple.* New York: Scholastic, 1991.
Udry, Janet. *A Tree Is Nice.* Harper Jr. Books, 1956.

The Mitten

Brett, Jan. *The Mitten: A Ukranian Folktale.* New York: Putnam, 1990.
Lippert, Margaret. (Reteller). *The Mitten.* New York: Macmillan Reading Program, 1989.
Poehlmann, Johanna. (Ill.). *The Mitten.* Racine, WI: Copycat Press, 1991.
Tresselt, Alvin. *The Mitten.* New York: Mulberry Books, 1964.

The Three Little Pigs

Celsi, Teresa. *The Fourth Little Pig.* Austin, TX: Steck-Vaughn, 1992.

Dahl, Roald. "The Three Little Pigs," in *Roald Dahl's Revolting Rhymes.* New York: Bantam, 1986.

Galdone, Paul. *The Three Little Pigs.* New York: Scholastic, 1970.

Hooks, William. *The Three Little Pigs and the Fox.* New York: Macmillan, 1989.

Scieszka, Jon. *The True Story of the Three Little Pigs, by A. Wolf.* New York: Viking Kestrel, 1989.

CHAPTER 6

Dramatizing Across the Curriculum— Grades 4 Through 8

Students in the middle years, grades 4 through 8, are growing rapidly, not only physically, but socially, emotionally, and academically as well. The majority of these young people are eager for more responsibility. They readily accept the challenge of working together and enjoy activities that require physical activity and creative thinking, such as composing a drama together. Such opportunities allow student leaders to develop their skills, while others learn the fine art of give-and-take, negotiating to have their suggestions accepted by the whole group. Some students are organizers and keep groups on task, while those with the most creative minds enjoy contributing their ideas to enhance the scene at hand.

Working on problem-solving situations in groups allows students to experience real "world of work" situations. Most of their future careers will involve working with others. Research has shown that most people are fired from their jobs due to the lack of ability to get along with others, *not* because of lack of job skills. Planning drama activities together in school during adolescence nurtures these skills and provides students with opportunities to be involved in a "slice of real life" in their formative years. In addition to the fun of creating a dramatization, the social and problem-solving skills developed here will be invaluable to these youngsters in the future.

DRAMA FOR SOCIAL STUDIES

The scope and sequence charts of most social studies curricula spiral upward and outward in ever-widening circles of knowledge (Schug & Beery, 1992). Primary school children usually begin with a study of their immediate families, progress to the neighborhood, and then learn about their communities and the occupations of people they have come to know as "community helpers." By the time they reach their intermediate years, boys and girls are ready to expand their understanding to peoples of their nation and the world at large, in both a contemporary and historical sense. The following social studies topics are not strictly followed by all local and state curricula, but in general they have been widely accepted throughout much of the United States.

Grade 4

To broaden their sense of the world but still maintain a foothold in the familiar, many fourth grades undertake a year's investigation of their own particular state. The historical aspect of this study generally begins with an examination of the various Native American tribes who lived there prior to the arrival of the European explorers. Dramatizations of elements of the tribes' cultures are appropriate means for "walking a day in another's moccasins" in order to understand the highly developed interdependence of tribal members. Age level, gender, and highly developed skills all played a vital part in the survival of the tribe, and children of the students' own age were important contributing members to the tribe's welfare. Such ideas are developed in many children's books, including *People of the Breaking Day* by Marcia Sewall (1990). The author uses first person narration to make this a more immediate reading experience for students.

The introduction of European culture into the Indian world provides additional possibilities for dramatic interpretation. New ideas and customs provided both positive and negative changes, and children need to be made aware of them. Again, enacting scenes where such changes occurred allows students to see both sides of the picture. Students might depict the impact that the introduction of the horse, rifle, metal tools, and even reservations had on the Native American population. A book that deals directly and candidly with the interaction of cultures is *The Tainos: The People Who Welcomed Columbus* by Francine Jacobs (1992), which describes the explorer's contact with the Bahamian Island Indians. These gentle farmers who originated in South America were wiped out in less than fifty years. Jacobs's book provides much stimulus to discussion and many opportunities to dramatize brief vignettes of interaction between the two cultures.

Students this age can take the abstract idea of government and make it come alive by enacting how a bill becomes a law. Making charts of this process from textbooks and encyclopedias is instructive, but a realistic drama will have a much more lasting impression. Select a topic that would have an immediate impact on students' lives. They have been informed many times of the need to wear protective helmets when riding their bicycles, so the idea of having a law to enforce the wearing of this type of headgear would be quite relevant to them on a daily basis. Once the class is familiar with the three branches of their government (legislative, executive, and judicial), students could be actively involved in dramatizing

1. A committee of "legislators" composing a bill that would require all riders of two wheeled bicycles to wear safety helmets. The bill would then come out of committee and be "debated" on the house floor. If passed when voted on, the bill would then proceed to the state senate for a similar debate.
2. Student "citizens" writing letters presenting arguments on both sides of the debate in an effort to influence their legislators. If both houses pass the bill, it would then go to the state "governor" for signature in order to become an actual law.
3. An elaborate signing ceremony with news reporters using videocameras attending and recording the event. An evening "news show" could play back this important news event on the classroom TV set, and reporters could give a news report. (The videotape could also be circulated to home television sets to share with parents.)
4. "Citizens" who vehemently oppose the passage of such a law could force a test case in the "courts" to see if the law could be repealed. The final opinion, of course, would be decided by the state court.

   Textbooks come alive and have so much more meaning when a realistic exercise like this one is implemented through drama. Although the students perform the actual roles in the presentation, the teacher *must* be very active behind the scenes, guiding, coaching, and helping the students organize their scenes. Acting out roles involved in government is a totally new concept to fourth graders, and they will need much assistance for this to be successful. For instance, a house debate will be a totally new experience, and the student playing the speaker of the house will have to become acquainted with some rudimentary rules of parliamentary procedure to make the debate seem authentic. A "staged" heated debate with a pounding gavel and demand for "order" would heighten the excitement.

   Other components of the study of a state include its history, agriculture, education, cultural diversity, transportation, parks, economy, and growth of big cities. Again, it is the teacher's decision as to how to incorporate different types of activities to inculcate important concepts into the class' understanding, but using creative drama as a teaching tool is well recognized. Not only do the students have to understand the "big picture" in order to interpret it dramatically; they have to organize the scene sequentially, decide who plays which roles, practice what will be said and what happens, and then present it. All of the skills involved—*interpretation, organization, sequencing, decision making, rehearsal*, and *performance*—are higher level learning skills needed in later life. A wise teacher encourages the development of these skills and fosters their use in the classroom as often as possible.

Grade 5

Fifth graders often study the entire United States. Sometimes this broad area is divided into a two-year study, the United States from 1492 to 1800 for fifth graders, and the United States from 1800 to the present for sixth graders.

The United States from 1492 to 1800 includes learning about different tribes of Native Americans, the European explorers, settlement of the Atlantic seaboard, the thirteen original colonies, the Revolutionary War, and the beginning of the nation the children now know as their own United States of America. Many children's books deal with various aspects of this large period of time. One of the best is the photo essay written by Kate Waters, *Sarah Morton's Day* (1989). Photographed in full color at Plymouth Plantation and featuring actors dressed in period costume, this is told, as if written in 1627, by nine-year-old Sarah.

The advent of the European explorers, whether here for land acquisition or to spread religion, had a profound impact on the peoples on both sides of the Atlantic Ocean. To commemorate the 500th anniversary of Columbus's four voyages to the New World, many schools are enacting scenes depicting the impact of his discoveries. Drama can help students understand the importance of this time period from the perspective of the peoples on both sides of the encounter. Books are now available that show both the positive and negative aspects of this time of exploration. A comparison of these different books through creative drama would involve utilizing the higher elements of Bloom's taxonomy. Explore such questions as

- Where did Columbus think he had landed?
- What were his impressions of the native population?
- How did he treat them?
- What did the West Indies inhabitants think of Columbus?
- How did they receive him?
- Did Columbus really prove, by his voyages, that the world was round?
- How did King Ferdinand and Queen Isabella treat Columbus after he returned to Spain from his first voyage? After his fourth voyage?
- What impact did Columbus's voyages have on the Western world?

A valuable culminating activity after the drama presentations is to create a large classroom chart comparing and contrasting the major ideas in each book. Nancy Smiler Levinson's book, *Christopher Columbus* (1990), full of large black and white maps and illustrations of art about the explorer, is a useful resource. See list at the end of this chapter for some other books about Christopher Columbus.

The Revolutionary War period is fascinating to children of this age level and is filled with many possibilities for dramatization. Biographies of key historical figures such as George Washington, Ben Franklin, Thomas Jefferson, Paul Revere, and Dolly Madison are available for upper elementary readers. Try dramatizing one of the following events:

1. An event leading to the Revolutionary War, such as Washington's march under British General Braddock to capture Fort Duquesne from the French. This event highlights the important differences in military tactics between Indian guerilla warfare and the massed force engagement traditionally used by the English and other European troops. Braddock was killed and the British were defeated in this particular skirmish, but Washington emerged as an expert commander and would later use a combination of both the old and new warfare against the British.
2. The signing of the Declaration of Independence
3. The Boston Tea Party
4. The quartering of British troops in people's homes
5. The high-handed search and seizure rule used by British customs officers to invade private homes and businesses
6. The winter at Valley Forge

Not only biographies of famous people of the time, but historical novels, too, are ready sources for dramatization. *My Brother Sam Is Dead* by James Collier (1974) and *Johnny Tremain* by Esther Forbes (1971) are two of many stories depicting different events and perspectives from the Revolutionary War period. The first book, based on a real event, portrays a family of Tories loyal to England. The eldest son runs away to join the Revolutionary army, but is subsequently caught and shot as a traitor. Many scenes can be dramatized from this book.

1. The conflict between the Tory father and his eldest son
2. The trial of the eldest son by the Tories
3. The younger son's perception of both the family's and colonies' conflicts

The second novel, *Johnny Tremain*, about a fictional character set in pre-Revolutionary times, centers mainly on the events in Boston leading up to the Revolutionary War. The Boston Tea Party, secret meetings with Sam Adams and other revolutionaries, Paul Revere's involvement, and other events are seen through the eyes of the main character, young Johnny, who is present at many of the prewar scenes. An orphaned apprentice whose hand is burned in a terrible accident in Paul Revere's silversmith shop, Johnny deals with both his own inner turmoil and the larger conflict of the period.

Grade 6

If sixth graders are studying the history of the United States from 1800 to the present, they have a myriad of possibilities for dramatic interpretation.

1. The westward movement
2. The Civil War
3. Immigration
4. The Industrial Revolution
5. World Wars I and II
6. The wars in Korea, Vietnam, and the Persian Gulf
7. The growth of major cities
8. The development of modern technology

Activity 1. A sixth-grade social studies class has been studying the westward expansion in the United States in the 1850s. The boys and girls have studied their social studies texts, read several trade books on the subject, and enjoyed the Oregon Trail program on their classroom computers. As a culminating activity try the following:

1. Going through the decision process of whether to stay in the east or move west
2. Planning what possessions to take and what to leave behind
3. Getting ready to set out on the trail after arriving in St. Louis
4. Troubles and hardships on the trail
5. What occurs once they arrive at their destination

This creative drama activity would probably take several days.

Day 1:
   Divide the class into five groups, each selecting one of the five topics listed above. Allow time for the groups to use their textbooks, notes, such novels as Kathryn Lasky's *Beyond the Divide* (1983), and other research to *discuss* what they'd like to portray in their drama presentation.

Day 2:
- Plan *how to dramatize* the ideas discussed the previous day.
- Decide who will play the characters selected.
- Determine what types of activities will take place.
- Determine what the sequence of events will be.
- Discuss how the dramatization might end.

Day 3: Use this session to work on those aspects as children refine their dramatizations.

Day 4: Have the groups present their dramatizations to the rest of the class.

This particular activity in its entirety could easily last a week or more. It is an activity for a class that is used to creative drama being an integral part of the learning process. In a school where students have been exposed to drama since kindergarten, this culminating activity is quite feasible. However, you should not jump into such a project without providing the class with a great deal of earlier drama training such as that suggested in the beginning chapters of this book. This full-scale improvisation will involve incorporating key concepts learned, decision making, and group cooperation, as well as creative drama skills. At this point drama has truly become an integral part of the educational process.

Activity 2. Another possibility for sixth-grade dramatization is the study of the immigrants who came by the thousands to seek a better life in the United States in the last half of the 1800s. Most students have ancestors, or perhaps parents, who emigrated from different countries to come here, or they may be immigrants themselves. Research will reveal that people emigrated due to scarcity of land, such as in Switzerland; religious persecution in Poland; forced conscription into the military in Germany; the law of primogeniture in Norway; and the lack of food—the potato famine in Ireland in the 1840s, for instance. Excellent possibilities for dramatization include

1. The decision to leave and what to pack in the one trunk allowed aboard the steamship
2. The crowded voyage across the ocean
3. The sighting of the Statue of Liberty
4. The examination process at Ellis Island
5. Trying to reach a certain destination in the United States

A parent back in Europe reading aloud a homesick "letter" from a young son or daughter who has left home for America could be a very poignant moment as these sixth graders realize the permanent separation immigration caused in many families. Don't hesitate to use such picture books as *A Peddler's Dream* by Janice Shefelman (1992) with children of this age. Picture books of this type, which include a longer text than is usual, provide a rich resource of ideas about complex topics that can lead into drama. A very personalized account of how one immigrant came from Lebanon to make his fortune in America, Shefelman's book brings large ideas into sharp focus for youngsters in ways that generalized textbooks rarely do. Children will empathize with Solomon, his wife Marie, and their drive to succeed, which helps them overcome the very real threat a fire in their store poses to the new life they've built for themselves.

Grade 7

By seventh grade, students are ready for a beginning study of the history of the Western world. This often begins with the Fertile Crescent area of Mesopotamia between the Tigris and Euphrates Rivers. It then expands to the Greco-Roman period, the Medieval era, and the Renaissance period, with the advent of city-states, and then progresses to the development of the modern European nations. The expansion of European influence into North and South America may also be included in this year's study, and, with time permitting, students may also examine the effects of World Wars I and II on the modern world.

Activity. While studying the Medieval period in Europe, students will encounter all the ramifications of the development of classes of society in and around fortified castles. The lords of these castles and their surrounding fiefdoms developed their own special worlds within a world, and students will be fascinated with the ideas of heraldry, the feudal system, the Crusades, knighthood, and castle attack and defense methodology. A dramatic enactment culminating this unit of study and involving a day (or week) in the life of a castle, including all the characters from the lowliest serf to the feudal lord himself, would be a fitting conclusion to such a unit. Students could enact

1. A holiday feast
2. A jousting tournament
3. A visiting relative, displaying a coat of arms
4. A thwarted siege of the castle
5. An honored son returning from the Crusades to a banquet celebration
6. A magician conjuring some enchantment for the ladies
7. A juggler performing

8. A bard singing or reciting some verses from a story poem about Robin Hood
9. Proposal of plans for an addition to the castle
10. Discussion of an upcoming hunt with ruling families from nearby castles

The variety of scenes will depend on the interests and capacities of the students as they work to make decisions about which scenes to enact. Although creative drama does not usually involve costumes or stage properties, this might be an exception; students could design and display their own coats of arms or draw an actual building plan for an addition to the castle to share with the players and with the audience, too, of course. Very practical suggestions about simple costuming are given by Lynn Edelman Schnurnberger in *Kings Queens Knights and Jesters* (1978).

David Macaulay's book, *Castles* (1977), is an excellent source showing the planning and construction of castles of that period. His black and white illustrations show the care and research he's taken to present an accurate account of the engineering skills of the time between 1277 and 1305. *Medieval Knights* by M. Trevor Cairns (1991) covers the concept of knighthood in the Middle Ages, and Aliki's book, *A Medieval Feast* (1983), shows how people of the time held a banquet (see Figure 6.1). See the list at the end of the chapter for additional resources on this time period.

Grade 8

Eighth graders often study cultures other than the Western world. They may explore the history of the continent of Asia, especially the Indian, Chinese, and Japanese peoples, and also the continent of Africa, with an emphasis on the civilization of ancient Egypt. The differences in history, societal beliefs, ideas of family, religion, government, contributions to science and the arts, languages, and so on, are monumental.

Activity 1. After studying the differences in Asian societies, it might be interesting to have a week or more of creative drama presentations depicting important aspects of each culture. Divide the class into groups dealing with a particular major Eastern culture, and, after discussion, research, and practice, children can present their findings to the class in a dramatization. For instance, students responsible for the Chinese culture could select one student to be Marco Polo, who, in role, learns about the Chinese by observing and speaking with different characters such as

- The chief gunpowder manufacturer
- The person in charge of paper making

FIGURE 6.1. Aliki's *A Medieval Feast* (1983) contains a wide variety
of pantomime possibilities to challenge children: setting up tents for
the horsemen, fencing the fields, turning wild boar on spits, and
sounding the trumpets, among others. All this and more, to welcome
the king and his traveling entourage.

- The great Khan himself, ruler of China at the time Polo lived there
- A Chinese "scribe," who demonstrates some of the characters used
  in Chinese writing
- The manager of a silk-making establishment (as part of a "tour" of
  the establishment). The entire process, from silkworm to finished
  kimono, is fascinating and worthy of dramatization.

The possibility of scenes to be enacted are limited only by time constraints and the imaginations of the eighth graders themselves.

Activity 2. Delving into the history of ancient Egypt is equally captivating. A multitude of books are available on the subject (see a partial listing at the end of this chapter). Topics for possible dramatization include

- Egyptian daily family life
- Farming and the trades of different craftsmen
- Religion
- The clothing and cosmetics worn during that time
- Hieroglyphics
- The pyramids
- The entombment of the boy king Tutankhamun

Again, a thoroughly researched study of the different aspects of Egyptian society by the students could lead to "A Week in the Life of the Ancient Egyptians" as portrayed in several dramatic scenes with the students "in character."

For instance, students could build a pyramid using a square base attached at the corners to four pieces of lumber of equal length. Those pieces of lumber would rise and meet to form the apex of a prism. This could be covered by cotton sheeting or paper and decorated to look like a pyramid. An "entrance" could be made in one wall to allow students inside to peer at the tomb contents. Students could explain how a pyramid was built, how a body was mummified, and the purposes of the many artifacts that were included in the tomb.

A "scribe" might conduct business in another part of the classroom. He could have a chart showing the different signs used in hieroglyphic writing and offer to make a cartouche, or name inscription, for class members. He might even have a drawn replica of the Rosetta stone to explain how hieroglyphics were finally deciphered. The stone contains one message written in three different languages, and it was through the study of this stone that the ancient Egyptian language was finally translated. Catharine Roehrig's *Fun with Hieroglyphs* (1990) provides fascinating information about this complex writing system; the book comes packaged with stamps and an ink pad so students can create their own messages.

These are only two examples of a culminating activity on ancient Egypt. Many others could be listed. Eighth graders are very capable of handling projects of this magnitude, but the teacher's role is critical in keeping the momentum going and the focus centered on the topics and dramatizations at hand. A clipboard containing a chart of which group is portraying which aspect of Egyptian life, together with a checklist of steps accomplished, is a lifesaver for the teacher. Not only does the teacher have to keep the students on task, but it is also the teacher's responsibility to visit each group for a brief period each day, listening and offering succinct suggestions for additions and improvements to the formulation of the dramatizations in progress. A partial listing of resources appears at the end of the chapter.

DRAMA FOR SCIENCE

Grade 4

School systems across the country have been coping with difficult budget constraints. Often the first items deleted from budgets are class supplies, among them hands-on items for science experiments. How can students learn scientific concepts solely from reading textbooks? That's like trying to learn to swim from an encyclopedia! Creative drama can assist in demonstrating scientific concepts, using little more than the students' own creative minds and bodies. Let us suppose that a fourth grade is examining different kinds of pressure and the effects pressure has when applied to various items. Such a study might focus on air pressure, water pressure, and the energy released from a coiled spring under pressure (see Figure 6.2).

Activity 1. Demonstrate air pressure by having a student "be" a deflated bicycle inner tube. This student lies on his side on the floor, curling up, grabbing his ankles, and lying as quietly and limply as possible. Another student can enact holding a hand-operated air pump, "attaching" the hose to the first student's feet, and then "pumping" the handle up and down, inserting air into the deflated inner tube. As the air begins to inflate the inner tube, the student slowly puffs up and rises from the floor until he is upright in the shape of a circle, still grabbing his ankles. The finishing touch, of course, is to screw down the cap on the inner tube's nozzle so the air doesn't escape. This simple demonstration is highly effective because most children can relate to the process of inflating a bicycle tire. The teacher can take the experiment one step further by having the children enact pumping too much air pressure in the tire until it "explodes." The same idea can be used with a balloon, an inexpensive way to have children explore the concept of too much air pressure.

FIGURE 6.2. After studying the scientific concept of air pressure, children are translating what they know from words about the idea to an enactment of the idea.

Activity 2. Demonstrate water pressure by having four pupils squat on the floor forming the letter X, backs together and facing outward, in the shape of a common garden sprinkler. Another student can "attach" a garden hose to the sprinkler and turn the water on. If she verbalizes the steps in this procedure, the students who are acting the part of the sprinkler will know exactly when the water is turned on, and they can begin to rotate clockwise on the floor, making the sounds of water spraying out in four directions as they spin around. When the water is shut off, they will no longer have the power (or pressure) necessary to rotate and spray, so they must resume their beginning inert position. Again, this is a simple but effective method of explaining applied water pressure in a situation with which all children are familiar.

Activity 3. To further demonstrate what occurs when a coiled spring is under pressure, the teacher could pose the question, "How might you show a simple household toaster with toast springing up?" Two students stand facing each other, arms extended at shoulder height and hands clasped. It doesn't take much imagination for the mind's eye to envision this as an electric toaster. A third student could be the "slice of bread" about to be toasted, squatting between the first two students. A fourth could be the lever, attached to a spring facing the back of one of the two "toaster" students. When a final student "depresses" the lever, setting the timer and spring into action, it won't be long before the spring releases and the "toast" jumps up, done to a turn. Additional items such as alarm clocks, a screen door, a "Slinky," and other springloaded objects can also be dramatized. A little research on the part of the students could result in a list of possibilities. David Macaulay's delightfully illustrated book, *The Way Things Work* (1988), shows how different types of springs work. Throughout, Macaulay uses his sense of humor and knowledge of mechanics to explain the functions of various machines to upper elementary and middle school students.

Grade 5

Fifth graders may have studied the three states of water—liquid, solid, and gas—in previous grades, but the more complicated concept of water as a renewable resource is appropriate for students of this age. To make this a realistic scientific study, they might study the effects modern industry has on the environment of a specific area. Dramatizations could be constructed around scenes dealing with such questions as:

- What political conflicts might arise at the suggestion that a nuclear power plant might be built near a small river town?
- What might happen if local nearby wetlands were drained for a new factory or shopping center complex?
- What could happen to the river if a nuclear power plant was constructed on its banks?

Pupils could choose to portray certain viewpoints, research the facts, and be interviewed on a "TV show" or participate in a panel discussion at a "town meeting." The teacher could moderate the panel, if necessary, but older students can usually handle all the parts in the drama, both pro and con, and would prefer to do so. A town vote could be held after the discussion of the issues, and the results could be "posted" or written in a news article, a tie-in to the writing program.

Grade 6

Sixth graders often study the basic concepts involved in the flow of the electrical current. They can design and implement several versions of switch-controlled open and closed electrical circuits, usually by testing small light bulbs. They may also use a variety of wet and dry cell batteries. Rather than consider this study closed at this point, why not reinforce the concepts just learned by allowing students to

- Build simple telegraph sets
- Learn the Morse Code
- Actually use the sets to communicate with each other

Directions for the construction of a simple code practice light are readily available in encyclopedias or basic "how-to" books on electricity.

Once these transmitters are assembled and ready for use, students can begin learning the Morse Code. A system of dots and dashes, or long and short flashes of the electric light bulb on the code practice light model, constitutes the basis for identifying letters and numbers. This code system is easily located in encyclopedias or books on codes. All the students have to do is copy it down and become familiar with it. With a bit of concentrated practice, they will soon enjoy sending simple messages to each other.

To make this more realistic, it would be fun for students to stage a situation where an emergency SOS message is received from a ship in trouble. For some reason, it can't reach the Coast Guard telegraph officer, so it sends out a general Mayday alarm. A group of sixth-grade students is having a sleep over in a home with a telegraph transmitter and the students receive the message. It is up to them to alert the proper authorities quickly, but first information on location coordinates must be obtained from the ship.

- How do they do this promptly and efficiently?
- What steps need to be taken?
- Whom do they contact with this information if, in reality, the Coast Guard is not available?

Additional factors could be added to the dramatization, or different story lines could involve more groups of students, but each group would focus on the use of its code practice light.

Grade 7

Somewhere in every science curriculum there should be space for a unit titled "Inventions." Most students have played with Lego blocks, or some variation of that toy. Many have also used modern versions of Erector sets, and miniature motors to make a "machine" do some work. A few students may have built model airplanes, cars, or boats and controlled their movements by hand held radio operated devices. While projects of this kind are cost prohibitive for the majority of school systems, students can still "invent" a simple machine capable of doing some kind of work. The teacher can ask students to design such an invention at home and bring it in on a specified date for a "Class Expo Day." Each student, or pair of students, will explain the function of the machine and the steps taken to build it, and demonstrate it for the rest of the class.

The one major criterion is that from the moment a human hand trips a lever, pushes a button, or turns a crank, there must be two more functions or steps that occur before the machine actually performs its designated function. For instance, if a student designs an "automatic" egg cracker, there must be at least *three* steps involved in the process.

- A human hand could roll a golf ball down an inclined chute.
- The ball would then trip a lever releasing a miniature toy wagon.
- Containing a fresh egg, the wagon would roll backwards to the rim of a frying pan.
- The frying pan would stop the wagon from rolling any further, but the egg would still be in motion and bump open the wagon's gate, allowing the egg to fall into the frying pan and crack open.

It isn't necessary to create a truly usable machine; the objective is to join in the spirit of the project and have a good time sharing the inventions. The beginning section of the Walt Disney film, "Chitty Chitty Bang Bang," has several zany innovative inventions for the class to see and discuss.

The teacher could make the day of sharing these devices as elaborate as desired. There could be a cloth-covered table in front of the room used strictly by the student demonstrating an invention to the class at an assigned time. The demonstration can be as elaborate and dramatic as the student wishes. Students could use a 5″ × 8″ card to write their names, the names of their inventions, and the sequence of steps needed to make them function. The building custodian could be invited to "judge" the design and function of the inventions. Often custodians are the most mechanically inclined people in the school building, due to the maintenance problems they have had to solve. Wouldn't this be a delightful, fun filled day of learning and sharing? The second author has used this project many times with middle schoolers, and it was a resounding success on each occasion.

Grade 8

Eighth graders may be introduced to beginning botany. A main component they can study is the world of bacteria and their two-sided features of being both beneficial and destructive to humankind. In the introductory phase, the class learns to identify the fundamental shapes of bacteria and how they reproduce. If classroom microscopes aren't available, or if there are too few for a total class demonstration, a form of drama could be used. Most classrooms *do* have an overhead projector, and the lighted table platform is a ready-made "theater screen" for visually pointing out the differences in the three fundamental shapes of bacteria. Before class some of the students could prepare "visual aid" shapes of bacteria attached to a thread that could be moved about on the screen. The rod-shaped *bacilli* are the largest group of bacteria, followed by the spherical *cocci*, and smallest in number of species are the *spirilla*, or spiral-shaped bacteria. The differences in the three main types of bacteria could be easily and compellingly shown by using color, shapes, and movement.

Two groups of bacteria, bacilli and spirilla, are motile, or able to move independently. Again, some students could prepare ahead of time an enlarged version of each of these two, complete with hairlike flagella, perhaps shown by many pieces of thread attached to the outer edges all around the cell wall. When the form is wiggled on the overhead projector, it will appear as though the cell is actually propelling itself, or "swimming" in its environment. A bit of research will tell the students that some bacteria have a single terminal flagellum, while others have one or a cluster of flagella at one or both ends of the cell. The flagella are usually as long as or longer than the bacterial cell itself, which makes for an interesting display to the students observing this miniature dramatization. How much more interesting to take notes from a "moving" organism whose attributes are explained by one of their peers than to listen to a teacher's lecture or copy a diagram from a textbook! To our visually oriented youngsters, raised on TV and videos, this type of demonstration is much more entertaining, and therefore more easily remembered for recall later on a test.

To indicate the miniscule size of bacteria, an enlarged chart could be constructed, showing that it would take more than a thousand of one of the largest bacteria, placed end to end, to equal an inch. Use a paper punch to collect a thousand paper dots so a giant "inch" could be made with the dots pasted side by side to indicate how small they really are. This would be a good project for mainstreamed learning disabled students who function best when learning with hands-on activities. Some middle schools or junior high schools have a student enrollment as high as one thousand. If the class could mentally envision a thousand students standing side by side in a straight line, that too would equal the number of the largest type of bacteria per inch. Such comparisons are mentally mind-boggling and help students understand the microscopic world of bacteria. When students study further and learn that one drop of liquid can contain up to 50 million bacteria, they will begin to realize the infinitesimal size of these one-celled organisms.

Once the introductory information explaining the characteristics of bacteria has been explored, the class can move on to cell structure and cell division. Cell division, in which a cell divides into two equal parts, or daughter cells, can be dramatized.

- Give all the students in the classroom certain lettered cards.
- The entire group of students huddles together to form one bacteria cell.
- At a signal from the teacher, all students with the letter A would stretch backward in one direction to form a separate huddle on one side of the room.
- Those with a B do the same, but stretch toward the opposite side.
- Those with a C, D, E, or F divide again into the four corners of the room into ever smaller groups, demonstrating how bacterial cells manage to reproduce so quickly.

After this is over, tell students that, under favorable conditions, bacteria divide as often as once every 20 minutes. At this rate, a single cell gives rise to nearly 70 billion cells in 12 hours. Fortunately, this rate of division can be maintained for only a short time! Crowding, the exhaustion of food materials and water, and the accumulation of toxic waste products limit the bacterial population.

As their knowledge base increases, students could make charts categorizing bacteria that are helpful and those that are destructive. For example, "good" bacteria eliminate waste materials such as sewage, forest debris, and garbage, and aid in the process of tanning hides, the manufacture of butter and cheese, and the production of sauerkraut, vinegar, and silage. However, "bad" bacteria spoil food and milk, pollute water, and spread diseases such as cholera. Students will add to their "good guy" and "bad guy" lists through further research, and this information then becomes a ready-made vehicle for a debate or skit differentiating between the positive and negative effects of bacteria in the environment. Another approach would be to put "A. Bacterium" on trial and decide whether his split personality should be allowed to survive. Mock trial "lawyers" could cross examine him and other witnesses, the rest of the class in the "audience" could play the part of the jury; a secret ballot could be taken and tabulated to see if he remains or is banished. In such a context, students find that searching out the facts is much more enjoyable, and the information is likely to be retained much better.

DRAMA FOR MATHEMATICS

Grade 4

By the time children reach fourth grade they have been taught the concepts of multiplication (speedy addition) and division (accelerated subtraction).

They are proud when they've mastered their multiplication and division facts and can zip through a set of flash cards as fast as they can deal them out.

However, it is quite another story to apply this knowledge to word problems. When it comes to understanding the concept of "factor times factor equals product" and "product divided by factor equals factor," the situation becomes much more complicated. One way to facilitate the internalization of these two important ideas is through the use of dramatization.

Activity. You could write a series of simple word problems on $3'' \times 5''$ cards for children to use in demonstrating their strategies. It takes at least three children to demonstrate each problem, since at least two factors and a product will be involved. This becomes a nice-sized group for thinking and solving a problem together. Suppose a card reads: "Four students receive $3.00 each for raking a neighbor's lawn. What is the total amount that the neighbor must pay for having his yardwork done?" Students have to go through the problem-solving process and realize that here is an $F \times F = P$ situation, and that the **total** (key word) will be larger than $3.00, or four times $3.00 which equals $12.00. Deciding whether the solution should involve *putting together* or *taking apart* groups is what this whole process is about. Acting out a story problem, then solving it in a group situation, expedites and facilitates understanding of key concepts. Once the groups have successfully solved their problems, they share the problems and solutions with the rest of the class. Dramatizing them and then writing the mathematical problem and solution on the board and verbalizing them will reinforce the thinking that was involved. It is fun as well as instructive to have different groups dramatize and solve their problems with each other.

In division, or the "product divided by one factor equals the remaining factor" situation, students must realize that the answer must be smaller, since groups are being taken apart. An example could be written on a card: "Seven students must divide 21 sheets of paper equally among themselves. How many sheets would each student receive?" By thinking together, the group should decide on a "product divided by a factor equals the missing factor." Again, dramatizing the problem in front of the class, and writing it on the board and verbalizing it, reinforces the mathematical concepts being studied.

Grade 5

Decimals can be confusing for 10-year-olds. Up to this point, most of their dealings with the number system have been in whole numbers or in fractions. To equate fractions with decimals is very difficult for concrete thinking students. The teacher can make this comparison by being the "Ruler of Numberland" and create a reality/fantasy scene to help explain the correlation between the two ideas.

"The decimal point is critical," the teacher might begin in the reality phase of the lesson. "It marks the place where whole numbers stop and decimal fractions begin. You've learned that whole numbers increase by multiples of ten as you move from right to left. As you recall, we have the ones place, then to its immediate left is the 10×1 or tens place, followed by the $10 \times 10 \times 1$ or hundreds place. Therefore, we could also say in reverse that the value of the numbers decrease as we move from left to right. Now let's look at the other side of the decimal point to see what happens here. This isn't as new as you think, because we have previously worked with money problems involving dollar signs and a decimal point. Mentally put on your best thinking cap and see if you can understand what I'm about to share with you. The number just to the right of the decimal point is *less* than one. In fact, it's only worth ¹⁄₁₀ of one, or one divided by ten. When we wrote ¹⁄₁₀ as a fraction, we used a numerator and denominator to show its value. Here's a new way to write it: .1—see it on the board where I just wrote it? I could change the number if necessary and have .2 or .5 or .9, or whatever, and they would still be measured in tenths, ²⁄₁₀, ⁵⁄₁₀, and ⁹⁄₁₀. This is a second way to show the same amount, just as we say that a penny is the same as one cent. Raise your hand if you understand so far. Good. Now let's add a number two places to the right of the decimal point. How about .01? In that position the one stands for ¹⁄₁₀₀ or one part of a hundred. How did we write one cent using a dollar sign and decimal point last month? Right—as $ .01. Doesn't that mean we have one penny out of a hundred in a dollar? Isn't that the same as ¹⁄₁₀₀? You bet it is. What if we wrote $ .10? Yes, that's ten cents, or ¹⁰⁄₁₀₀, or ¹⁄₁₀ in simplest form. Great, we're beginning to make a connection here. One of the hardest, yet craziest, things to remember is that the difference between the words ten and tenth is only the *th* ending. You really have to be careful to see those two little letters. The same goes for hundreds and hundredths—a *th* is used again to end the word."

At this point the teacher writes down a variety of hundreds, tens, ones, tenths, and hundredths numerals on the board and quizzes the class until it's clear that they see the difference between the whole number and fractional representations.

Activity. Now for the fantasy part. The teacher tells the class:

- Draw a series of three boxes in a row on the board, followed by a decimal point, and then two more boxes.
- Put a "roof" over each of the five boxes to represent five "houses" in Numberland.
- The house furthest on the left is subtitled hundreds, the next house is tens, and so on through hundredths.
- The class copies the exact same chart on their papers.
- The teacher continues: In the tens house there lives a 6; in the tenths house lives a 2. In the ones house is a 4, while the hundredths house has a 7. Last of all, a 3 lives in the hundreds house. Reading from left to right, what large magical numeral do I have?
- The class should respond with 364.27, or three hundred sixty-four *and* (for the decimal point) twenty-seven hundredths.

Once the class catches on, students can take turns presiding and have others try to guess their special magic numerals. Not only is this fun, it solidifies place value, and makes children aware of the necessity to listen hard for the *th* endings. It's also a game two students can play together during free time. In addition, the game increases in difficulty as more places in the decimal system are learned.

Grade 6

Sixth-grade students are often introduced to the idea of plotting graphs. Once the basic idea of locating a point on a graph has been established, it would be fun to incorporate creative drama to reinforce the concept. The teacher, or a couple of reliable students, could tape equal lengths of brightly colored heavy yarn to the floor in the gymnasium, measuring off a vertical line (or *y* axis, also called the ordinate) and a horizontal line (or *x* axis, also known as the abscissa). Depending on the number of students in the class, yarn placed at three-foot intervals in both vertical and horizontal directions to include the numerals from 0 to 5 would accommodate a class of 25 pupils with room to spare. Large index cards could be taped on the outer edges of the vertical and horizontal axes to indicate where the numerals from 0 to 5 are actually located. The entire class then enters the gymnasium for a game of "Graphic Goofiness." Each child would select a spot to sit on where a vertical and horizontal line intersect. Since graph coordinates are always stated with the horizontal value first, a student located at 5.3 would be seated at x axis $= 5$ and y axis $= 3$.

Activity. Now the game begins. The teacher could say zany things like

- 4,1—Stand up and crow like a rooster.
- 0,3—Stand up and do 6 jumping jacks.
- 2,4—Change places quickly with 4,2.
- 1,1—Show us your best monster face, voice, and body motion.

The ideas are endless, but it would help the teacher to have a list of suggestions handy. After students have caught on to the game, volunteers could be the callers and the teacher could join in the game as a part of the graph or be an observer, checking to make sure the students understand how to locate points on a graph.

Grade 7

Working with the laws of probability or chance is a fascinating aspect of studying numbers in math class. Seventh graders will learn it is difficult to beat the "odds" after being involved in a few simple problems involving probability. Most students are familiar with the idea of flipping a coin and yelling "heads" or "tails" while the coin is still in the air, to make a decision such as which baseball team will bat first. A few math sessions devoted to predicting the outcome of how many heads or tails will occur is enjoyable, but it is also a realistic method of proving the high rate of risk taken when gambling.

Activity. To conduct this drama session:

1. Give each pair of students a penny and a paper numbered from 1 to 100 on which to record coin tosses.
2. Have the pair of students agree before tossing the coin how many each of heads and tails will occur between them. The laws of probability say that 50 of each would be likely.
3. Students take turns flipping and recording the results of their tosses. They will soon discover that none, or very few, of the student pairs achieved exactly 50 tosses each for heads and tails.

The second author recalls observing pairs of students scattered all over the floor in the classroom, each pair totally concentrating and oblivious of the other boys and girls equally absorbed in flipping coins and recording the results.

To further demonstrate the laws of probability, a single die can be thrown, and the results recorded for a predetermined number of tosses. It won't take long for students to discover that the chances of achieving any specific quantity of the number from 1 to 6 are even less than those of predicting the outcome of the coin toss. A discussion of the probability of selecting winning numbers on state lotteries could be an eye-opening finishing touch to this lesson.

Grade 8

Beginning geometry concepts are often taught at this level. For instance, the idea of time zones around the globe introduces the concept that the earth is round and therefore contains 360 degrees, equivalent to the amount in any circle.

Activity. To further explore this reasoning process

1. Ask students about "doing a 360," and they will immediately equate it with turning a bicycle or skateboard around in a circle, fast! They already know there are 24 hours in a day, and this is a number important to remember. Since the earth rotates past the sun one time zone per hour, it is a simple matter to find out how many degrees there are per time zone by dividing 24 into 360. The resulting answer, 15, indicates there are 24 equal time zones of 15 degrees each.
2. Have students use the International Date Line on a globe to begin a "new" day. They can begin to relate the addition and subtraction of time by moving west *or* east as far as 180 degrees between time zones. (Two times 180 degrees = 360 total degrees.)

As a final activity to check for mastery

* Have the students push back their desks and form a huge circle of 24 boys and girls on the floor, as equidistant from each other as possible.
* One person would be selected to be the International Date Line and the rest of the class would receive a number of degrees divisible by 15 in order east and west from that line.
* The teacher could then ask questions of students not in the circle, such as, "Jack, it is now 8:00 A.M. Begin at 45 degrees west, move east two time zones. Now what time is it?"
* Similar questions can be asked of other pupils, and those not a part of the circle should soon select someone they'd like to replace so all eventually have an opportunity to find out what time it is at some particular point on the earth.

If the class is clever enough, the teacher could even ask someone to move two and a half time zones and see if a student comprehends that half past a certain hour is the correct response. The idea of time passing becomes a reality rather than an abstraction for students as they physically move from one time zone to another, and the concept is much more likely to be retained accurately.

DRAMA FOR LANGUAGE ARTS

Grade 4

Folktales are a favorite genre for many children of this age. A visit to the library by the students and/or teacher will produce many books of folktales in no time at all. *Going to Squintum's: A Foxy Folktale* by Jennifer Westwood (1985) is a good example of a story with well-defined separate episodes. A wily fox tricks the different people he meets as he tries to secure the best possible meal for himself.

Some children may be starting to enjoy historical fiction at this point, while others continue their earlier love of poetry. Boys and girls in the fourth grade are able to use puppetry to share stories and poems with each other. Simple paper bag puppets are easy and quick to make. More elaborate cloth puppets involving cutting material and sewing are too frustrating and time consuming for most fourth graders: Besides, the children are anxious to *use* the puppets, not spend a great deal of effort creating them.

Activity. Choose a story or poem and divide students into small groups of two or three. Groups will need to divide the story characters up, sketch and paint the scenery, and make the puppets. A trip to the school or local library will provide a variety of books on how to make puppets.

The story dialogue has to be rehearsed and tape recorded. Some stories need a narrator, but in others a narrator is superfluous. The teacher needs to supervise several rehearsal sessions. Students can record their story lines on audiocassette tapes so that they can concentrate on puppet movement and scene changes without the additional responsibility of reading or remembering character parts. The tape recording alleviates a lot of stress and ensures a higher quality performance. Besides, tapes can be erased and re-recorded as often as necessary to get the best character voice and mood a child can achieve. If the teacher sidecoaches during the taping session, it will help bring out voice and mood effectively.

The teacher needs to meet with each group several times as the groups proceed to the performance. Students learn to handle a long-range project and also how to work in a group, build on each other's strengths, and attempt to negotiate peaceably with each other. Social skills acquired during such a project need to be developed step by step, just as the puppets do. The teacher's role is to gently arbitrate, allowing the group members to reach satisfactory conclusions to disagreements or other hurdles they encounter.

Although the children won't agree, the actual puppet performance is almost an anticlimax for the teacher. Some days it seems like the groups are making no progress whatsoever, but a bit of advice and nurturing from the teacher makes all the difference. The group forgives each other minor infractions, wipes away the tears and pouts, and moves forward. The proud faces of the puppeteers after a successful performance makes such a learning experience well worth the hassle. All teachers should allow their students to share in such a project. It's a real "growing up" time in their lives.

Grade 5

Historical fiction is effective as a vehicle for dramatizing events from the past. A teacher who wants to coordinate the social studies curriculum with language arts will find many stories from U.S. history from 1800 to the present that allow for excellent character interviews. Mary Jett-Simpson (1989) suggests that

1. Teachers identify spots in the story where students' comprehension of character will increase by assuming the role of the character. Interviews can be conducted during or after reading the story.
2. Teachers summarize the context of the situations at these points to set the scene for the interviews.
3. Teachers ask students to assume the roles of characters. Several students can dramatize the character at the same point as a basis for discussing different interpretations.

While these shorter dramatizations don't cover a story from beginning to end, they can act as an intermediate step in drama skill development, which would lead nicely to a complete story line enactment later. Some excellent stories with strong characters to use for character interviews are included in the list of related reading at the end of the chapter.

Grade 6

Sixth grade seems to be a year when many skills are finally refined and ready to be used at will. These students are still intrigued by biographies of famous people and historical fiction, and are increasingly aware of the beauty and complexity of poetry.

Dramatizations of entire story plots are undertaken with much more ease at this age. The story structure can be discussed and written on the board, including elements of setting (time and place), characters, problem, goal, episodes in sequence, climax, resolution, and theme. Next, the class can select groups of students to dramatize the different story episodes. When the groups meet, they make decisions about

- Who will portray the characters involved.
- What will be said.
- What actions need to be dramatized.
- How they will show the action in their particular scene.

If necessary, one student or the teacher can provide a verbal connection between scenes to keep the story line flowing. It is often enlightening to have the whole dramatization videotaped for the students to view afterward. This offers an opportunity for students to reflect on all the different aspects of the drama. Positive constructive criticism of their efforts will lead to even better dramatizations in the future.

For teachers who wish to use literature depicting events in the United States from 1800 to the present, a listing of appropriate books is provided at the end of this chapter.

Grade 7

In seventh grade, boys and girls are expanding their knowledge base and studying the history of the Western world. Greek, Roman, and Norse mythology is rife with stories begging to be dramatized. The legends of Beowulf, Ulysses, Joan of Arc, El Cid, Don Quixote, Roland, Robin Hood, William Tell, and others of similar stature are larger than life representations of the conflicts humans face within themselves and against humankind, nature, and the supernatural. Additional hero tales such as Julius Caesar, King Nebbudkudnezzar, Charlemagne, and William the Conqueror place famous people in the context of their historical time, lending credence to the fact that people, as well as natural events, definitely *do* change the course of history.

Character interviews are a good way to present the lives of these people. Another possibility is to have students dress up in the costumes of the characters they've chosen and give a monologue remembering certain crucial events in the characters' lives. Simple props could be added, such as an apple for the story William Tell presents. The students have to do some in-depth research on the lives of their characters to give a thorough presentation, but seventh graders are fully capable of such a task. They've been using the library's research facilities for years by this age, and this is a research project with a different conclusion. Instead of the traditional written report, they enjoy presenting their findings through drama. The entire class benefits by learning about the lives of many famous people, not just the ones they researched themselves. They could call their monologues "This is Your Life, William Tell," or whatever name needs to be supplied.

Students who are uncomfortable with a solo dramatization can create a model of a castle, a cottage, an inn, or other building of the era. Although a time-consuming, hands-on project, it necessitates much research to build an accurate model. Explaining the features of a prop to the class is much less threatening for students with lower self-esteem.

A third possibility is to let another group of students plan an enactment of *Shrek!* by William Steig (1990). This story is a spoof on quest stories, and middle schoolers just love dramatizing it! Shrek, the main character, is an ugly monster sent out into the world to seek his fortune. A witch tells him he will meet a dragon, and then search for a princess in a castle and marry her. Of course, the dragon is no match for ugly Shrek, and the princess is just as ugly as he is, so they make a perfect pair and live "horribly ever after."

Grade 8

Eighth graders, who are interested in science fiction and satire, could use creative drama to great advantage. If a class has been studying different science fiction novels and wishes to have an interesting culminating activity, why not let a panel of peers act out a quiz game like Jeopardy? This panel would use elements of the science fiction stories studied and their authors to answer questions asked by the game host. Some of the more famous science fiction stories are included in the annotated listing at the end of this chapter.

Satire is often exciting to eighth graders. They are mature enough to understand its purpose and derive a great deal of satisfaction when they've studied and understood a satirical literary work. One book that can be used to introduce satire is David Macaulay's *Motel of the Mysteries* (1979). Because students have studied ancient Egypt and the famous archeological digs of the tombs in the Valley of the Kings in that country, this book will be especially hilarious. It takes place in the year 4022 A.D. in the ancient area of the world known to the people of the present time as "Usa." Due to a massive deluge of pollution and waste materials back in 1985, the area has been buried for centuries. An amateur archeologist, Howard Carson, is sent to search for whatever he can find, and he unearths the remains of a motel of the time. The students will love the name of the motel, the Toot "n" C'mon, a paraphrase of Tutankhamun. Carson thinks the DO NOT DISTURB sign on the motel room door marks the entrance to a still-sealed burial chamber. When he explores the interior of the motel room and tries to suggest what the contents were used for by the ancient people, the story gets zanier by the minute. Two skeletons are found, one of them (see Figure 6.3) lying in a "porcelain sarcophagus" (labeled No. 9) in the Inner Chamber, which in reality is the bathroom. Carson further suggests that No. 1 and No. 4 were used to prepare the body for its final journey. His hilarious, bumbling conclusions will tickle the funny bone of any eighth grader.

Activity. After a thorough study of satire and how it can be used not only to teach but also to take a good look at ourselves, eighth graders might improvise some original scenes using satire.

- They *must* select a topic with which they are very familiar, because satire is grounded on a thorough understanding of the subject being ridiculed. For instance, they might come from the future to dig up a mall, complete with a huge central fountain, an ancient video arcade, a kitchen accessory shop, a fishing equipment store, and a toy store, to name just a few possibilities.
- Different groups of students could each describe the contents of one of the discoveries and create suggestions as to what the objects might have been used for by the ancient civilization that lived there.

This type of improvisation is totally creative. There is no prior script or story to follow. The students must be imaginative, yet use background knowledge to design a believable dramatization. When satire is well done, it is thoroughly enjoyable. Such an improvisation will elevate the eighth graders to a height they've never before experienced.

DRAMA FOR ART

Grade 4

Making puppets is perfect activity for fourth graders. Children can create a recognizable puppet with a personality by using a basic paper lunch bag as a base, the addition of pipe cleaners, yarn, cut out colored construction paper, and other materials. Some basic partner type of puppet presentations are a good introduction to the use of voice and puppet movement. A book of riddles will provide a ready-made series of very short scripts for the children to use as they experiment with handling a puppet correctly. You might use *A Basket Full of White Eggs* by Brian Swann (1988), which includes riddle poems from several different countries and cultures. The oversized, double-spread illustrations are an elegant context in which children can think about the movement possibilities the riddles contain.

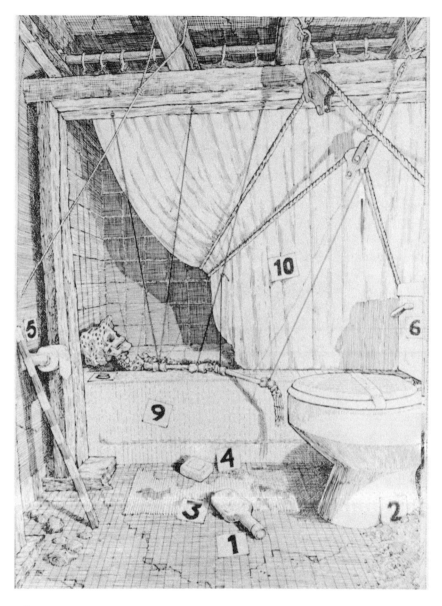

FIGURE 6.3. David Macaulay's tongue-in-cheek treatment of an archae-
ological dig in *Motel of the Mysteries* (1979), as shown here in his black
ink drawings, provides many opportunities for scene development by
older students.

Fables are also an excellent source of material conducive to the use of puppetry. There are many versions of these fables available: The edition with pictures by Heidi Holder (1981) features full-page, formally bordered illustrations done in mostly sepia tones; the one by Mitsumasa Anno (1989) embeds the fables into a story the illustrator wrote about Mr. Fox and Freddy; the edition by Tom Paxton (1990) features pictures by Robert Ray-evsky full of details worth studying. Any of these would work well as a lead-in to dramatizing.

Grade 5

Fifth graders studying U.S. history could create a frozen pantomime of some famous American paintings. An example would be the popular artistic ren-dering of Washington crossing the Delaware, a picture that has hung in many classrooms across our nation. After studying the painting, students could use their bodies to create a silhouette of this scene. Then they may wish to take it a step further and let each of the characters "step out" of the painting and tell a little bit himself. The Broadway play "Sunday Afternoon in the Park with George," based on the painting "An Afternoon at La Grande Jatte" by Georges Seurat, did exactly that, and audiences loved seeing those familiar figures step out of the scene and dramatize who they were. Fifth graders would enjoy the research and creativity necessary, and the end result would be well worth the effort. The series "Art for Children" by Ernest Raboff (e.g., 1987, 1988) contains over a dozen titles featuring the work of older artists like Michelangelo and more contemporary painters like Pablo Picasso. Large-size, full-color reproductions make it easy for students to see the drama possibilities in the paintings.

Grade 6

Students enjoy creating art, and by sixth grade they have the skills neces-sary to produce a complex art project. It would be fun to research the street life of New York in the late 1800s when many different immigrant populations crowded into that city. Pop-up street scenes could be designed depicting different vendors, street games the children played, and crowded tenement buildings with laundry hanging from the windows. *How to Make Super Pop-ups* by Joan Irvine (1992) will help children create a three-dimensional scene. Books that present the flavor of the time include *A Tree Grows in Brooklyn* by Betty Smith (1947), *Immigrant Kids* by Russell Freedman (1980), and *Rollerskates* by Ruth Sawyer (1986).

Thomas Hart Benton painted a series of murals for the New School for

Social Research in Manhattan in 1930. His scenes are crammed with muscular, energetic views of America. They portray the oil industry, mining, steel manufacturing, the Old South, and city scenes. Students could study and discuss these paintings with their teacher, and then use them as a point of departure to create a dramatization telling what happened before, during, and after a particular scene occurred. By making this bit of American history reflect reality, students will understand more about life in the early part of this century. The story of Benton's life is told by Wilma Yeo and Helen K. Cook in *Maverick with a Paintbrush* (1977), which details his life in engrossing fashion, but includes only a few full-color reproductions of his paintings.

Grade 7

Seventh graders would enjoy a class project creating a mural depicting the many trials and tribulations Ulysses and his men encountered on their journey home from The Trojan War. Their narrow escape from Polyphemus, the one-eyed Cyclops, his meeting with the Siren, and other adventures tell the story in one massive viewing. Part of this adventure is told in *Cyclops*, illustrated in heavily painted, darkly rich illustrations by Leonard Everett Fisher (1991). If the children really become involved in this, they might enjoy presenting a dramatization for other classes on the day their mural is "unveiled." Groups of students could present scenes in sequence from the mural to show others not involved in the project what particular adventure each scene represents. One student could give an introduction, present a unifying narrative to provide a smooth transition from one scene to the next, and give closure to the dramatization.

Grade 8

After a thorough study of the elements of science fiction, eighth graders might create their own science fiction creatures, perhaps using papier maché for this project. Students enjoy searching for weird accoutrements to add to their basic body shapes to make their particular creature unique. A search through the garage, the home workshop, the old toy box, and the basement at home should produce quite a variety of original objects d'arte. Once the characters have been created, students can give them names and personalities, and either speak for them to the class or carry on a monologue about their new creation. Writers of science fiction for this age include H. M. Hoover and Louise Lawrence, among others. Each has written many books that feature episodes full of dramatic possibilities.

DRAMA FOR MUSIC

Grade 4

Activity. Folk songs with a story line, such as "Froggy Went A-Courting" or the "Ballad of Davy Crockett," present great opportunities for pantomimed drama. Children enjoy looking at the oversized, formal, full-color pictures by Chris Conover (1986) for her version of Froggie. These are in vivid contrast to the illustrations by Feodor Rojankovsky (1955) for a book of the same title. It would stimulate interesting discussion to ask children to

- Identify how these illustrations are alike and different
- Decide which ones they prefer
- Discuss the reasons for their preferences

After the children have learned the songs and discussed the story line, they can suggest ways to enact different verses. Groups of children can each be assigned verses to work on, and when the whole class meets again the verses can be pantomimed while the rest of the class sings.

Grade 5

"Hiawatha's Childhood," from *The Song of Hiawatha* by Henry Wadsworth Longfellow, tells in poetry form about the boyhood of the Indian hero, Hiawatha. One good version is entitled *Hiawatha*, and is illustrated by Susan Jeffers (1983). Children need to study the poem and become familiar with some of the Indian words, such as *wah-wah-taysee*, meaning "little firefly." The class may wish to use choral reading, synchronized with a drummed cadence, to tell the story in unison. One or more students could act out the part of Hiawatha in pantomime as the poem is read. This is a good vehicle to work on the element of voice. One's voice must blend in with all the others in a choral reading, and this isn't easy for all children to do. Practice will help, and the children will become familiar with vocal inflection, such as pitch, stress, and juncture. A good performance helps children feel good about themselves as a cohesive unit.

Grade 6

Sixth graders can learn and dramatize many famous Civil War songs. "When Johnny Comes Marching Home Again" is a favorite of generations and can be found in most books of patriotic songs. One source is *The Golden Book of Favorite Songs* (John Beattie et al., 1946), a book that has been reprinted for years. The bittersweet message of planning what will happen when a son, brother, husband, or grandson returns from the War Between the States might create a lasting impression of the futility of war for this age level. The actual celebrations of such occurrences are left to the imagination, which makes many creative drama interpretations possible. Different students could be family groups and plan how they would welcome a family member home. They need to consider how he might be changed, minus an arm or a leg, or sick, or blind, or changed in personality. This is a good opportunity to use improvisation techniques. Students need to ask themselves

- What family members do we wish to characterize?
- Where do we live—on a farm, in a city, or elsewhere?
- What kind of a celebration will we plan for him?
- What physical and mental changes will have occurred in his life during all these years?
- What will we say to him?
- What will he say to us?
- How will our lives change having him home again?

This could be a very poignant and revealing situation for adolescent twelve-year-olds.

Grade 7

While studying Medieval Europe, students might be introduced to ballads of the time. One of the more famous ones is "The Ballad of Robin Hood," a story poem in verse, with a chorus between verses. A balladeer usually traveled from castle to castle, singing and entertaining the inhabitants in exchange for room and board. He usually sang alone, accompanying himself by strumming on a lyre or mandolin. Versions of "The Ballad of Robin Hood" have been passed down and recorded, so students could listen to it on a tape to become acquainted with this style of singing. The verses are filled with the action-packed adventures of the hero, Robin Hood. A book now out of print, but worth searching for in libraries, is *The Song of Robin Hood* by Anne Malcolmson (1947). It is full of exquisitely detailed black pen drawings by Virginia Lee Burton, which show in minute detail, using a stylized approach, the adventures that can lead to drama. Using the song, movie versions of the story, and research from the library, students could form groups to dramatize different adventures of Robin and his merry men.

Grade 8

Eighth graders studying the cultures of the Eastern hemisphere might read George Orwell's *Animal Farm* (1986) as an introduction to communism.

Once the book has been studied and analyzed, the class might create a rap song to underscore the basic ideas it presents. Different animals with different movements and voices would be an interesting addition, and students could choose which animal they would most like to dramatize. Someone is sure to have a tape with different rhythms already preprogrammed on it, or perhaps a class member is a drummer in the school band and willing to accompany the group. Eighth graders love doing this type of scene, and they would certainly put their hearts and souls into the performance.

If this exercise is a success, the class might create a second rap song, perhaps even adding a dance routine for King Tut, the boy king of ancient Egypt. There's a lot of useful background information, told interestingly and accompanied by many full-color photographs, in *Into the Mummy's Tomb* by Nicholas Reeves (1992).

SUMMARY

Adolescent students vary greatly in physical development, social maturity, cognitive ability, and emotional growth. The key word in their lives at this time is *change*. Good peer relationships are essential to their well-being. Teachers can use this knowledge to good advantage by providing group learning experiences allowing for guided interactive communication. Using language skills and drama in the arts and content areas enhances social development, fosters academic interest, and promotes the self-confidence so important to this age group.

RELATED READING

Bagert, B. (1992). Act it out: Making poetry come alive. In B. Cullinan (Ed.), *Invitation to read: More children's literature in the reading program* (pp. 14–23). Newark, DE: IRA.

This "teacher friendly" book provides many suggestions for making reading come alive for children. The chapter on poetry by Brad Bagert suggests a sequential process for introducing children to poetry, and drama is a large part of making this happen.

Cottrell, J. (1987). *Creative drama in the classroom: Grades 4–6.* Lincolnwood, IL: National Textbook.

In this and in her similar text for grades 1–3, Cottrell discusses using creative drama as an educational tool, the teacher as drama leader, how to build drama skills, and integrating drama with content areas. A big plus is how to write practical drama plans.

Heinig, R. B. (1988). *Creative drama for the classroom teacher* (3rd ed.). Englewood Cliffs, NJ: Prentice-Hall.

A college teacher of creative drama for many years, Heinig presents a very workable plan for teachers who wish to use creative drama in their classrooms. Beginning with simple drama activities and games, and progressing through a carefully sequenced program of drama activities, she guides teachers new to creative drama to ever-higher levels of skills. She relies heavily on the wealth of wonderful children's literature available as source material.

Jett-Simpson, M. (1989). Creative drama and story comprehension. In J. W. Stewig & S. L. Sebesta (Eds.), *Using literature in the elementary classroom* (pp. 91–102). Urbana, IL: National Council of Teachers of English.

Using examples from literature that can be dramatized to enhance children's reading comprehension, Jett-Simpson presents another way to evaluate students' learning. She presents a step-by-step procedure to incorporate drama into the school reading program and use it as a viable assessment tool.

Salisbury, B. (1986). *Theatre arts in the elementary classroom: Grades 4–6.* New Orleans, LA: Anchorage Press.

Designed as a theatre arts textbook for the elementary classroom teacher, Salisbury's book describes the drama process, provides strategies and management for using it, and gives a scope and sequence for developing skills. She incorporates students' bodies and voices in drama, and suggests ways to use drama with all the subject areas typically found at these grade levels.

Spolin, V. (1986). *Theater games for the classroom: A teacher's handbook.* Evanston, IL: Northwestern University Press.

Spolin has compiled an entire book of games to use in developing creative drama techniques. She uses a step-by-step process to help teachers plan and present these games to students. Beginning with warm-up games and progressing to public performance plays, she gives a wide variety of drama activities, complete with directions and readily usable.

RELATED CHILDREN'S BOOKS

Christopher Columbus

Bains, Rae. *Christopher Columbus.* Mahwah, NJ: Troll Associates, 1985.
Fradin, Dennis B. *The Nina, the Pinta and the Santa Maria.* New York: Watts, 1991.

Fritz, Jean. *Where Do You Think You're Going, Christopher Columbus?* New York: Putnam, 1981.

Goodnough, David. *Christopher Columbus*. Mahway, NJ: Troll Associates, 1979.

Haskins, Jim. *Christopher Columbus, Admiral of the Sea*. Jefferson City, MO: Scholastic, 1991.

Humble, Richard. *The Voyages of Columbus*. New York: Watts, 1991.

Levinson, Nancy S. *Christopher Columbus: Voyage to the Unknown*. New York: Dutton Children's Books, 1990.

Roop, Peter, and Roop, Connie (Eds.). *I—Columbus: My Journal*. New York: Walker, 1990.

Stone, Elaine M. *Christopher Columbus*. Wheaton, IL: Tyndale, 1991.

Revolutionary War Days

Bulla, Clyde. *Pocahontas and the Strangers*. Jefferson City, MO: Scholastic, 1988.

Collier, James L. *My Brother Sam Is Dead*. New York: Four Winds Press, 1974.

Edmonds, Walter. *The Matchlock Gun*. Mahwah, NJ: Troll Associates, 1991.

Forbes, Esther. *Johnny Tremain*. Boston: Houghton Mifflin, 1971.

Fritz, Jean. *And Then What Happened, Paul Revere?* New York: Putnam, 1973.

Fritz, Jean. *Can't You Make Them Behave, George?* New York: Putnam, 1982.

Fritz, Jean. *The Great Little Madison*. New York: Putnam, 1989.

Fritz, Jean. *What's the Big Idea, Ben Franklin?* New York: Putnam, 1982.

Krensky, Stephen. *George Washington, the Man Who Would Not Be King*. Jefferson City, MO: Scholastic, 1991.

O'Dell, Scott. *Sarah Bishop*. Jefferson City, MO: Scholastic, 1991.

Roop, Peter, and Roop, Connie. *Buttons for General Washington*. Minneapolis, MN: Lerner, 1987.

Speare, Elizabeth. *Sign of the Beaver*. Boston: Houghton Mifflin, 1983.

United States History, 1800 to the Present

Ashabranner, Brent. *Always to Remember: The Story of the Vietnam Veterans Memorial*. New York: Putnam, 1988.

Davidson, Margaret. *Frederick Douglass Fights for Freedom*. Jefferson City, MO: Scholastic, 1989.

Davidson, Margaret. *The Story of Thomas Alva Edison, Inventor*. Jefferson City, MO: Scholastic, 1990.

Freedman, Russell. *Lincoln, A Photobiography*. New York: Clarion, 1987.

Keith, Harold. *Rifles for Watie*. New York: HarperCollins Children's Books, 1987.

Sobol, Donald J. *The Wright Brothers at Kitty Hawk*. Jefferson City, MO: Scholastic, 1987.

Spinelli, Jerry. *Maniac Magee*. Boston: Little, Brown, 1990.

Sterling, Dorothy. *Freedom Train: The Story of Harriet Tubman*. Jefferson City, MO: Scholastic, 1987.

Sullivan, George. *The Day Pearl Harbor Was Bombed: A Photo History of World War II*. Jefferson City, MO: Scholastic, 1991.

Sullivan, George. *The Day We Walked on the Moon: A Photo History of Space Exploration*. Jefferson City, MO: Scholastic, 1990.

Medieval References

Aliki. (1983). *A Medieval Feast*. New York: HarperCollins Children's Books, 1983.
Berenstain, Michael. *The Armor Book*. New York: David McKay, 1979. now o.p.
Bulla, Clyde. *The Sword in the Tree*. New York: Harper and Row, 1962.
Cairns, Conrad. *Medieval Castles*. Minneapolis, MN: Lerner, 1989.
Cairns, M. Trevor. *Medieval Knights*. England: Cambridge University Press, 1991.
Cairns, M. Trevor. *The Middle Ages*. Minneapolis, MN: Lerner, 1975.
Clarke, Richard. *Castles*. New York: Watts, 1986.
de Angeli, Marguerite. *The Door in the Wall*. Jefferson City, MO: Scholastic, 1984.
Gee, Robyn. *Living in Castle Times*. Tulsa, OK: EDC, 1982.
Gray, Elizabeth. *Adam of the Road*. New York: Puffin, 1987.
Hastings, Selina. *Sir Gawain and the Green Knight*. New York: Morrow, 1987.
Jones, Madeline. *Knights and Castles*. Batsford, UK: Trafalgar Square, 1991.
Lasker, Joe. *Merry Ever After*. New York: Puffin, 1978.
Macaulay, David. *Castles*. Boston: Houghton Mifflin, 1977.
MacDonald, Fiona. *A Medieval Castle: Inside Story*. New York: P. Bedrick Books, 1990.
Morgan, Gwyneth. *Life in a Medieval Village*. Minneapolis, MN: Lerner, 1982.
Scarry, Huck. *Looking Into the Middle Ages*. New York: HarperCollins, 1985.
Smith, Beth. *Castles*. New York: Watts, 1988.
Steig, William. *Shrek!*. Toronto, Canada: HarperCollins, 1990.
Unstead, R. J. (Ed.). *See Inside a Castle*. New York: Watts, 1979.

Egyptian References

Allen. *Pharaohs and Pyramids*. Tulsa, OK: EDC, 1977.
Burland, Cottie. *Ancient Egypt*. Chester Springs, PA: Dufour, 1974.
Egypt: Quest for Eternity. Video #51294 available from the National Geographic Society, P. O. Box 2118, Washington, DC 20013–2118.
Ferguson, Sheila. *Growing Up in Ancient Egypt*. London: Anchor Brendon Ltd., 1980.
Giblin, James. *The Riddle of the Rosetta Stone: Key to Ancient Egypt*. New York: HarperCollins, 1990.
Glubok, Shirley, and Tamarin, Alfred. *The Mummy of Ramose*. New York: Harper & Row, 1978.
Hart, George. *Ancient Egypt*. San Diego, CA: Harcourt Brace Jovanovich, 1989.
Morley, Jacqueline. *An Egyptian Pyramid: Inside Story*. New York: P. Bedrick Books, 1991.
Payne, Elizabeth. *The Pharaohs of Ancient Egypt*. New York: Random House, 1981.
Reiff, Stephanie. *Secrets of Tut's Tomb and the Pyramids*. Austin, TX: Raintree, 1983.
Stead, Miriam. *Ancient Egypt*. New York: Watts, 1985.
Unstead, R. J. *An Egyptian Town*. New York: Watts, 1986.

Other

Beattie, John, Breach, William, Glenn, Mabell, Goodell, Walter, Gordon, Edgar, Hall, Norman, Hesser, Ernest, and Wisenal, E. Jane (Eds.). *The Golden Book of Favorite Songs.* Minneapolis, MN: Schmitt, Hall and McCreary, 1946.

Conover, Chris. *Froggie Went A-Courting.* New York: Farrar, Straus & Giroux, 1986.

Rojankovsky, Feodor. *Frog Went A-Courtin.* San Diego: Harcourt Brace Jovanovich, 1955.

Shefelman, Janice. *A Peddler's Dream.* Boston: Houghton Mifflin, 1992.

Smith, Betty. *A Tree Grows in Brooklyn.* New York: Harper & Row, 1947.

Waters, Kate. *Sarah Morton's Day.* New York: Scholastic, 1989.

Westwood, Jennifer. *Going to Squintum's: A Foxy Folktale.* New York: Dial Books for Young Readers, 1985.

References

Anderson, P. S., & Lapp, D. (1988). *Language skills in elementary education.* New York: Macmillan.

Barnfield, G. (1968). *Creative dramatics in schools.* New York: Hart Publishing.

Barsky, M., & Mozenter, G. (1976). The use of creative drama in a children's group. *International Journal of Group Psychotherapy, 26,* 105–114.

Barton, R., & Booth, D. (1973). Do swans really eat fudgesicles? (The picture book and child drama). *Children's Literature in Education, 11,* 13–24.

Blackie, P., Bullough, B., & Nash, D. (1972). *Drama.* New York: Citation Press.

Blair-Clough, I., & Wheeler, B. (1979). In the shadow of Three Mile Island. *Instructor, 89,* 115–116 ff.

Blank, W. E. (1954). The effectiveness of creative dramatics in developing voice, vocabulary and personality. *Speech Monographs, 21,* 251.

Bolton, G. (1980). Theatre form in drama teaching. In K. Robinson (Ed.), *Exploring theatre and education* (pp. 71–87). London: Heinemann.

Booth, D., & Martin-Smith, A. (1988). *Re-cognizing Richard Courtney: Selected writings on drama and education.* Ontario: Pembroke.

Bordan, S. D. (1970). *Plays as teaching tools in the elementary school.* West Nyack, NY: Parker Publishing.

Boyd, G. (1975). Role playing. *Social Education, 21,* 267–269.

Brown, K. L. (1967). Speech and listening in language arts textbooks. *Elementary English, 44,* 336–341.

Brown, V. (1992). Assessment of preschool drama programs. *The Drama/Theatre Teacher, 4*(3), 5–9.

Brownlie, F., & Gilchrist, D. (1989). Extending collective experience into and beyond the text. *The Reading Teacher, 42*(8), 618–622.

Burke, J. J. (1980). The effect of creative dramatics on the attitudes and reading abilities of seventh grade students. *Dissertation Abstracts International, 41*(12), 4887A.

Campbell, J. (1991). 1990–1991 research: Youth drama theatre, and education. *Youth Theatre Journal, 6*(1), 18–21.

Carlton, L., & Moore, R. H. (1968). *Reading, self-directive dramatization and self-concept.* Columbus, OH: Charles E. Merrill.

Chaparro, J. L. (1979). From the cradle to the classroom. *Language Arts, 56,* 256–261.

Cheifetz, D. (1971). *Theatre in my head.* Boston: Little, Brown.

Cole, N. R. (1940). *The arts in the classroom.* New York: John Day.

Cole, N. R. (1966). *Children's arts from deep down inside.* New York: John Day.

Complo, J. M. (1974). *Dramakinetics in the classroom.* Boston: Plays.

Cottrell, J. (1984). *Teaching with creative dramatics.* Lincolnwood, IL: National Textbook.

Cottrell, J. (1987). *Creative drama in the classroom: Grades 1–3* and *Grades 4–6.* Lincolnwood, IL: National Textbook.

Craig, T., & Edwards, J. (1992). Creating the story in drama. *Youth Theatre Journal, 6*(4), 3–6.

Cullum, A. (1967, now o.p.). *Push back the desks.* New York: Citation Press.

Currell, D. (1987). *The complete book of puppet theatre.* Totowa, NJ: Barnes & Noble Books.

Dillon, D. A. (1981). Drama as a sense of wonder—Brian Way. *Language Arts, 58*(3), 356–362.

Dumas, W. (1970). Role playing: Effective technique in the teaching of history. *Clearing House, 44,* 468–470.

Ehrlich, H. W. (1974). *Creative dramatics handbook.* Philadelphia: Office of Early Childhood Programs.

Fast, J. (1970). *Body language.* New York: M. Evans.

Feericks, M. (1980). Mime. *Instructor, 89,* 60–67.

Fisher, C. J., & Terry, C. A. (1990). Dramatic expression. In *Children's language and the language arts* (pp. 287–288). Boston: Allyn & Bacon.

Fitzgerald, B. S. (1962). *World tales for creative drama and storytelling.* Englewood Cliffs, NJ: Prentice-Hall.

Flower, C., & Fortney, A. (1983). *Puppets: Methods and materials.* Worcester, MA: Davis Publications.

Fowler, C. (1989, November). The arts are essential to education. *Educational Leadership, 47,* 61–63.

Fox, M. (1987). *Teaching drama to young children.* Portsmouth, NH: Heinemann Educational Books.

Glazer, J. I. (1986). *Literature for young children.* Columbus, OH: Charles E. Merrill.

Goodman, K. (1986). *What's whole in whole language?* Ontario: Scholastic.

Goodridge, J. (1970). *Creative drama and improvised movement for children.* Boston: Plays.

Graham, G., Holt/Hale, S. A., & Parker, M. (1987). *Children moving.* Palo Alto, CA: Mayfield Publishing.

Haley-James, S. (Ed.). (1981). *Perspectives on writing in grades 1–8.* Urbana, IL: National Council of Teachers of English.

Hall, R. (1973). Educational drama in England. *Children's Theatre Review, 22,* 17.

Hammill, D., & Bartel, N. (1975). *Teaching children with learning and behavior problems.* Boston: Allyn & Bacon.

Hayes, J. F., & Schindel, D. N. (1992). Museum education through drama: Blazing a new trail. *The Drama/Theatre Teacher, 4*(2), 12–15.

Heathcote, D. (1970). How does drama serve thinking, talking, and writing? *Elementary English, 47,* 1077–1081.

Heathcote, D. (1980). From the particular to the universal. In K. Robinson (Ed.), *Exploring theatre and education* (pp. 7–50). London: Heinemann.

Heinig, R. B. (1992). *Improvisation with favorite tales*. Portsmouth, NH: Heinemann.

Henderson, L. C., & Shanker, J. L. (1978). The use of interpretive dramatics versus basal reader workbooks for developing comprehension skills. *Reading World, 17,* 239–243.

Hennings, D. G. (1977). *Words, sounds, and thoughts*. New York: Citation Press.

Henry, M. W. (Ed.). (1967). *Creative experiences in oral language*. Champaign, IL: National Council of Teachers of English.

Hentoff, N. (1966, January 22). Among the wild things. *New Yorker*, pp. 39 ff.

Hillman, A. (1975). The play's the thing. In G. I. Brown (Ed.), *The live classroom* (pp. 276–291). New York: Viking Press.

Hirsch, E. D., Jr. (1987). *Cultural literacy. What every American needs to know*. Boston: Houghton Mifflin.

Hodgson, J. (1981). Drama—At the core of the curriculum. In N. McCaslin (Ed.), *Children and drama* (pp. 238–246). New York: Longmans.

Hoetker, J. (1969). *Dramatics and the teaching of literature*. Champaign, IL: National Council of Teachers of English.

Holt, J. (1969, now o.p.). *The underachieving school*. New York: Pitman.

Hopkins, L. B., & Arenstein, M. (1990). *Do you know what day tomorrow is?* New York: Scholastic.

Hornbrook, D. (1991). *Education in drama*. Bristol, PA: Falmer Press.

Jalongo, M. R. (1992). *Early childhood language arts*. Boston: Allyn & Bacon.

Jenkins, P. D. (1980). *The magic of puppetry: A guide for those working with young children*. Englewood Cliffs, NJ: Prentice-Hall.

Jennings, S. (Ed.). (1987). *Dramatherapy: Theory and practice for teachers and clinicians*. Beckenham, UK: Croom Helm.

Jensen, W., Sloane, H., & Young, K. (1988). *Applied behavior analysis in education*. Englewood Cliffs, NJ: Prentice-Hall.

Jett-Simpson, M. (1989). Creative drama and story comprehension. In J. W. Stewig & S. L. Sebesta (Eds.), *Using literature in the elementary classroom* (pp. 91–102). Urbana, IL: National Council of Teachers of English.

Joyce, M. (1980). *First steps in teaching creative dance to children*. Palo Alto, CA: Mayfield Publishing.

Juliebo, M. F. (1989). Role-play and citizenship education. In K. A. McLeod (Ed.), *Canada and citizenship education* (pp. 169–174). Toronto: Canadian Educational Association.

Kase-Polisini, J. (1989). *Drama as a meaning maker*. New York: University Press of America.

Klein, M. L. (1988). *Teaching reading comprehension and vocabulary: A guide for teachers*. Englewood Cliffs, NJ: Prentice-Hall.

Last, E. (Ed.). (1990). *A guide to curriculum planning in classroom drama and theatre*. Madison: Wisconsin Department of Public Instruction.

Leavitt, H. D., & Sohn, D. A. (1985). *Look, think and write*. Lincolnwood, IL: National Textbook.

Lefevre, C. A. (1970). *Linguistics, English and the language arts*. Boston: Allyn & Bacon.

Lewis, C. D. (1968). The poem and the lesson. *English Journal, 55*, 321–327.

Linek, W. (1991). Grading and evaluation techniques for whole language teachers. *Language Arts, 68*(2), 125.

MacDonald, J. B. (1986). Understanding communication patterns through playmaking. *Youth Theatre Journal, 1*(2), 3–9.

May, R. (1975). *The courage to create.* New York: Norton.

McCaslin, N. (1987). *Creative drama in the intermediate grades: A handbook for teachers.* New York: Longman.

McCaslin, N. (1990). *Creative drama in the classroom* (5th ed.). White Plains, NY: Longman.

McCracken, R. A., & McCracken, M. J. (1987). *Reading is only the tiger's tail: A language arts program.* Winnipeg, Canada: Peguis Publishers Limited.

McGinnis, E., & Goldstein, A. (1984). *Skillstreaming the elementary school child.* Champaign, IL: Research Press.

McIntyre, B. M. (1974). *Creative drama in the elementary school.* Itasca, IL: F. E. Peacock.

Meek, A. (1990). Recurring rhythms. *Educational Leadership, 47*(6), 3.

Mehrabian, A., & Ferris, S. R. (1967). Inference of attitudes from non-verbal communication in two channels. *Journal of Consulting Psychology, 31*, 248–252.

Merina, A. (1992). Made to measure. *NEA Today, 11*(2), 15.

Mitchell, M. (1985). Creative drama: Bridging the gap between the elementary school and the art museum. *Children's Theatre Review, 34*(3), 5–7.

Moffett, J., & Wagner, B. J. (1992). *Student-centered language arts, K–12.* Portsmouth, NH: Boynton/Cook.

Monson, R., & Pahl, M. (1991). Charting a new course with whole language. *Educational Leadership, 46*(6), 52.

Murphy, K. B. (1976). On the trail of Lewis and Clark. *Teacher, 94*, 42–45.

National Council of Teachers of English. (n.d.). *Informal classroom drama.* Urbana, IL: NCTE.

Noble, G., Egan, P., & McDowell, S. (1977). Changing the self-concepts of seven-year-old deprived urban children by creative drama or videofeedback. *Social Behavior and Personality, 5*, 55–64.

Norton, D. E. (1989). *The effective teaching of language arts.* Columbus, OH: Charles E. Merrill.

O'Neill, C. (1988). Exploring a topic through role-play and drama. *Voices, 13*(3), 6–9.

O'Shea, C., & Egan, M. (1978). A primer of drama techniques for teaching literature. *English Journal, 67*, 51–55.

Oster, G. (1969). Structure in creativity. *Elementary English, 46*, 438–443.

Pangrazi, R. P., & Dauer, V. P. (1992). *Dynamic physical education for elementary school children.* New York: Macmillan.

Pappas, C. C., Kiefer, B. Z., & Levstik, L. S. (1990). *An integrated language perspective in the elementary school.* New York: Longman.

Pearson, D. (1989). Reading the whole-language movement. *The Elementary School Journal, 90*(2), 234.

Petty, W. T., Petty, D. C., & Becking, M. F. (1981). *Experiences in language: Tools and techniques for language arts methods.* Boston: Allyn & Bacon.

Pflaum, S. W. (1986). *The development of language and literacy in young children.* Columbus, OH: Charles E. Merrill.

Pratt, C. (1990). *I learn from children.* New York: HarperCollins.

Robinson, K. (1980). Drama, theatre and social reality. In K. Robinson (Ed.), *Exploring theatre and education* (pp. 141–175). London: Heinemann.

Salisbury, B. (1986). *Theatre arts in the elementary classroom.* New Orleans: Anchorage Press.

Sanders, N. M. (1966). *Classroom questions: What kinds?* New York: Harper & Row.

Schmidt, T., Goforth, E., & Drew, K. (1975). Creative dramatics and creativity. *Educational Theatre Journal, 27,* 111–114.

Schug, M. C., & Beery, R. (1992). *Teaching social studies in the elementary schools: Issues and practices.* Prospect Heights, IL: Waveland Press.

Shaw, A. (1968). *The taxonomy of objectives in creative dramatics.* Unpublished doctoral dissertation, Columbia University.

Shuman, R. B. (1978). Educational drama and the creative process. In R. B. Shuman (Ed.), *Educational drama for today's schools* (pp. 41–61). Metuchen, NJ: Scarecrow Press.

Siks, G. B. (1958). *Creative dramatics: An art for children.* New York: Harper & Row.

Siks, G. B. (1968). Perceiving through creative dramatics. In V. Littlefield (Ed.), *English encountered* (pp. 1–5). Madison: Wisconsin Department of Public Instruction.

Silberman, C. (1970). *Crisis in the classroom.* New York: Random House.

Sklar, D. J. (1991). *Playmaking: Children writing and performing their own plays.* New York: Teachers and Writers Collaborative.

Sterling, M. E. (n.d.). Thematic units: Apples, #266. Huntington Beach, CA: Teacher Created Materials, Inc.

Stewart, M. (1979). Puppets in education: A developing science. *Sunrise Semester,* Drama in Education, *Newsletter No. 1,* New York University, Office of Off-Campus Programs.

Stewig, J. W. (1977). Creative drama: More than story dramatization. *Communication Education, 26,* 189–196.

Stewig, J. W. (1979). Nonverbal communication: "I *see* what you say." *Language Arts, 56,* 150–155.

Stewig, J. W. (1986). Elementary school principals and creative drama. *Youth Theatre Journal, 1*(2), 15–18.

Stewig, J.W., & Jett-Simpson, M. (in press). *Teaching language arts in early childhood.* Belmont, CA: Wadsworth.

Sutherland, Z. (Ed.). (1976). *The Arbuthnot anthology of children's literature* (4th ed., rev.). New York: Lothrop, Lee and Shepard.

Sutherland, Z., & Livingston, M. C. (Eds.). (1984). *The Scott, Foresman anthology of children's literature.* Glenview, IL: Scott, Foresman.

Swartz, L. (1992). How far can you see with your eyes? Some thoughts about a drama curriculum. *The Drama/Theatre Teacher, 4*(2), 6–11.

Tarlington, C., & Verriour, P. (1991). *Role drama.* Portsmouth, NH: Heinemann.

Torrance, E. P. (1962). *Guiding creative talent.* Englewood Cliffs, NJ: Prentice-Hall.

VanTassel, K., & Greimann, M. (1973). *Creative dramatization.* New York: Macmillan.

Vawter, J., & Vancil, M. (1980). Helping children discover reading through self-directed dramatization. *The Reading Teacher, 34,* 320–323.

Wagner, B. J. (1976). *Dorothy Heathcote: Drama as a learning medium.* Washington, DC: National Education Association.

Wagner, B. J. (1979). Using drama to create an environment for language development. *Language Arts, 56,* 268–274.

Wagner, B. J. (1983). The expanding circle of classroom drama. In B. Busching & J. I. Schwartz (Eds.), *Integrating the language arts in the elementary school* (pp. 155–164). Urbana, IL: National Council of Teachers of English.

Wagner, B. J. (1990). Dramatic improvisation in the classroom. In S. Hynds & D. L. Rubin (Eds.), *Perspectives on talk and learning* (pp. 195–211). Urbana, IL: National Council of Teachers of English.

Wagner, P. (1978). Elusive notion of creativity and pedagogical practice. *Clearing House, 51,* 204–205.

Walker, B. (1975). *We made a story.* Chicago: The Coach House Press.

Wall, J., & Murray, N. (1990). *Children and movement.* Dubuque, IA: William C. Brown.

Ward, W. (1933). Creative dramatics as a medium for teaching literature. *The Elementary English Review, 10,* 40–44.

Ward, W. (1952). *Stories to dramatize.* Anchorage, KY: Children's Theatre Press.

Ward, W. (1957). *Playmaking with children.* New York: Appleton-Century-Crofts.

Watson, D. (1989). Defining and describing whole language. *The Elementary School Journal, 90*(2), 136.

Weissman, "Miss Jackie." (1988). The apple seed song. *Instructor, 97*(7), 69.

Wells, G. (1990). Creating the conditions to encourage literate thinking. *Educational Leadership, 47*(6), 13.

White, M. (1987). *The Japanese educational challenge.* New York: Free Press.

Williams, H. M. (1991). *The language of civilization: The vital role of the arts in education.* Washington, DC: President's Committee on the Arts and the Humanities.

Yawkey, T. D., Askov, E. N., Cartwright, C. A., Dupuis, M. M., Fairchild, S. H., & Yawkey, M. L. (1981). *Language arts and the young child.* Itasca, IL: F. E. Peacock.

Ziskind, S. (1976). *Telling stories to children.* New York: H. W. Wilson.

Recommended Children's Books

Adoff, Arnold. *Eats. Poems.* New York: Lothrop, Lee and Shepard Books, 1979.

Aliki. *The Story of Johnny Appleseed.* New York: Trumpet Book Club, 1963.

Aliki. *A Medieval Feast.* New York: Crowell, 1983.

Anno, Mitsumasa. *Anno's Aesop.* New York: Orchard Books, 1989.

Bacmeister, Rhoda. "Galoshes," in *A New Treasury of Children's Poetry.* Garden City, NY: Doubleday, 1984, p. 28.

Bantock, Dick (Ill.). *There Was an Old Lady.* New York: Puffin, 1989.

Baum, L. Frank. *The Wizard of Oz.* New York: Holt, Rinehart and Winston, 1982.

Becvar, Patsy. *Who Was John Chapman?* Chicago: Nystrom, 1991.

Brett, Jan. *Beauty and the Beast.* New York: Clarion Books, 1989.

Brett, Jan. *The Mitten.* New York: Putnam, 1990.

Brown, Marcia. *Stone Soup.* New York: Charles Scribner's Sons, 1947.

Browne, Anthony (Ill.). *Alice's Adventures in Wonderland.* New York: Alfred A. Knopf, 1988.

Carle, Eric. *The Tiny Seed.* Saxonville, MA: Picture Book Studio, 1987.

Cathon, Laura E., and Schmidt, Thusnelda. *Perhaps and Perchance: Tales of Nature.* Nashville: Abingdon, 1962.

Celsi, Teresa. *The Fourth Little Pig.* Austin, TX: Steck-Vaughn Co., 1992.

Cole, Joanna. *A New Treasury of Children's Poetry.* New York: Doubleday, 1984.

Colum, Padraic. *The Girl Who Sat by the Ashes.* New York: Macmillan, 1968.

Conover, Chris (Ret.). *Froggie Went A-Courting.* New York: Farrar, Straus & Giroux, 1986.

Cooney, Barbara. *Miss Rumphius.* New York: Viking Press, 1982.

Cresswell, Helen. *Bagthorpes Abroad.* New York: Macmillan, 1984.

Crossley-Holland, Kevin. *British Folk Tales.* New York: Orchard Books, 1987.

Dahl, Roald. "The Three Little Pigs," in *Roald Dahl's Revolting Rhymes.* New York: Bantam, 1986.

de Angeli, Marguerite. *Thee, Hannah.* Garden City, NY: Doubleday, 1940.

dePaola, Tomie. *The Comic Adventures of Old Mother Hubbard and Her Dog.* New York: Harcourt Brace Jovanovich, 1981.

de Regniers, Beatrice Schenk. *Jack and the Beanstalk*. New York: Atheneum, 1985.

de Regniers, Beatrice Schenk (Sel.). "April Rain Song," in *Sing a Song of Popcorn*. New York: Scholastic, 1988, p. 20.

de Regniers, Beatrice Schenk. *Red Riding Hood*. New York: Aladdin, 1990.

Farjeon, Eleanor. *The Glass Slipper*. New York: Viking Press, 1981.

Farjeon, Eleanor, and Mayne, William. "The Midas Touch," in *Calvacade of Kings*. New York: Henry Z. Walck, 1965, pp. 113–132.

Fisher, Leonard Everett. *Cyclops*. New York: Holiday House, 1991.

Fitzhugh, Louise. *Harriet the Spy*. New York: Harper & Row, 1964.

Fowles, John. *Cinderella*. London: Jonathon Cape, 1974.

Frank, J. (Ed.). *Poems to Read to the Very Young*. New York: Random House, 1982.

Freedman, Russell. *Immigrant Kids*. New York: Dutton, 1980.

Galdone, Paul. *The Three Little Pigs*. New York: Scholastic, 1970.

Galdone, Paul. *The Three Bears*. New York: Seabury Press, 1972.

Galvino, Italo. *Italian Folktales*. New York: Pantheon Books, 1981.

George, Jean Craighead. *The Moon of the Gray Wolves*. New York: HarperCollins, 1991.

Gibbons, Gail. *The Seasons of Arnold's Tree*. New York: Harcourt Brace Jovanovich, 1984.

Gibbons, Gail. *The Milk Makers*. New York: Macmillan, 1985.

Gibson, Michael. "Midas, the Golden King," in *Gods Men and Monsters*. New York: Schocken Books, 1982, pp. 126–128.

Giganti, Paul, Jr. *Each Orange Had 8 Slices*. New York: Greenwillow, 1992.

Grahame, Kenneth. *The River Bank*. New York: Viking Press, 1983.

Haley, Gail E. (Ret.). *Puss in Boots*. New York: Dutton Children's Books, 1991.

Heins, Paul. *Snow White*. Boston: Atlantic–Little, Brown, 1974.

Hennessy, B. G. *The Missing Tarts*. New York: Puffin, 1989.

Hinton, S. E. *That Was Then, This Is Now*. New York: Viking Press, 1971.

Holder, Heidi. *Aesop's Fables*. New York: Viking Press, 1981.

Hooks, William. *The Three Little Pigs and the Fox*. New York: Macmillan, 1989.

Hopkins, Lee Bennett (Sel.). *The Sky Is Full of Song*. New York: Harper & Row, 1987.

Hopkins, Lee Bennett (Sel.). *On the Farm*. Boston: Little, Brown, 1991.

Hopkins, Lee Bennett (Sel.). *Ring Out, Wild Bells*. San Diego: Harcourt Brace Jovanovich, 1992.

Hopkins, Lee Bennett (Sel.). *To the Zoo. Animal Poems*. Boston: Little, Brown, 1992.

Huber, Miriam Blanton. *Story and Verse for Children*. New York: Macmillan, 1965.

Hutchins, Pat. *The Doorbell Rang*. New York: Greenwillow, 1986.

Hyman, Trina Schart (Ill.). *Little Red Riding Hood*. New York: Holiday House, 1983.

Ingoglia, Gina. *Johnny Appleseed and the Planting of the West*. New York: Disney Press, 1992.

Irvine, Joan. *How to Make Super Pop-ups*. New York: Beechtree Books, 1992.

Isaka, Yoshitaro. *Hansel and Gretel*. Tokyo: Gakken, 1971.

Jacobs, Francine. *The Tainos: The People Who Welcomed Columbus*. New York: Putnam, 1992.

Jeffers, Susan (Ill.). *Hiawatha*. New York: Dial, 1983.

Jennings, Terry. *The Young Scientist Investigates Seeds and Seedlings.* Chicago: Children's Press, 1981, now o.p.

Johnson, Hannah. *From Apple Seed to Applesauce.* New York: Lothrop, Lee and Shepard, 1977.

Jones, Carol (Ill.). *Old MacDonald Had a Farm.* Boston: Houghton Mifflin, 1989.

Juenesse, Gallimard, and de Bourgoing, Pascale. *Fruit.* New York: Cartwheel Books, 1991.

Juster, Norton. *The Phantom Tollbooth.* New York: Random House, 1961.

Keats, Ezra Jack. *Peter's Chair.* New York: Harper & Row, 1967.

Keats, Ezra Jack. *A Letter to Amy.* New York: Harper & Row, 1968.

Koch, Michelle. *Hoot. Howl. Hiss.* New York: Greenwillow, 1991.

Lasky, Kathryn. *Beyond the Divide.* New York: Macmillan, 1983.

LeCain, Errol (Ill.). *The Snow Queen.* New York: Viking Press, 1979.

Lenski, Lois. *Strawberry Girl.* Philadelphia: J. B. Lippincott, 1945.

LeSieg, Theodore. *Ten Apples Up on Top.* New York: Random House, 1961.

Littledale, Freya (Ret.). *Snow White and the Seven Dwarfs.* New York: Four Winds Press, 1980.

Livingston, Myra Cohn. *A Circle of Seasons.* New York: Holiday House, 1982.

Lobel, Anita. *Alison's Zinnia.* New York: Greenwillow, 1990.

Low, Alice. *The Macmillan Book of Greek Gods and Heroes.* New York: Macmillan, 1985.

Macaulay, David. *Motel of the Mysteries.* Boston: Houghton Mifflin, 1979.

Macaulay, David. *The Way Things Work.* Boston: Houghton Mifflin, 1988.

Malcolmson, Anne (Ed.). *The Song of Robin Hood.* Boston: Houghton Mifflin, 1947.

Manning-Sanders, Ruth. *A Book of Witches.* New York: Dutton, 1966, now o.p.

Marcus, Leonard S., and Schwartz, Amy. *Mother Goose's Little Misfortunes.* New York: Bradbury Press, 1990.

Marks, Alan. *Ring-a-Ring O'Roses and a Ding-Dong Bell.* Saxonville, MA: Picture Book Studio, 1991.

Marshall, James. *A Summer in the South.* Boston: Houghton Mifflin, 1977.

Marshall, James. *Rats on the Roof and Other Stories.* New York: Dial Books for Young Readers, 1991.

Martin, Rafe. *The Rough-Face Girl.* New York: Putnam, 1992.

Marzollo, Jean. *Pretend You're a Cat.* New York: Dial Books for Young Readers, 1990.

Matthee, Dalene. *Circles in a Forest.* New York: Alfred A. Knopf, 1984.

McGough, Elizabeth. *Your Silent Language.* New York: Morrow, 1974, now o.p.

Mendoza, George. *The Marcel Marceau Alphabet Book.* Garden City, NY: Doubleday, 1970.

Metaxas, Eric. *King Midas and the Golden Touch.* Saxonville, MA: Picture Book Studio, 1992.

Mikaelsen, Ben. *Rescue Josh McGuire.* New York: Hyperion Press, 1991.

Miles, Miska. *Nobody's Cat.* Boston: Little, Brown, 1969.

Moore, Eva. *Johnny Appleseed.* New York: Scholastic, 1964.

Murphy, Jim. *The Call of the Wolves.* New York: Scholastic, 1989.

Noll, Sally. *Jiggle Wiggle Prance.* New York: Greenwillow, 1987.

Norton, Mary. *Bed-Knob and Broomstick*. New York: Harcourt Brace, 1957.

Numeroff, Laura Joffe. *If You Give a Mouse a Cookie*. New York: Harper & Row, 1985.

Orwell, George. *Animal Farm*. New York: New American Library, 1986.

Paxton, Tom. *Belling the Cat and Other Aesop's Fables*. New York: Morrow Junior Books, 1990.

Pincus, Harriet. *Little Red Riding Hood*. San Diego: Harcourt Brace Jovanovich, 1989.

Pizer, Vernon. *You Don't Say: How People Communicate Without Speech*. New York: Putnam, 1978, now o.p.

Pollack, Pamela (Sel.). *The Random House Book of Humor for Children*. New York: Random House, 1988.

Potter, Beatrix. *The Tale of Peter Rabbit*. London: F. Warne and Co., 1988.

Prelutsky, Jack (Sel.). *The Random House Book of Poetry for Children*. New York: Random House, 1983.

Raboff, Ernest Lloyd. *Pablo Picasso* (Art for Children Series). New York: J.B. Lippincott, 1987.

Raboff, Ernest Lloyd. *Michelangelo Buonarroti* (Art for Children Series). New York: J. B. Lippincott, 1988.

Reeves, Nicholas. *Into the Mummy's Tomb. The Real-Life Discovery of Tutankhamun's Treasures*. New York: Scholastic, 1992.

Roehrig, Catharine. *Fun with Hieroglyphs*. New York: Viking Press, 1990.

Rojankovsky, Feodor (Ill.). *Frog Went A-Courtin*. San Diego: Harcourt Brace Jovanovich, 1955.

Rounds, Glen. *I Know an Old Lady*. New York: Holiday House, 1990.

Sage, Alison (Ret.) *Rumplestiltskin*. New York: Dial, 1991.

Sawyer, Ruth. *Rollerskates*. New York: Puffin, 1986.

Scheer, Julian. *Rain Makes Applesauce*. New York: Holiday House, 1964.

Schnurnberger, Lynn Edelman. *Kings Queens Knights and Jesters: Making Medieval Costumes*. New York: Harper & Row, 1978.

Schroeder, Binette (Ill.). *Beauty and the Beast*. New York: Clarkson N. Potter, 1987.

Scieszka, Jon. *The True Story of the Three Little Pigs, by A. Wolf*. New York: Viking Kestrel Co., 1989.

Selsam, Millicent. *The Apple and Other Fruits*. New York: Morrow, 1973, now o.p.

Sendak, Maurice. *Where the Wild Things Are*. New York: Harper & Row, 1963.

Seuss, Dr. *The 500 Hats of Bartholomew Cubbins*. New York: Vanguard Press, 1938.

Sewall, Marcia. *People of the Breaking Day*. New York: Atheneum, 1990.

Sheldon, William D. *The Reading of Poetry*. Boston: Allyn & Bacon, 1966.

Sheppard, Jeff. *The Right Number of Elephants*. New York: Harper Trophy, 1990.

Shotwell, Louisa R. *Roosevelt Grady*. New York: Grosset and Dunlap, 1963.

Silverstein, Shel. *The Giving Tree*. New York: Harper & Row, 1964, now o.p.

Simon, Seymour. *Snakes*. New York: HarperCollins, 1992.

Sis, Peter. *Going Up!* New York: Greenwillow, 1989.

Smith, Janice Lee. *The Kid Next Door and Other Headaches*. New York: Harper & Row, 1984.

Smothers, Ethel Footman. *Down in the Piney Woods*. New York: Alfred A. Knopf, 1992.

Spicer, Dorothy Gladys. *The Owl's Nest*. New York: Coward-McCann, 1968, now o.p.

Steig, William. *The Amazing Bone*. New York: Farrar, Straus & Giroux, 1976.

Stevens, Janet (Ill.). *The Three Billy Goats Gruff*. San Diego: Harcourt Brace Jovanovich, 1987.

Stewig, John Warren. *The Fisherman and His Wife*. New York: Holiday House, 1988.

Stewig, John Warren. *Stone Soup*. New York: Holiday House, 1991.

Sutherland, Zena (Sel.). *The Orchard Book of Nursery Rhymes*. New York: Orchard Books, 1990.

Swann, Brian. *A Basket Full of White Eggs*. New York: Orchard Books, 1988.

Teacher Created Material Inc. *Thematic Unit—Apples* (#266, p. 62), n.d.

Thornton, Shelley (Ill.). *The Star in the Apple*. New York: Scholastic, 1991.

Thurber, James. *Many Moons*. New York: Harcourt Brace and World, 1943, 1990.

Udry, Janet. *A Tree Is Nice*. New York: Harper Jr. Books, 1956.

Walsh, Ellen Stoll. *Theodore All Grown Up*. Garden City, NY: Doubleday, 1981.

Waters, Kate. *Sarah Morton's Day*. New York: Scholastic, 1989.

Watson, N. Cameron. *The Little Pigs' First Cookbook*. Boston: Little, Brown, 1987.

Watts, Bernadette (Ret.). *Goldilocks and the Three Bears*. New York: North–South Books, 1984.

Weevers, Peter (Ill.). *Alice's Adventures in Wonderland*. New York: Philomel Books, 1989.

Weil, Lisl. *Pandora's Box*. New York: Macmillan, 1986.

Westcott, Nadine Bernard (Ill.). *I Know an Old Lady Who Swallowed a Fly*. Boston: Little, Brown, 1980.

Westwood, Jennifer. *Going to Squintum's. A Foxy Folktale*. New York: Dial Books for Young Readers, 1985.

Williams, Jay. *The King with Six Friends*. New York: Parents Magazine Press, 1968.

Williams-Ellis, Annabel. *Tales from the Enchanted World*. Boston: Little, Brown, 1986.

Willis, Val. *The Surprise in the Wardrobe*. New York: Farrar, Straus & Giroux, 1990.

Yeo, Wilma, and Cook, Helen K. *Maverick with a Paintbrush*. Garden City, NY: Doubleday, 1977.

Yeoman, John, and Blake, Quentin. *Old Mother Hubbard's Dog Dresses Up*. Boston: Houghton Mifflin, 1990.

Zwerger, Lisbeth (Ill.). *Hansel and Gretel*. New York: Morrow, 1979.

Index

About the Authors

John Warren Stewig is a professor of language arts in the Department of Curriculum and Instruction of the University of Wisconsin—Milwaukee. He taught kindergarten through sixth grade in public schools before completing a Ph.D. at the University of Wisconsin—Madison. He is a past president of both the Wisconsin and the National Council of Teachers of English. He is the author of 10 professional books for teachers and of articles in over 40 different periodicals. In addition, he writes for children. His most recent title, *The Moon's Choice*, is his fourth book for young readers.

Carol Buege is a teacher with 28 years classroom experience who currently works with middle school youngsters in Green Bay, Wisconsin, teaching English and reading. She is also a part-time instructor in the University of Wisconsin—Green Bay Education Department. In addition to helping found the Northeast Wisconsin Talented and Gifted organization in the area, Buege has published in educational periodicals and spoken at local, state, regional and national conventions. She was the recipient of a Delta Kappa Gamma scholarship which enabled her to take a sabbatical and complete her Ph.D.